The War Between the Unseen Kingdoms

Spiritual Warfare Extreme Series

H.A.Lewis
Patricia Lewis

Activate the Kingdom of God Within You
YOU are the Lion of Judah

The War between the Unseen Kingdoms

ISBN: 978-0-9988129-1-5 Soft cover

This book was printed in the United States of America.

The WAR Between The Unseen Kingdoms

H.A.Lewis
Patricia Lewis

War In The Heavens

Today there is a war raging stronger than ever before between the unholy and holy angels of the Lord as we draw near to HIS coming, due to Satans' rebellion which was cast out of the third heaven down into the **second heaven** – known as the **prince and power of the AIR** [**Ephesians 2:1-2**]

An unseen world of darkness from the second heavens
is bringing forth violence, wars, murder, witchcraft, drugs, gender confusion, hate against Jews etc. and blocking the Holy Spirit to abide in the church and revival to the land as the spirit of the serpent which influenced Adam and Eve leads the people away from the truth of God's word.

This influence rages against Israel and its people and the God of Israel

Any country who is in good terms with Israel and considers Israel its friend, surely will have the blessings of the Lord and his protection. And in the day God judges the nations, it will be considered a sheep nation and not a goat.

[**Numbers 24:9**] The nation is like a mighty lion; When it is sleeping, no one dares wake it. Whoever blesses Israel will be blessed, And whoever curses Israel will be cursed

[**Genesis 12:3**] Good News Translation (GNT)
[3] I will bless those who bless you, But I will curse those who curse you.
And through you I will bless all the nations

Stand UP, Gear UP, Move Forward in Prayer and Power

Heaven Waits for Earth to Move

"There must be a move on earth before there is a move in heaven. It is not heaven that binds first, but the earth. It is not heaven that looses first, but the earth

Scripture reveals that God waits on His people to pray before He will act
[Ezekiel 22:30, Jeremiah 33:3, Psalm 107]

When Heaven is silent and God is not moving mightily it always comes down to a failure on the earth and in the church to pray!

In Nazareth, Jesus' power was restricted and limited by unbelief.

[**Isa. 64:7**] "No one calls on your name or strives to lay hold of you."

Jesus told his disciples *"Ask, Seek, and Knock"* and heaven would answer!
[Matthew 7:7-12]

Table of Contents

Introduction   9

Chapter 1: What is Spiritual Warfare?   12
Lesson 1 ~ The Bigger Picture
Lesson 2 ~ Preparing For Spiritual Warfare

Chapter 2: We Are in A War   18
Lesson 1 ~ Do NOT Fear the Combat Zone
Lesson 2 ~ Know Who God Is - Our God
Lesson 3 ~ Dressed For Combat
Lesson 4 ~ Scriptures on Fighting the Enemy
Lesson 5 ~ We Must Be Fearless
Lesson 6 ~ We Must P.U.S.H.

Chapter 3: The Weapons of Our Warfare   34
Lesson 1 ~ Praying in Jesus Name
Lesson 2 ~ The Authority Abiding in Us
Lesson 3 ~ The Holy Spirit vs. the Spirit of Christ

Chapter 4: Activate the Kingdom of God Within You   43
Lesson 1: ~ Christ's Identity in Me
Lesson 2: ~ Who I Am in God
Lesson 3: ~ Pursue, Smite, and Consume
Lesson 4: ~ The Triumphant Walk
Lesson 5: ~ The Fight of Faith
Lesson 6: ~ The Cross and the Grave
Lesson 7: ~ Jesus in the Midst
Lesson 8: ~ Intercessory Prayer

Chapter 5: The Emotional Strongman   80
Lesson 1: Exposing the Names of the Different Emotional Strongman
Chart of the Emotional Strongmen

Chapter 6: Scripture to Combat Emotional Areas   91
           ~ Fear
           ~ Suicide
           ~ Terror
           ~ Worry
           ~ Forgiveness
           ~ Depression

Chapter 7: Overcoming Generational Curse   109
Lesson 1: ~ Examples of Generational Curses from the Bible
Lesson 2: ~ How to Break the Power of Curses Over our Family and Us
Lesson 3: ~ A Warfare Declaration ~ From Generational Curses
Lesson 4: ~ Scriptures Concerning Curses

Chapter 8: God and His Angels   117
Lesson 1 ~ Know What God's Angels Do
Lesson 2 ~ The Doctrine of Angels
Lesson 3 ~ Organization of Angels
Lesson 4 ~ His Angels Battle for You

Chapter 9: Satan and his Demonic Forces   126
Lesson 1 ~ Know Who Your Enemy Is ~ The Origin of Satan
Lesson 2 ~ Names of Demon Spirits
Lesson 3 ~ Origin of Demons
Lesson 4 ~ Demon Activity

Chapter 10: Principalities and Powers in High Places   137
The Second Heaven ~ Opposition to God's Kingdom
Lesson 1 ~ The Assignment of Principalities and Powers
     ~ First, Second, Third Heaven Chart
     ~ Satan's Influence on Man Chart
Lesson 2 ~ Wicked Spirits Counterfeit the Act of the Holy Spirit
Lesson 3 ~ False Religions & Their Foundation brings Deception
Lesson 4 ~ Test the Spirits that Speak
Lesson 5 ~ Wicked Spirits and Powers: Charismatic Witchcraft and Soul Ties
Lesson 6 ~ Names of Principalities
Lesson 7 ~ Warning - Engaging With Demons in the 2nd Heavens

Chapter 11: Spiritual Warfare Preparation   147
Lesson 1 ~ Religious Pride
Lesson 2 ~ Spirit of Legalism
Lesson 3 ~ Spirit of Sectarianism
Lesson 4 ~ Spirit of Lawlessness
Lesson 5 ~ Japhia, King Lachish
Lesson 6 ~ Spirit of Ritualism

Chapter 12: The Nephilim, the Anakim, and the Rephaim   163
Lesson 1 ~ Names of the Giants
Lesson 2 ~ Where the Giants Originated

Chapter 13: Do the Rephaims Exist Today?   172
Lesson 1 ~ Legends are Perversions of the Truth

Lesson 2 ~ The Tunnels of Belgium

Chapter 14: Secret Societies   175
    ~ Names & Political & Gov't Occult Charts

Chapter 15: The Characteristics and Assignment of the Serpent   179
Lesson 1 ~ Comparing the Serpent Physically and Spiritually
Lesson 2 ~ The Serpent's Snares/Traps

Chapter 16: Sins of the Fathers and Curses   188
Lesson 1 ~ David's Descendants
Lesson 2 ~ David's Ancestors
Lesson 3 ~ Scriptures Concerning Sins of the Fathers

Chapter 17: Spiritual Wickedness Against Believers   194
Lesson 1 ~ Paul's Writing About Spiritual Wickedness
Lesson 2 ~ We Fight Unseen Forces ~ Examples from Daniel and Job

Chapter 18: Spiritual Warfare Against Principalities   200
Lesson 1 ~ What is a Principality?
Lesson 2 ~ Our Lack of Discernment - Success for Satan

Chapter 19: God Is Saying To Us: "Fear NOT!"   206

Chapter 20: If the Strongman is NOT Bound   209
Lesson 1 ~ We Must Bind the Strongman
Lesson 2 ~ It Does Happen in the Natural as a Result of the Spiritual
Lesson 3 ~ Walking in Victory - Dying to Self
Lesson 4 ~ Jesus Bound the Strongman
Lesson 5 ~ Our Lives Become Prey for the Enemy When We Belong to Jesus
Lesson 6 ~ Christianity is not a Party or Picnic, but Warfare
Lesson 7 ~ What is Our Part in Deliverance

Chapter 21: Scriptures for Victorious Living   234
    ~ God's Favor
    ~ Guidance and Leading
    ~ Hearing God
    ~ Peace
    ~ Strengthen Your Faith

Introduction

This is written in an attempt to reveal a dimension of spiritual warfare, which to the best of my knowledge, is not often taught in the Church. It strikes a parallel between **Joshua 10** and **Ephesians 6:12**. It's simply comparing the enemy kings of Israel to the ruler spirits of new covenant warfare. Since the five Amorite kings united against Gibeon and Israel, who had made peace, we see that unity in the Holy Spirit is a must if these **strongmen** are to be bound.

Some of us, having practiced spiritual warfare for many years, have noticed that we seem to have short-lived success in that area of our Christian walk. One of the reasons for this is that we start in the wrong place – *putting the cart before the horse* so to speak. FIRST…the strongman or ruler spirit must be **bound** [**Matt. 12:29**]. Cutting off one branch at a time cannot kill a weed; the root must be severed.

These spirits do not seek to inhabit individuals but seek to inhabit corporate bodies of people. These five kings of **Joshua 10** got the battle started and then hid in the cave of Makkedah – meaning *sheepfold* in Hebrew. The names of the five kings and the nations they rule, according to my interpretation of the root meanings, are types of religious spirits that camouflage themselves inside the Church.

After being found (by the discerning of spirits), the men were told to *bind* them with large stones (Spirit-revealed word) and then to pursue the lesser in rank enemy until all were consumed. The key scriptures for this spiritual warfare are found in **Psalms 149**.

Psalms 149:6-9 Let the high praises of God be in their mouth, and a two-edged sword in their hand; To execute vengeance upon the heathen, and punishments upon the people; To bind their kings with chains, and their nobles with fetters of iron; To execute upon them the judgment written: this honour have all his saints. Praise ye the Lord.

In this study, you will find the scriptural depth as well as the practical application to accomplishing the goal of being a victorious, overcoming Church.

New and Old Spiritual Warfare Parallels

❖ Satan's kingdom operates in military ranks (i.e. legions, princes, etc.)

Matthew 12:25-29 And Jesus knew their thoughts, and said unto them, Every kingdom divided against itself is brought to desolation; and every city or house divided against itself shall not stand; And if Satan cast out Satan, he is divided against himself; how shall then his kingdom stand? And if I by Beelzebub cast out devils, by whom do your children cast them out? Therefore they shall be your judges. But if I cast out devils by the Spirit of God, then the kingdom of God is come unto you. Or else how can one enter into a strong man's house, and spoil his goods, except he first bind the strong man? And then he will spoil his house.

❖ This kind of spiritual warfare is that of an army against an army (or kingdom against kingdom).

Matthew 24:7 For nation shall rise against nation, and kingdom against kingdom; and there shall be famines, and pestilences, and earthquakes, in diverse places.

❖ The **battle plan for** both armies is the same -- to divide the ranks.

❖ Success of both armies depends upon the willingness and ability to march in rank and to carry out the orders from their commander in chief.

BATTLE PLAN

PRAY

WITHOUT CEASING

1 THESSALONIANS 5:17

SUIT UP

PUT ON THE FULL ARMOR OF GOD

EPHESIANS 6:11

HAVING DONE ALL

STAND

EPHESIANS 6:13

TURNING LAMBS INTO LIONS FOR THE KINGDOM OF GOD

Chapter 1
What is Spiritual Warfare?

~ Lesson 1 ~
The Bigger Picture

When we speak of spiritual warfare we are essentially speaking of the conflict between God and His heavenly host and Satan and his evil forces. To engage in this spiritual warfare is through prayer. Spiritual warfare is prayer warfare. We can only fight from two basic strategies: defensive or offensive. Consider this – those who fight offensively takes the initiative. Napoleon Bonaparte was asked, "How did you win all your battles?" His reply was, "I was always there a few minutes before they expected me."

We must discern the nature of Satan's lie. For instance you may have thoughts like: he will never get saved, he will never change, you will never get healed, or you will never have enough. We can exercise our authority in Jesus to stop Satan's activities. God's word says:

⇒ Take every lie into captivity of the word – **2 Corinthians 10:5**
⇒ Bind the strongman – **Mark 3:27**
⇒ Plunder his goods – **Mark 3:27**
⇒ Bind his rule and authority – **1 Corinthians 15:24**

Prayer can alter history by releasing legions of angels into action. Realizing this should motivate us to pray intently and constantly. **2 Chronicles 7:14** says, If my people, which are called by my name, shall humble themselves, and pray, and seek my face, and turn from their wicked ways; then will I hear from heaven, and will forgive their sin, and will heal their land

⇒ **What happens in the heavenlies when we engage in spiritual warfare?** Unseen to the natural eye, angels engage in battle in the spiritual world. Individually or collectively as we pray, they may guide the governments of the earth as well as events in our own personal lives.

We can see a glimpse into the continual battle raging in the spiritual realm between those angels protecting God's people and those angels trying to destroy God's people in **Daniel 10**. Daniel was praying for direction and clarification. After **twenty-one days**, angel came and told him God had heard his prayer the **very first day** and had dispatched the angel to him (Daniel) with the answer [**Daniel 10:12, 13, 20, 21**].

Contemplate the contrast between the natural and spiritual. A spiritual battle is happening in an effort to control the movement of the nations. In history (natural) several battles took place between Persia and Greece.

Ephesians 6:10-12 We do not wrestle with flesh and blood but with unseen spiritual forces.

We play a major part in the unseen battle by praying. Daniel prayed twenty-one days. He set his heart on understanding [**Daniel 10:12**]. Just like Daniel we need to be persistent and determined. We need to put on our armor [**Ephesians 6**] and pray the word cause angels hearken to the word of God [**Psalm 102:20**].

⇒ **There is a spirit called Antichrist, which is world domination without Christ.**⇐

It is the demonic spirit behind those like Napoleon Bonaparte or Adolf Hitler who had ambition to rule the world for their glory. They try to take over the place that only belongs to God [**Psalm 24:1**].

A praying church or body can bind the spirit and halt its activity.

~ Lesson 2 ~
Preparing For Spiritual Warfare

2 Corinthians 10:3-5 For though we walk in the flesh, we do not war after the flesh: (For the weapons of our warfare are not carnal, but mighty through God to the pulling down of strong holds;) Casting down imaginations, and every high thing that exalteth itself against the knowledge of God, and bringing into captivity every thought to the obedience of Christ.
James 1:12-14 Blessed is the man that endureth temptation: for when he is tried, he shall receive the crown of life, which the Lord hath promised to them that love him. Let no man say when he is tempted, I am tempted of God: for God cannot be tempted with evil, neither tempteth he any man: But every man is tempted, when he is drawn away of his own lust, and enticed.

If we put these two scripture references together, we find that the primary battlefield is in our minds. Yes! Satan exists. However, all Satan does is play upon what we already have in our minds and our natural desire to defy and rebel against God and to elevate and worship ourselves in God's place. All Satan does is present to us the lust of the flesh, the lust of the eyes, and the pride of life. We react according to our own internal desires to pleasure ourselves. The battle is not so much Satan as it is our own hearts.

Jeremiah 17:9 The heart is deceitful above all things, and desperately wicked: who can know it?

One of the things that our deceitful heart does is tell us that things are not sins when they clearly are. It also deceives us into believing that we are honoring God when in fact we honor ourselves. While the Holy Spirit is trying to convict us regarding our sin, our heart is trying to tell us that we are inherently good and righteous, and that we can honor God in our own way.

So, how do we win this battle?

Read the Bible and compare the truth of the Bible with the lies in our minds. If we reject the lies in our minds, then Satan will have nothing to grab on to. ***This is key to becoming a spiritual warrior.*** It is only when we succeed in driving Satan out of our heads by first becoming aware of exposing and opposing our own delusions and vanities that we are able to take the fight to Satan ourselves.
    Reading the Bible is an absolute must. Not only do we need to study all of the scriptures on a regular basis, but to be a spiritual warrior, we need to study Psalms and Proverbs. The *Proverbs* of wisdom help us distinguish between the foolishness of our own minds and the righteousness of God's Spirit when we are discerning thoughts. Once we have done that, the *Psalms* of praise show us how to make prayers of confession to ask God to cast down imaginations, and every high thing that exalts itself against the knowledge of God, and bringing into captivity every thought to the obedience of Christ for us.

Proverbs $\Rightarrow$ Identify the imaginations
Psalms $\Rightarrow$ Teaches how we should pray and ask God to cast them down

Keep in mind, spiritual warfare is NOT salvation, which only happens once. It is NOT the infilling of the Holy Spirit, which should happen from time to time. Spiritual warfare is a continual basis

– the battle never ends. Even though we are saved and our spirits were cleansed and the Holy Spirit indwells us, our flesh still exists and we still live in a sinful world.

The very notion that we can be as Christ on the cross and say, "It is finished", and move on to bigger and better things is in itself a vain imagination of our own inherent righteousness and desire to reject God's rule over our lives. In addition, so are the notions that just because we recently received an anointing or infilling of the Holy Spirit, or that we have done a lot of Bible reading lately, or that we have had a revelation from God or a great blessing or miracle, or we just feel so good inside and are so excited, that we are ready to turn on our praise music and go break down strongholds and take on prince demons.

These kinds of '**religious**' notions are when we are the most susceptible to the temptation of our own flesh. Why would that be? We actually start to become convinced of some notion of righteousness or power within ourselves instead of relying on God and giving Him the praise.

We've seen this among prominent preachers on television. They cavort about and carry on by saying, "Oh, I **feel** the anointing on me this evening. The Holy Spirit is moving in this place tonight. Because of <u>HOW I FEEL RIGHT NOW</u>, the blind are going to see, prophecies and visions are about to come down from heaven, the lame are going to walk, and the captives are going to be set free."

When the preacher screams that out, everyone begins thinking about what they want from God and how God has to give it to them because they are so righteous and because they are following a pastor that is so anointed so they get 'slain in the spirit' in anticipation of receiving their bounty from heaven. Then they get up again in the same condition they were in before. When we read all the accounts of healings and miracles in the Bible, how many of these accounts match the <u>spiritual activity</u> that we witness from preachers on television?

Truthfully, very little of it does. If we read the scriptures, we will see the people who God used to do these great healings and miracles often under extreme duress beforehand and often receiving great persecution afterwards. Jesus Christ was sent to the cross after raising Lazarus from the dead. Stephen was martyred after working miracles [**Acts 6 – 7**], and Paul and Silas were viciously beaten and cast into prison after casting a demon out of the slave girl [**Acts 16:16-24**].

Whenever we do something for God it comes at a cost, so the people that we see acting in such a manner are either not showing us the cost or they are not paying a cost because God is not whom they serve. Therefore, the next time we feel that the time is ripe for us to go cast out some devil because we **feel** so mighty, powerful, and good inside, consider the book of Lamentations. It will remind us of whom we are serving and the cost of serving Him.

God is **NOT** an action movie, fantasy novel, or video game. He is our master, and He alone has the right to either destroy us for eternity or permit us to worship and serve Him forever in Heaven. ***Spiritual warfare is a serious endeavor for the truly committed and sincere of heart only.*** Our goal in spiritual warfare should not be to glorify self, to help or free people, or to battle Satan. Instead it should be to glorify God.

If that is not your only goal, then you will be as Simon the sorcerer [**Acts 8:9-24**] or the seven sons of Sceva [**Acts 19:13-16**]. This does not apply to spiritual warfare alone. Anything that we do should be for the glory of God alone. If we have any other motivation, we are only doing harm to others and ourselves despite our many works.

For those who are serous about spiritual warfare you must:
- ✓ On a daily basis measure your mind against the Bible's wisdom
- ✓ Pour your heart out to God in confession (the prophets such as Jeremiah, Isaiah, and Habakkuk also had outstanding confessional prayers),
- ✓ THEN go about the business of binding, rebuking, and casting out demons.

We must do this so that our minds will be made suitable to the work of God in spiritual warfare, both in discerning what God wants done AND how God wants it done. If we do not know what God wants us to do and how God wants us to do it, we will certainly fail.

>>We must know His will.<<

When coming into the Promised Land, the children of Israel had to know that it was God's will for them to take Jericho, **AND** they had to know it was to be done by marching around the city blowing trumpets. Why? Simple, this was the manner in which God wanted to be glorified, lest it be said that the children of Israel overcame Jericho because of their many numbers and with Joshua's military strategy.

Believe it or not but there are skeptics who try to claim that the walls of Jericho were knocked down by a timely and fortuitous earthquake. This is why it's extremely important that before we initiate any warfare activity, we cast down our imaginations. If not, what we do will be done by our own power or righteousness and that is disastrous.

NOTES

Chapter 2
We Are in A War

We are in a war and ALL Christians are involved in this war [**Philippians 1:30**].

~ Lesson 1 ~
Do NOT FEAR the Combat Zone

According to Paul it is a good warfare and charges Timothy to wage it [**1 Timothy 6:18, 19**]. It is a fight of faith [**1 Timothy 6:12**] and it is not a natural war but a spiritual one [**2 Corinthians 10:3**].

There are two forces in this war. Each force has a strategy and both are highly organized with ranks, levels, and divisions. One force is the devil, the evil angels, and demons. *These forces are intent on destroying God's people.*

1 Peter 5:8, 9 Be sober, be vigilant; because your adversary the devil, as a roaring lion, walketh about, seeking whom he may devour: Whom resist steadfast in the faith, knowing that the same afflictions are accomplished in your brethren that are in the world.

The other force is God, God's angels, and God's people. God's angels help God's faithful people fight against the demonic forces. We are to fight with truth, righteousness, peace, faith, salvation, the Word and prayer.

Ephesians 3:13-18 Wherefore I desire that ye faint not at my tribulations for you, which is your glory. For this cause I bow my knees unto the Father of our Lord Jesus Christ, of whom the whole family in heaven and earth is named, that He would grant you, according to the riches of His glory, to be strengthened with might by His Spirit in the inner man; that Christ may dwell in your hearts by faith; that ye, being rooted and grounded in love, may be able to comprehend with all saints what is the breadth, and length, and depth, and height.

There are battles that CAN only be won by prayer
~No Double Mindedness & No Unbelief Allowed~

This is why we need to know how to pray effectively. Praying **faith-filled** words to the Father activate the angels, who battle the evil spiritual forces.

Psalm 35:1-3 Plead [my cause], O Lord, with them that strive with me: fight against them that fight against me. Take hold of shield and buckler, and stand up for mine help. Draw out also the spear, and stop [the way] against them that persecute me: say unto my soul, I [am] thy salvation.

Like all wars, the war we are engaged in has soldiers. US! Our captain is Jesus Christ [**Hebrews 2:10**]. **2 Timothy 2:1-26** gives us the characteristics of a good soldier in God's army.

⇒ Verses 1, 2: Soldiers are *strong* in belief.
⇒ Verses 3, 4: Soldiers are *single-minded* [sold out to God].
⇒ Verses 5-10: Soldiers are *strict* [disciplined].
⇒ Verses 11-13: Soldiers are *secure* [in their righteousness].

⇒Verses 14-19: Soldiers are *sound* in faith [founded in faith].
⇒Verses 20-23: Soldiers are *sanctified* [set apart from the world, holy living]
⇒Verses 24-26: Soldiers are *servants*.

2 Timothy 2:3, 4 Thou therefore endure hardness, as a good soldier of Jesus Christ. No man that warreth entangleth himself with the affairs of [this] life; that he may please him who hath chosen him to be a soldier.

As good soldiers under the command of our captain, Jesus Christ, we must understand that full-time service is required. Once you have enlisted, your voluntary commitment is for life. It is important that you are also very disciplined and strict obedience to orders is required.

Be **aggressive** towards the devil and his forces [like **LIONS**] – spiritual, yet peacemakers [like **LAMBS**] to others around you – natural.

Read The Dispensation of the Lion & the Lamb by H. A. Lewis
Each dispensation between the lion and lamb dresses differently

Matthew 5:9 Blessed [are] the peacemakers: for they shall be called the children of God.

Be a fighter marked by a driving forceful energy in the spirit. [**Matthew 16:18, 19; Romans 12:11**] And be ready to declare war against Satan's army to help bring the peace of God.

Natural soldiers have a special uniform for wartime. Likewise spiritual soldiers also have a special uniform. We find it listed in [**Ephesians 6:13-18**], where Paul takes the pieces of armor worn by the Roman soldier of his time and made spiritual application from it.

Lesson 2
Know Who God Is - Our God

It is beneficial to know your God. Why? Because there is no sign of weakness in the soldier [us] when we know our Commanding Officer. The key to knowing God is fellowship [**Hebrews 11:6; 1 John 1:3; 1 Corinthians 1:9; Psalm 68:1, 2**]. Moses had a desire to know God and see His glory [**Exodus 33:11-18**].

WHO is God?
- My salvation → **Isaiah 12:2**
- Awesome, Great King → **Psalm 47:2**
- My refuge → **Psalm 27:1-6**
- My Provider (Jehovah Jireh) → **Philippians 4:19**
- My Banner (Jehovah Nissi) → **Exodus 17:15**
- My Father → **Romans 8:14-17; Galatians 4:6, 7**
- My faithful God → **Hebrews 13:5, 6**
- Grace and Peace → **2 Peter 1:2, 3**

WHAT does God have?
- Angels at our disposal → **Psalm 103:20; Hebrews 1:14**
- His Mighty Word → **Hebrews 4:12; John 8:31, 32**
- Undefeated record → **Luke 10:18**
- A secret place for us → **Psalm 91:1, 2**
- A Guide for us (Holy Ghost) → **John 16:13**
- Strategy: uproot the gates of hell → **Matthew 16:18, 19**
- Love → **1 Corinthians 13:8**
- Gifts of the Holy Ghost → **1 Corinthians 12:4-11**
- Tongues, mysteries, secrets → **1 Corinthians 14:2**
  [Amplified Bible says 'secret truths and hidden things']

WHAT can God do?
- He stripped Satan of his power. → **Colossians 2:15**
- He redeemed us and adopted us. → **Galatians 4:4, 5**
- He has empowered us. → **Mark 16:15-18; Ephesians 1:19-22**
- He has delivered us. → **2 Peter 2:9**
- He rose up. → **Isaiah 42:13, 14**
- He avenges us. → **Psalm 18:47**
- He goes with us to battle. → **Deuteronomy 20:4**
- He saves His anointed. → **Psalm 20:6**

~ Lesson 3 ~
Dressed For Combat

The night is far spent, the day is at hand: let us therefore cast off the works of darkness, and let us put on the armor of light. **Romans 13:12**

THE ARMOR OF GOD

❖ The **first** piece of the armor is *the belt of truth* [**Ephesians 6:14**]. **Truth** signifies honesty and correctness. In the ancient garments of Paul's day, the girdle [belt] about the waist held in place every other part of the uniform. If the girdle [belt] was lost, everything else was lost.

Since it is the belt of truth then falsehood forfeits the very thing that holds the other pieces of armor together. Lying and deceit in your life will forfeit the protection of your spiritual armor. As soldiers of Almighty God, we are girded with truth in the face of the enemy. Remember, we will never go wrong telling the truthful thing.

❖ The **second** piece of the armor is *the breastplate of righteousness* [**Ephesians 6:14**]. On the Roman soldier the breastplate protected his heart.

1 Thessalonians 5:8 But let us, who are of the day, be sober, putting on the breastplate of faith and love.

Unrighteous acts will rob us of this vital protection and exposes our hearts to Satan. We cannot have sin in our lives and expect to be victorious when waging warfare with the enemy.

Hebrews 10:22 Let us draw near with a true heart sprinkled from an evil conscience, and our bodies washed with pure water.

❖ The **third** piece of the armor is that *feet are fitted with the Gospel of Peace* [**Ephesians 6:15**]. The Romans wore sandals that were bound by thongs over the instep and around the ankle. The soles were thickly studded with nails. This implies a firm-footed stability in the time of attack. This foundation (Gospel of Peace) for our feet will also keep us from slipping and sliding.

❖ The **fourth** piece of the armor is *the shield of faith* [**Ephesians 6:16**]. A Roman soldier's shield was a large, oblong piece of metal that covered the whole body. Our faith should be a force moving deep down in our spirits. It is not a mystery; it is a power beyond us.

A natural example would be the building of a skyscraper. If we wanted it to last, the footings must be dug deep in the ground to remain firm. Now if the footings were built on sand, the skyscraper would collapse.

It is the same with faith. If we build our faith on 'sand footings', the devil can easily knock us off our faith. We must have it rooted firmly in the Word of God where it remains firm and our whole bodies are completely covered.

Two faith footings, which cannot be moved, are found in [**Hebrews 11:6**]. The first is: knowing that there is a God and the second is: knowing that He is a rewarder of those who diligently seek Him.

❖ The **fifth** piece of the armor is *the helmet of salvation* [**Ephesians 6:17**]. A helmet refers to the protection for the head and brain. It implies the understanding and knowledge you get from reading the Bible so that your eyes are not blinded, your ears are not deafened, nor is your mind confused with attacks from the world, the flesh, or the devil. Watch out! The devil always tries to enter through the thought realm. If we don't control our thoughts, our thoughts will control us. We lead our thoughts by the Word of God.

❖ The **sixth** piece of the armor is what can be used for **both defense and offense**. It is *the sword of the spirit* [**Ephesians 6:17**], which is really the Word of God. Jesus showed us how to wield the sword of the spirit. He used the Word in doing battle with Satan when He was being tempted by him in the wilderness after a forty day fast. He deflected a potential blow by responding with, "It is written…" He proved victory is gained with the sword.

❖ The **final** piece is actually an action on our part. It is *praying always* [**Ephesians 6:18**]. This is how we keep in touch with our superiors. Through prayer the Holy Spirit guides us, gives us our orders and helps us to lay hold of spiritual resources.

2 Corinthians 6: 4, 7 But in all [things] approving ourselves as the ministers of God…by the armor of righteousness on the right hand and on the left,

Imagine it! The shield in your left hand guarding against the fiery darts and the sword in your right hand: speaking and praying the Word. Every piece in place, not worn or frayed but pristine in its care and in working order.

Would we be called 'O Valiant Warrior' as Gideon was?

Lesson 4
God Is Saying To Us: "Fear NOT!"

Luke 10:19 Behold I give unto you power to tread on serpents and scorpions, and over all the power of the enemy.

⇒GOD IS RAISING UP A FEARLESS GENERATION⇐

God is going to have a people today who are STRONG, COURAGEOUS and FEARLESS even in the midst of great opposition, trial and danger…during the fiercest onslaughts of the enemy, and even in the face of death. FEAR NOT. BE STRONG AND OF GOOD COURAGE are not simply words of encouragement; they are given as a COMMAND by God to His people. FEAR NOT!

- God told Abram: **Fear not**, Abram: I am thy shield, and they exceeding great reward. [**Genesis 15:1**]

- He told Isaac: **Fear not,** for I am with thee, and will bless thee, and multiply thy seed for my servant Abraham's sake. [**Genesis 26:24**]

- God said to Jacob: **Fear not** to go down into Egypt; for I will there make of thee a great nation. [**Genesis 46:3**]

- He told Moses: **Fear ye not**, stand still, and see the salvation of the Lord. [**Exodus 14:13**]

- God told Joshua: Have I not commanded thee? Be strong and of a good courage; **be not afraid,** neither be thou dismayed: for the LORD thy God, is with thee whithersoever thou goest. [**Joshua 1:9**]
- God told Jehoshaphat and the children of Israel as they went to fight their enemies: Ye shall not need to fight in this battle: set yourselves, stand ye still, and see the salvation of the LORD with you, O Judah and Jerusalem: **fear not**, nor be dismayed; tomorrow go out against them: for the LORD will be with you. [**2 Chronicles 20:17**]

- God said to Israel: **Fear not**: for I have redeemed thee, I have called thee by they name; thou art mine. When thou passest through the waters, I will be with thee; and through the rivers, they shall not overflow thee; when thou walkest through the fire, thou shalt not be burned; neither shall the flame kindle upon thee. For I am the LORD thy God, the Holy One of Israel… [**Isaiah 43:1-3**]

- He told Daniel, **Fear not**: peace be unto thee, be strong, yea, be strong. [**Daniel 10:19**]

Lesson 5
We Must P.U.S.H

Pray Until Something Happens

Paul told the Romans, "The God of peace will soon crush Satan under your feet."
[**Romans 16:20** (NIV)]

Whose feet was Paul referring to? THE CHURCH!

Through Christ we have been given the *dunamis* power of God, and it is OUR FEET God wants to use to tread on Satan. It is OUR FEET He is going to use to CRUSH Satan!

God wants us to GET SPIRITUALLY VIOLENT…PURSUE Satan and the evil spirits that are attacking us in our minds…and FIGHT against them until they are totally destroyed. He wants us to expose them, one by one, and put our feet on their necks.

As we go out onto the battlefield of our hearts and minds to destroy the spirit of fear,

I want everyone to see themselves as the captains of Joshua's army. By faith take the victory Christ has already won over Satan and his demon spirits.

We must put our feet where Christ's is…on the neck of every enemy...every fear in our lives.

As Commander in Chief over God's army, Christ's command to us as we go into battle is the same as Joshua's was to his soldiers – FEAR NOT!

~ Lesson 6 ~
Scriptures on Fighting the Enemy

The following are scriptures to used in fighting an enemy, be it the devil, a demon, etc.:

❖ **The Attitude of Battle – Humility and Obedience to God**

Proverbs 24:17 Do not rejoice when your enemy falls, and do not let your heart be glad when he stumbles; lest the Lord see it, and it displeases Him, and He turn away His wrath from him.

Proverbs 25:21 If your enemy is hungry, give him bread to eat; and if he is thirsty, give him water to drink; for so you will heap coals of fire on his head, and the Lord will reward you.

James 4:7 Therefore submit to God. Resist the devil and he will flee from you.

Leviticus 26:3 If you walk in My statutes and keep My commandments, and perform them … you shall eat your bread to the full, and dwell in your land safely. I will give you peace in the land, and you shall lie down, and none will make you afraid; I will rid the land of evil beasts, and the sword will not go through your land. You will chase your enemies, and they shall fall by the sword before you. Five of you shall chase a hundred, and a hundred of you shall put ten thousand to flight; your enemies shall fall by the sword before you.

Deuteronomy 23:14 For the Lord your God walks in the midst of your camp, to deliver you and give your enemies over to you; therefore your camp shall be holy, that He may see no unclean thing among you, and turn away from you.

❖ **God's Anointing for an Offensive Approach to Battle**

Luke 10:19 Behold, I give you the authority to trample on serpents and scorpions, and over all the power of the enemy, and nothing shall by any means hurt you.

Luke 9:1 Then He called His twelve disciples together and gave them power and authority over all demons, and to cure diseases.

Mark 6:7, 13 And He called the twelve to Him, and began to send them out two by two, and gave them power over unclean spirits … and they cast out many demons, and anointed with oil many who were sick, and healed them.

Matthew 10:1 And when He had called His twelve disciples to Him, He gave them power over unclean spirits, to cast them out, and to heal all kinds of sickness and all kinds of disease.

Matthew 10:6 But go rather to the lost sheep of the house of Israel. And as you go, preach, saying, "The kingdom of heaven is at hand. Heal the sick, cleanse the lepers, raise the dead, cast out demons. Freely you have received, freely give."

Isaiah 54:17 No weapon formed against you shall prosper, and every tongue which rises against you in judgment you shall condemn. This is the heritage of the servants of the Lord, and their righteousness is from me," says the Lord.

Psalm 44:5 Through You we will push down our enemies; through Your name we will trample those who rise up against us. For I will not trust in my bow, nor shall my sword save me. But You have saved us from our enemies, and have put to shame those who hated us. In God we boast all day long, and praise Your name forever.

2 Chronicles 16:9 For the eyes of the Lord run to and fro throughout the whole earth, to show Himself strong on behalf of those whose heart is loyal to Him.

Daniel 11:32 … but the people who know their God shall be strong, and carry out great exploits.

Zechariah 4:6 This is the word of the Lord to Zerubbabel: 'Not by might, nor by power, but by My Spirit,' says the Lord of Hosts.

Acts 1:8 But you shall receive power when the Holy Spirit has come upon you; and you shall be witnesses to Me in Jerusalem, and in all Judea and Samaria, and to the end of the earth.

1 Thessalonians 1:5 For our gospel did not come to you in word only, but also in power, and in the Holy Spirit…

1 Corinthians 4:20 For the kingdom of God is not in word but in power.

Romans 15:19 … in mighty signs and wonders, by the power of the Spirit of God …
2 Corinthians 12:12 Truly the signs of an apostle were accomplished among you with all perseverance, in signs and wonders and mighty deeds.

Hebrews 2:4 God also bearing witness both with signs and wonders, with various miracles, and gifts of the Holy Spirit…

Mark 16:20 And they went out and preached everywhere, the Lord working with them and confirming the Word through the accompanying signs. Amen.

Acts 4:33 And with great power the apostles gave witness to the resurrection of the Lord Jesus. And great grace was upon them all.

1 John 2:27 But the anointing which you have received from Him abides in you…

1 John 2:20 But you have an anointing from the Holy One, and you know all things…

Acts 2:43 Then fear came upon every soul, and many wonders and signs were done through the apostles.

Joshua 1:5 No man shall be able to stand before you all the days of your life; as I was with Moses, so I will be with you. I will not leave you nor forsake you. Be strong and of good courage…

Psalm 144:1 Blessed be the Lord my Rock, who trains my hands for war, and my fingers for battle – my loving kindness and my fortress, my high tower and my deliverer, my shield and the One in whom I take refuge, who subdues my people under me.

2 Samuel 22:29 For You are my lamp, O Lord; the Lord shall enlighten my darkness. For by You I can run against a troop; by my God I can leap over a wall. As for God, His way is perfect; the word of the Lord is proven; He is a shield to all who trust in Him.

Psalm 18:32 It is God who arms me with strength, and makes my way perfect. He makes my feet like the feet of deer, and sets me on high places. He teaches my hands to make war, so that my arms can bend a bow of bronze … I have pursued my enemies and overtaken them; neither did I turn back again till they were destroyed, I have wounded them, so that they were not able to rise; they have fallen under my feet. For You have armed me with strength for the battle; you have subdued under me those who rose up against me.

❖ **God's Strength, Boldness and Courage for Battle**

Philippians 4:13 I can do all things through Christ who strengthens me.

Psalm 28:7 The Lord is my strength and my shield…

Psalm 138:3 In the day when I called out, You answered me, and made me bold with strength in my soul.

Psalm 68:35 O God, You are more awesome than Your holy places. The God of Israel is He who gives strength and power to His people.

Isaiah 40:29 He gives power to the weak, and to those who have no might He increases strength.

Proverbs 3:26 For the Lord will be your confidence, and will keep your foot from being caught.

Job 17:9 Yet the righteous will hold to his way, and he who has clean hands will be stronger and stronger.

Hosea 11:10 They shall walk after the Lord. He will roar like a lion. When He roars, then His sons shall come trembling from the west…
Proverbs 24:10 If you faint in the day of adversity, your strength is small.

❖ **God's Protection During the Battle**

Job 1:10 Have you not made a hedge around him, around his household, and around all that he has on every side?

2 Samuel 22:2 The Lord is my rock, my fortress and my deliverer; the God of my strength, in Him I will trust, my shield and the horn of my salvation, my stronghold and my refuge, my Savior, You save me from violence.

Psalm 62:1 Truly my soul silently waits for God; from Him comes my salvation. He only is my rock and my salvation; He is my defense; I shall not be greatly moved.

2 Thessalonians 3:3 But the Lord is faithful, who will establish you and guard you from the evil one.

Psalm 34:19 Many are the afflictions of the righteous, but the Lord delivers him out of them all. He guards all of his bones; not one of them is broken.

2 Timothy 4:18 And the Lord will deliver me from every evil work and preserve me for His heavenly kingdom.

Psalm 18:2 The Lord is my rock and my fortress and my deliverer; my God, my strength, in whom I will trust; my shield and the horn of my salvation, my stronghold. I will call upon the Lord, who is worthy to be praised; so shall I be saved from my enemies.

Psalm 37:39 But the salvation of the righteous is from the Lord; He is their strength in time of trouble. And the Lord shall help them and deliver them; He shall deliver them from the wicked, and save them, because they trust in Him.

Psalm 121:1 I will lift up my eyes to the hills – from whence comes my help? My help come from the Lord, who made heaven and earth. He will not allow your foot to be moved; He who keeps you will not slumber. Behold, He who keeps Israel shall neither slumber nor sleep. The Lord is your keeper; the Lord is your shade at your right hand. The sun shall not strike you by day, nor the moon by night. The Lord shall preserve you from all evil; He shall preserve your soul. The Lord shall preserve your going out and your coming in from this time forth, and even forevermore.

Psalm 31:2 … Deliver me speedily; be my rock of refuge, a fortress of defense to save me. For You are my rock and my fortress; therefore, for Your name's sake, lead me and guide me. Pull me out of the net which they have secretly laid for me, for You are my strength. Into Your hand I commit my spirit; You have redeemed me, O Lord God of truth.

Psalm 31:19 Oh, how great is Your goodness, which You have laid up for those who fear You, which you have prepared for those who trust in You in the presence of the sons of men! You shall hide them in the secret place of Your presence from the plots of man; You shall keep them secretly in a pavilion from the strife of tongues.

Psalm 27:1 The Lord is my light and my salvation; whom shall I fear? The Lord is the strength of my life; of whom shall I be afraid? When the wicked came against me to eat up my flesh, my enemies and foes, they stumbled and fell. Though an army should encamp against me, my heart shall not fear; though war should rise against me, in this I will be confident.

Psalm 118:6 The Lord is on my side; I will not fear. What can man do to me? The Lord is for me among those who help me; therefore I shall see my desire on those who hate me. It is better to trust in the Lord than to put confidence in man. It is better to trust in the Lord than to put confidence in princes. All nations surrounded me, but in the name of the Lord I will destroy them.

Romans 8:31 If God is for us, who can be against us?

Psalm 46:1 God is our refuge and strength, a very present help in trouble. Therefore we will not fear, though the earth be removed, and though the mountains be carried into the midst of the sea … God is in the midst of her, she shall not be moved; God shall help her, just at the break of dawn.

Psalm 56:3, 11 Whenever I am afraid, I will trust in You. In God I will praise His word, in God I have put my trust; I will not fear. What can flesh do to me? … In God I have put my trust; I will not be afraid. What can man do to me?

Psalm 105:13 When they went from one nation to another, from one kingdom to another people, He permitted no one to do them wrong; Yes, He reproved kings for their sakes, saying "Do not touch my anointed ones, and do My prophets no harm.

Psalm 60:11 Give us help from trouble, for vain is the help of man. Through God we will do valiantly, for it is He who shall tread down our enemies.

Isaiah 50:7 For the Lord God will help me; therefore I will not be disgraced; therefore I have set my face like a flint, and I know that I will not be ashamed. He is near who justifies me; who will contend with me? Let us stand together. Who is my adversary? Let him come near me. Surely the Lord God will help me; who is he who will condemn me? Indeed they will all grow old like a garment; the moth will eat them up.

Psalm 125:1 Those who trust in the Lord are like Mount Zion, which cannot be moved, but abides forever. As the mountains surround Jerusalem, so the Lord surrounds His people from this time forth and forever.

Psalm 66:8 Oh, bless our God, you peoples! And make the voice of His praise to be heard, who keeps your soul among the living, and does not allow our feet to be moved.

Isaiah 46:4 Even to your old age, I am He, and even to gray hairs I will carry you! I have made, and I will bear; even I will carry, and will deliver you.

Psalm 91:1-16 He who dwells in the secret place of the Most High shall abide under the shadow of the Almighty. I will say of the Lord, "He is my refuge and my fortress; my God, in Him I will trust. Surely He shall deliver you from the snare of the fowler and from the perilous pestilence. He shall cover you with His feather, and under His wings you shall take refugee; His truth shall be your shield and buckler. You shall not be afraid of the terror by night, nor of the arrow that flies by day, nor of the pestilence that walks in darkness, nor of the destruction that lays waste at noonday.

A thousand may fall at your side, and ten thousand at your right hand; but it shall not come near you.

Only with your eyes shall you look, and see the reward of the wicked. Because you have made the Lord, who is my refuge, even the Most High, your habitation, no evil shall befall you, nor shall any plague come near your dwelling; for He shall give His angels charge over you, to keep you in all your ways. They shall bear you up in their hands, lest you dash your foot against a stone. You shall tread upon the lion and the cobra, the young lion and the serpent you shall trample. Because he has set his love upon Me, therefore I will deliver him; I will set him on high, because he has known My name. He shall call upon Me, and I will answer him; I will be with him in trouble; I will deliver him and honor him. With long life I will satisfy him, and show him My salvation.

> ❖ **God Is the One Who Fights the Battles**

Exodus 15:3, 6 The Lord is a Man of War; the Lord is His name … Your Right Hand, O Lord, has become glorious in power; Your right hand. O Lord, has dashed the enemy in pieces. And in the greatness of Your excellence you have overthrown those who rose against You; You sent forth Your wrath which consumed them like stubble.

Isaiah 42:13 The Lord shall go forth like a mighty Man; He shall stir up His zeal like a Man of War. He shall cry out, yes, shout aloud; He shall prevail against His enemies.

Isaiah 45:2 I will go before you and make the crooked paths straight; I will break in pieces the gates of bronze and cut the bars of iron.

Isaiah 52:12 For you shall not go out with haste, nor go by flight; for the Lord will go before you, and the God of Israel will be your rear guard.

Deuteronomy 9:3 Therefore understand today the Lord your God is He who goes before you as a consuming fire. He will destroy them and bring them down before you; so you shall drive them out and destroy them quickly, as the Lord has said to you.

Exodus 14:14 The Lord will fight for you, and you shall hold your peace.

2 Chronicles 32:7 Be strong and courageous; do not be afraid nor dismayed before the king of Assyria, nor before all the multitude that is with him; for there are more with us than with him. With him is an arm of flesh; but with us is the Lord our God, to help us and to fight our battles.

Isaiah 49:25 … For I will contend with him who contends with you.

2 Thessalonians 1:6 … since it is a righteous thing with God to repay with tribulation those who trouble you.

Deuteronomy 33:27 The eternal God is your refuge, and underneath are the everlasting arms; He will thrust out the enemy from before you, and will say, "Destroy!"

Proverbs 20:22 Do not say, "I will recompense evil," wait for the Lord, and He will save you."

Genesis 12:3 I will bless those who bless you, and I will curse those who curse you.

Psalm 129:2 Many a time they have afflicted me from my youth; yet they have not prevailed against me … The Lord is righteous; He has cut in pieces the cords of the wicked.

Psalm 18:47 It is God who avenges me, and subdues the peoples under me; He delivers me from my enemies. You also lift me up above those who rise against me; You have delivered me from the violent man.

Psalm 35:1 Plead my cause, O Lord, with those who strive with me; fight against those who fight against me. Take hold of shield and buckler, and stand up for my help. Also draw out the spear, and stop those who pursue me. Say to my soul, "I am your salvation."

Psalm 9:3 When my enemies turn back, they shall fall and perish at your presence. For You have maintained my right hand and my cause; You sat on the throne judging in righteousness.

Jeremiah 1:8 "Do not be afraid of their faces, for I am with you to deliver you," says the Lord.

Psalm 7:11 God is a just judge, and God is angry with the wicked every day. If He does not turn back, He will sharpen His sword; He bends His bow and makes it ready. He prepares for Himself instruments of death; He makes His arrows into fiery shafts.

1 Samuel 2:9 He will guard the feet of His saints, but the wicked shall be silent in darkness. For by strength no man shall prevail. The adversaries of the Lord shall be broken in pieces; from heaven He will thunder against them. The Lord will judge the ends of the earth. He will give strength to His king, and exalt the horn of His anointed.

2 Chronicles 20:12-17 … For we have no power against this great multitude that is coming against us; nor do we know what to do, but our eyes are upon You … Then the Spirit of the Lord came upon Jahaziel … thus says the Lord to you: 'Do not be afraid nor dismayed because of this great multitude, for the battle is not yours, but God's … You will not need to fight in this battle. Position yourselves, stand still and see the salvation of the Lord, who is with you, O Judah and Jerusalem!" Do not fear or be dismayed; tomorrow go out against them, for the Lord is with you."

Isaiah 41:11 Behold, all those who were incensed against you shall be ashamed and disgraced; they shall be as nothing, and those who strive with you shall perish. You shall seek them and not find them – those who contend with you. Those who war against you shall be as nothing, as a nonexistent thing. For I, the Lord your God, will hold your right hand, saying to you, "Fear not, I will help you."

Isaiah 59:19 When the enemy comes in like a flood, the Spirit of the Lord will lift up a standard against him.

Psalm 20:6 Now I know that the Lord saves His anointed; He will answer him from His holy heaven with the saving strength of His right hand.

Psalm 138:7 Though I walk in the midst of trouble, You will revive me; You will stretch out Your hand against the wrath of my enemies, and You right hand will save me. The Lord will perfect that which concerns me…

Isaiah 43:2 When you pass through the waters, I will be with you; and through the rivers, they shall not overflow you. When you walk through the fire, you shall not be burned, nor shall the flame scorch you.

Psalm 44:3 For they did not gain possession of the land by their own sword, nor did their arm save them; but it was Your right hand, Your arm, and the light of Your countenance, because You favored them.

Habakkuk 3:12 You marched through the land in indignation; You trampled the nations in anger. You went forth for the salvation of Your people, for salvation with Your anointed. You struck the head from the house of the wicked.

Psalm 34:17 The righteous cry out, and the Lord hears, and delivers them out of all their troubles.

Deuteronomy 3:21 And I commanded Joshua at that time, saying, "Your eyes have seen all that the Lord Your God has done to these two kings; so will the Lord do to all the kingdoms through which you pass. You must not fear them, for the Lord Your God Himself fights for you."

❖ **His Angels Battle for You**

Psalm 34:7 The angel of the Lord encamps all around those who fear Him, and delivers them.

Psalm 91:11 For He shall give His angels charge over you, to keep you in all your ways.

Psalm 35:5-8 And let the angel of the Lord chase him … And let the angel of the Lord pursue him … Let the destruction come upon him unexpectedly.

Exodus 23:20 Behold, I send an angel before you to keep you in the way and to bring you into the place which I have prepared.

Hebrews 1:14 Are they not all ministering spirits sent forth to minister for those who will inherit salvation?

1 Chronicles 21:27, 29 Then the Lord commanded the angel, and he returned his sword to its sheath … but David could not go before it to inquire of God, for he was afraid of the sword of the angel of the Lord.

2 Kings 19:35 And it came to pass on a certain night that the angel of the Lord went out, and killed in the camp of the Assyrians one hundred and eighty-five thousand; and when the people arose early in the morning, there were the corpses – all dead.

Acts 12:23 Then immediately an angel of the Lord struck him, because he did not give glory to God. And he was eaten by worms and died.

Hebrews 13:2 Do not forget to entertain strangers, for by doing so some have unwittingly entertained angels.

NOTES

Chapter 3
The Weapons of Our Warfare

Now that we are fitted with our armor we need weapons for warfare. We cannot go to war without a well-stocked arsenal. And what our General gives us are powerful and will insure our victory.

The first is the *Word of God*, the sword of the Spirit [**Ephesians 6:17**], or the Gospel of Christ for it is the power of God [**Romans 1:16, 17**]. To use this weapon we must have confidence in it. How do we gain that confidence? We have to read it DAILY. [**Jeremiah 23:29**] It is proven that we only retain only about 10% of what's read after 3-5 days [**Romans 10:17; Joshua 1:8; Psalm 1:1-3**].

The second is the *Name of Jesus*. His name is powerful [**1 Samuel 17:45**]. In fact if we can't think of anything else to do in danger, yell out the name of Jesus. Trust me, it will be effective.

Philippians 2:9, 10 Wherefore God also hath highly exalted him, and given him a name which is above every name: that at the name of Jesus every knee should bow, of [things] in heaven, and [things] in earth, and [things] under the earth;
Colossians 3:17 And whatsoever ye do in word or deed, [do] all in the name of the Lord Jesus, giving thanks to God the Father by Him.

The third is the *blood of Jesus*. It is His blood that covers our sins before the eyes of God. We can cover every room in our homes with the blood by saying, "I plead (request) the blood…"

Revelation 12:11 And they overcame him by the blood of the Lamb, and by the word of their testimony; and they loved not their lives unto death.

The **fourth** is *relying on the presence of the Holy Spirit*. When we rely on Him, He is there to help and to guide us [**John 16:13; 1 John 4:4**]. This means we must admit our weakness and stop relying on our own abilities. We cannot overcome the spiritual with the natural. Therefore, we lose if we don't have the Holy Spirit's assistance.

To remain sensitive to the Holy Spirit we must live a life of fasting, meditate in the Word, walk in love, pray in tongues regularly, and obey instantly the voice of our spirit.

The **fifth** is *prayer*. Prayer is a force to be used, a tool to be utilized – a MIGHTY WEAPON.

Praying in the Spirit and asking God for the right words in our mouth will help us to speak boldly for Christ and lead us into triumph through Christ.

2 Corinthians 2:14 Now thanks [be] to God, who always leads us in triumph (victory) in Christ,…

James 5:17 Elias was a man subject to like passions as we are, and he prayed earnestly that it might not rain: and it rained not on the earth by the space of three years and six months.

2 Corinthians 10:4, 5 For the weapons of our warfare [are] not carnal, but mighty through God to the pulling down of strong holds; Casting down imaginations, and every high thing that exalteth itself against the knowledge of God, and bringing into captivity every thought to the obedience of Christ.

We are to speak boldly for Christ.
Acts 4:29-31 And now, Lord, behold their threatenings: and grant unto thy servants, that with all boldness they may speak thy word, by stretching forth thine hand to heal; and that signs and wonders may be done by the name of thy holy child Jesus. And when they had prayed, the place was shaken where they were assembled together; and they were all filled with the Holy Ghost, and they spake the word of God with boldness.

Praying in the Spirit and asking God for the right words in our mouth will lead us into triumph through Christ.
Romans 8:26, 27 Likewise the Spirit also helpeth our infirmities: for we know not what we should pray for as we ought: but the Spirit itself maketh intercession for us with groanings which cannot be uttered. And he that searcheth the hearts knoweth what is the mind of the Spirit, because he maketh intercession for the saints according to the will of God.

? What are the strongholds?
Strongholds are basically **thought patterns** that over a period of time have become so engraved in your soul (your mind) that they become part of you. They are like molten iron poured in a cast, which solidifies to form a permanent shape. In the same way, your thought patterns determine who you really become.

Proverbs 23:7 For as he thinks in his heart, so is he…
This thought becomes so established in you that it **has the power to resist any thing that is contrary** to it, and it seeks more and more to **fortify** itself against any form of attack.

>*If you confess the negative, you will possess it.*<

>Arguments in our minds are put there by the devil.<

>Every high thing that exalts itself against the knowledge of God is unbelief.<

~ Lesson 1~
Praying in Jesus Name
A Powerful Weapon

All Authority that was given to Jesus IS given to US
Matthew 28:18

Matthew 28:18 (KJV) And Jesus came and spake unto them, saying, All power is given unto me in heaven and in earth.

God the Father gave all authority to Jesus and then He sat down on His throne. Like wise Jesus gave the Church (us) all power and authority [**Ephesians 1:19-21**] and He sat down at the right hand of God. Now we have the authority on earth through the name of Jesus. The more we understand this authority the stronger our faith becomes and the more effective our weapon becomes.

John 14:12-14 (KJV) Verily, verily, I say unto you, He that believeth on me, the works that I do shall he do also; and greater works than these shall he do; because I go unto my Father. And whatsoever ye shall ask in my name, that will I do, that the Father may be glorified in the Son. If ye shall ask any thing in my name, I will do it.

His **name carries the authority** because authority was given to Him. And we've been given His name and pray *in Jesus' name* because His name is above every name.

>> Correct Praying >>

We do **NOT** pray to Jesus but we pray to the Father in Jesus' name [**John 16:23**]. Essentially we are to walk by the Spirit and when the Spirit leads us, we can speak with the same authority Jesus did.

Satan and his demon spirits know whether or not we have the authority and power over them and they react accordingly. They either flee at our command or they will ignore us. The seven sons of Sceva did not have the authority to cast out demons [**Acts 19:13-15**]. We are given authority to the degree we are under authority. Basically, the more we submit to the Lordship of Jesus, the more power and authority we have. When we do this and use His name in prayer, this is the authority Satan bows to.

>>Rebelling against God's authority<<

Satan was cast out of heaven because he rebelled against God's authority. We too can rebel against God's authority by going our own way instead of doing His will. When this happens we are not under authority; therefore, we have no authority. Jesus had authority because He did the will of the Father. The seven sons of Sceva used the name of Jesus but they had no power or authority because they were not under the Lordship of Jesus.

>>Faith works where God directs it<<

Jesus did what the Father showed Him to do. In [**Acts 10:38**] we find Peter is at Caesarea and he is talking to Cornelius and his household. He is telling them that Jesus was anointed with the Holy Spirit and then healed all who were oppressed by the devil. And we have this same anointing when we speak the will of God in Jesus' name, God will make it happen,

The lame man in [**Acts 3:1-8**] had been at the temple when Jesus was still here on earth. In fact Jesus walked by him every day when He went into the temple; however, Jesus never healed him. Why not? Jesus didn't heal him because the Holy Spirit never directed Him to do so.

When the words written in the Bible become real to us and we know inside without a doubt the words are true, God makes things happen.[**Hebrews 11**] is full of the accounts of people who believed the word in this way. By reading the word, we determine the will of God. By prayer, the written word becomes real to us. Doing this we will walk in His authority to accomplish God's will on the earth, and our joy will full when our prayers are answered.

~ Lesson 2 ~
The Authority Abiding in Us

Everyone wants to walk in power and authority by healing the sick, casting out devils, doing the works of Jesus, dominating the circumstances of life, and ruling and reigning with Christ in the here and now. There is only one way in which this can happen. WE HAVE TO DIE! The new birth (being saved) is death to the old man [**Romans 6:1-19; 2 Corinthians 5:17; Colossians 3:3**]

In other words we are now dead to sin and alive to God. He has raised us up together and made us sit together in heavenly places in Christ [**Ephesians 2:6**]. So…does hell know who we are? If they do, do we know who we are?

Dead Men Walking

1 Peter 4:1, 2	When Christ died…	We died.
Galatians 2:20	When Christ was raised from the dead…	We were raised from the dead.
1 Peter 3:18, 19	When Christ went to Hell and suffered…	We went to Hell and suffered.

Christ died a substitutionary death. He took our place. Because of this we can identify with Christ because **WE ARE IN HIM!**

The reason the wicked one cannot touch us is because he can't find us. Our lives are hidden with Christ in God [**Psalm 91, Proverbs 18:10**]. If we desire to exercise God's authority here on the earth as Jesus did, then we must lay down our lower life and take up His higher life. [**1 Corinthians 9:24-27; 1 Peter 2:21-24**]

To have **authority means to have power**, to take charge or to take dominion. From the very beginning God who has ALL authority gave man dominion and authority [**Genesis 1:26-28; Psalm 8:4-8**]. However Adam allowed Satan to deceive him in the Garden. As a result of Adam's sin, man failed to walk in authority and lost the image of Christ.

Great news! Jesus regained man's authority by dying on a cross and getting the keys to the kingdom [**Matthew 16:19; 18:18, 19**]. He exercised this kind of authority here on earth and showed us how to operate in this authority [**Luke 8:22-25; Hebrews 2:16, 17; Philippians 2:5-8**]. Now we can unlock heaven's treasures and those who are bound. We can also lock out Satan's activities in our lives. Our authority has to be exercised [**Matthew 28:18-20**]. And the only thing keeping us from having authority is allowing Satan to deceive us.

> **SIX AREAS** we have authority over are:
> ➢ Sin [**Romans 6:14**]
> ➢ Sickness [**1 Peter 2:24**]
> ➢ Thought life [**2 Corinthians 10:5**]
> ➢ Fear [**2 Timothy 1:7**]
> ➢ Confusion [**1 Corinthians 14:33**]
> ➢ The enemy [**Luke 10:19**]

Authority begins with submission. To be effectual, we need to be submitted to God's word and His will [**James 4:7, 10**]. In **Luke 7:2-9**] the Roman centurion understood how authority operated. God who has ALL authority delegated authority to us. When we speak with His authority, we speak for Him. Who should we be submitted to?

♦ We should be submitted to one another [**Ephesians 5:21**].
♦ We should be submitted to those in authority over us [**Hebrews 13:7**].
♦ When children, we should be submitted to our parents [**Ephesians 6:1**].
♦ We should be submitted to human institutions and authority [**1 Peter 2:13**].
♦ We should be submitted to elders [**1 Peter 5:5**].
♦ We should not be conformed to this world [**Romans 12:1, 2**]
♦ Wives should be submitted to husbands [**Ephesians 5:22**].
♦ We should buffet ourselves [**1 Corinthians 9:27**].

Great authority can only be given to those who have an understanding of submission and a servant's heart. Jesus, the Word, knew servant hood and gave us the example by taking on the form of a bondservant [**Philippians 2:7; Luke 22:24-27; John 13:4-17; Matthew 20:25-28**].

In the Greek the right to act is *exousia* and the ability or the power is *dunamis*. We are to be strong in this delegated authority given to us by the Word.

When Satan sees us using our authority, he must flee [**James 4:7**].

We exercise this authority by using Jesus' name [**Philippians 2:9**], the Word of God [**Luke 4:32; Matthew 8:5, 8; John 15:7; Ephesians 6:17; Hebrews 4:12**], and His blood [**Matthew 26:28; 1 Peter 1:19; Hebrews 10:19; Psalm 91:5-7**].

The devil is scared of the authority given to us and that is why he will try to keep us from learning the truth about our authority in Christ. When we discover our authority as believers, Satan is defeated and overcome.

Imagine if every believer understood their authority and stood together in unity! There is a spiritual power in unity that we need to understand. At the Tower of Babel [**Genesis 11: 1-9**], the people tapped into the power of unity. However, they were operating under their own will and not in submission to the Lord so this power could have been very destructive. This is why God intervened and shattered their ability to come into one voice.

Amazing! If people not submitted to God could wield such power, what would happen if there were those submitted to God? I am speaking of the power of unity that is available to the church that walks as Jesus spoke about in [**John 17**] – in a oneness that mirrors that of the Father and the Son.

[**Acts 2:1-6**] shows God's divine redemption and restoration of the true unity that had been defiled by human will at Babel. One hundred twenty believers were gathered in the upper room to wait upon Him. Unlike the people at the Tower of Babel, they were not trying by their own strength to reach their own goals. They were simply submitted to the Lord and waiting for the promise of the Holy Spirit.

As they did, they experienced a supernatural visitation where the Holy Spirit filled them. As they spoke only what the Spirit gave them to speak, the Lord supernaturally enabled all the people around them to hear the same message – God being praised – each in their own language. For the first time since Babel, the power of true unity was realized and the result was a harvest of three thousand souls and an explosion of the church in a single day.

In many ways the church is still functioning in an Old Testament model when it comes to authority. In the Old Testament, God would anoint an individual – a prophet, a priest, or a king – who would be given the authority by the Lord to lead. However in Acts we see the Spirit of God rested not on just one man but on a corporate body of one hundred twenty.

As we move more into a model of the kingdom, we should expect to see a body of believers, carrying the same spirit, passion and heart that will rise in unity to walk together. It is my personal belief that the early church walked in a revelation of this corporate anointing.

Over time as religious rules replaced relationship with God and one another, the church entered a period where many truths the Lord had poured in at its inception were lost, including the principle of corporate unity that releases authority.

Although the church has the potential to exercise an authority to address powers and principalities at city, region, or nation-wide levels, we have not yet seen this authority demonstrated. This is because no one individual, ministry, or denomination no matter how anointed they are, or how much revelation they have, can exercise this level of authority alone. It is a corporate authority that is required that can only be released through true unity.

The key to corporate unity is corporate death, humility, and brokenness that bring us into a place of submission to the Lord and to one another. We need to come to the place of being willing to die even to the gifts and visions the Lord has given us. It's **not** about laying down our giftings and **not** using them, but it's about **dying** to our **right** to use them to build our own vision or ministry. It's not about canceling what we do but it's about allowing the Holy Spirit to channel it for the corporate when and how He sees fit.

If a remnant of believers will humble themselves to walk in true unity they can operate in a spiritual authority far more powerful than any amassing of human strengths.

By 'laying down our crowns' at the feet of the Lord Jesus, we submit ourselves as a corporate body to seek the Lord together, refusing to move until He speaks. And once we have heard Him and come into agreement of a clear witness (it seems right to us and the Holy Spirit) as to His direction and timings, then will we begin to move with the authority of heaven and to address principalities and powers over our cities, regions, and nations.

~ Lesson 3 ~
The Holy Spirit vs. The Spirit of Christ
Question: Who is the Holy Spirit? **Answer:** He is as much God as the Father is.

For there are three who bear record in Heaven: the Father, the Word and the Holy Ghost and these are the three in one. [**I John 5**]

In **Genesis 1** we see the Holy Spirit moving on the face of the earth to prepare it for the restoration. It was by the power of the Holy Spirit that the Father raised Christ from the dead.

In every man who is born again, we have three spirits in us.

The first is the ***reborn spirit***, which must feed on the word daily to grow strong. If we don't draw near to God and rebuke the devil and resist the social life of the world then we can lose our relationship with God. God sent us a Helper to teach us what we should do. Remember Jesus' word before he ascended on high, **"**behold I send the promise of my Father upon you, But tarry ye in the city of Jerusalem until ye be endowed from power from on high." [**Luke 24:49**] We know we are to seek the Holy Spirit and allow Him to fill us completely.

Here are some of things He does.

- He brings all things all things to remembrance.
- He gives gifts to men.
- He reveals truth to us.
- He gives us the ability to accept and confess Christ as Lord.
- He creates a new mind in us.
- He transforms us into the image of the second Adam.

The Holy Spirit is very gentle and can be grieved.

He can give us understanding. It seems that the Holy Spirit is the person of the trinity who sends messengers to man, like He did to Gabriel and who He sent to Daniel, the mother of Sampson, Elizabeth, and Mary.

Remember the Holy Spirit will come to you and fill you completely.

What does the Spirit of Christ do for us?
It gives us the authority to overcome the enemy of your soul like Jesus had.

The spirit of Christ gives you the ability to stand. "It is NO longer I that lives but Christ that lives in me. I live this life by Christ who strengthens me." [**Galatians 2:20**]

The spirit of Christ that is within us gives us the **strength to stand** against the enemy and his allies.

The Holy Spirit renews our mind daily through the word of God so we can obtain wisdom, understanding, and knowledge.

NOTES

Chapter 4
Activate the Kingdom of God Within Us

~ Lesson 1 ~
Christ's Identity in Me

[1 Peter 2:9] But you are a chosen people, a royal priesthood, a holy nation, and God's special possession, that you may declare the praises of him who called you out of darkness into his wonderful light.

You are God's masterpiece, His tapestry.
[Ephesians 2:10]
You are one who He desires to trust in and use to bring change.

God Dwells in Us

All these things that God has done for our lives are too wonderful for us! The good news is that we do not have to rely upon ourselves to accomplish all of these great things in God for it is Christ in us that will do the work. God works in us, lives in us, speaks through us and acts through our lives. [Matthew 10:20]

We can say that He sees through our eyes and hears through our ears. We may be insensitive to the living presence of God in us, but if we are willing to yield ourselves completely over to the instruction of the Holy Spirit we will become aware of all that God would do in and through our members. We have been given the mind of Christ and the Spirit of the Son.

The foundation of the faith is that Christ dwells in us. [Ephesians 3:17] He is the greater One, Jesus, who along with the Father have made their dwelling in us by the Holy Spirit, who was given to us by the Father. He is both with us and in us. And we are to walk in Him, live in Him and conduct ourselves by His desires. We are joined to the Lord and are one Spirit with Him. We are called the temple of the Holy Ghost. We have received the same glory that the Father gave to Jesus. We are made one with Him just as He is One with the Father: Jesus is in us and the Father in Jesus so that we can be perfect in this oneness.

Walking in the New Covenant to Represent Him

One of the absolutes of the New Covenant is that we are to be those that represent God and stand in the place of Jesus. In order to fully represent Jesus, we have been given the power and authority that we need; Christ in us our confidence of glory. It was by the Holy Ghost that Jesus was incarnated into the womb of Mary and it is by the same Spirit of the Lord that we have been born again.

Jesus was baptized in the Holy Spirit to preach the gospel of the kingdom and so we too have been baptized with the same Spirit to preach this gospel of the dear Son. We are both commissioned and empowered to represent the kingdom. We are not of this world and are just like Him because we have been translated into His kingdom and baptized in His power.

The closer we draw to Him we discover our true identity.

God created human beings to have unique characteristics and purposes. The more closely we are drawn to Him, the more we discover our true identity and the more we allow God to weave us into a beautiful tapestry of His image and His ways.

Activate the Kingdom of God Within You
YOU are the Lion of Judah

Proverbs 19:21 Many are the plans in a person's heart, but it is the Lord's purpose that prevails.

Use these Bible verses to understand more about our identity in Christ, and how to not lose sight of who we are destined to be.

Jeremiah 29:11 (NIV) "For I know the plans I have for you," declares the LORD, "plans to prosper you and not to harm you, plans to give you hope and a future.

John 1:12 Yet to all who did receive him, to those who believed in his name, he gave the right to become children of God

Ephesians 1:5 he predestined us for adoption to sonship through Jesus Christ, in accordance with his pleasure and will

Romans 8:29-30 For those God foreknew he also predestined to be conformed to the image of his Son, that he might be the firstborn among many brothers and sisters. And those he predestined, he also called; those he called, he also justified; those he justified, he also glorified.

Colossians 2:9-10 For in Christ all the fullness of the Deity lives in bodily form, and in Christ you have been brought to fullness. He is the head over every power and authority.

1 Corinthians 6:17 But whoever is united with the Lord is one with him in spirit.

Jeremiah 1:5 Before I formed you in the womb I knew you, before you were born I set you apart; I appointed you as a prophet to the nations.

1 Corinthians 12:27 Now you are the body of Christ, and each one of you is a part of it.

Galatians 3:27-28 for all of you who were baptized into Christ have clothed yourselves with Christ. There is neither Jew nor Gentile, neither slave nor free, nor is there male and female, for you are all one in Christ Jesus.

1 Corinthians 6:19-20 Do you not know that your bodies are temples of the Holy Spirit, who is in you, whom you have received from God? You are not your own; you were bought at a price. Therefore honor God with your bodies.

1 John 3:1-2 See what great love the Father has lavished on us, that we should be called children of God! And that is what we are! The reason the world does not know us is that it did not know him. Dear friends, now we are children of God, and what we will be has not yet been made known. But we know that when Christ appears, we shall be like him, for we shall see him as he is.

Colossians 3:1-3 Since, then, you have been raised with Christ, set your hearts on things above, where Christ is, seated at the right hand of God. Set your minds on things above, not on earthly things. For you died, and your life is now hidden with Christ in God

~ Lesson 2 ~
Who I Am in God

Speak His Word out of your mouth. Sow His Word in your heart and build it into your walk.

Our hearts may fail us due to doubt, fear, unbelief, faintheartedness etc.
By proclaiming God's word out loud, it will remove the obstacles out of the way and be aligned with God's word which will NOT come back void. [Isaiah 55:11]

Please Note: Your brain knows your voice.

➢ I am born of God [**1 John 5:1**]. I am OF God [**1John 4:6**]. I am a spirit being – born of God!

➢ I am a spirit. I have a soul, and I live in a body, but I am first a spirit being – BORN OF GOD. [**1 Thessalonians 5:23**]

➢ I am a new creature in Christ, old things have passed away, behold all things have become new. [**2 Corinthians 5:17**]

➢ I have a new nature. It's the nature of God. It's the nature of love, for love is of God. [**1 John 4:7**]

➢ I have a nature of faith, because faith works by love, and the love of God has be SHED ABROAD in my heart by the Holy Ghost, who has been given to me. [**Romans 5:5**]

➢ I have been given the privilege of becoming a child of God. I am God's very own child and God is my very own Father. [**John 1:12; Romans 8:15**]

➢ Because I am His child, I am an heir of God and a joint heir with Jesus Christ. [**Romans 8:17**]

➢ Because I am in Christ Jesus – right now – there is no spirit of condemnation in me. [**Romans 8:1**]

➢ I have faith in God. I believe in Him, and I am in Him. I believe He is able and faithful.

➢ I am justified by FAITH; therefore, I have peace with God. [**Romans 5:17**]

➢ I am in Christ and He has made unto me wisdom, righteousness, sanctification, and redemption. Therefore, I am righteous in Christ Jesus and I have His wisdom. I am sanctified and redeemed by His blood. [**1 Corinthians 1:30**]

➢ I have the wisdom of God. I fear Him and His wisdom has been given to me.

➢ I have received an abundance of grace and the gift of righteousness and I reign in this life through Jesus Christ. [**Romans 5:17**] I receive and reign through Jesus Christ.

➢ I have been delivered from the power and the dominion of darkness (Satan) and I have been translated into the kingdom of God's dear Son. [**Colossians 1:13**]

➤ I have been crucified with Christ and I have been raised up together with Him and made to sit down together in heavenly places in Christ Jesus, far above all principalities, powers, might, and dominion. [**Ephesians 2:5, 6; 1:21**]

➤ I am presented to God as holy, without blame and reproof in His sight. Right now He freely accepts me through His grace. [**Colossians 1:22; Ephesians 1:6; 2:8**]

➤ I am blessed with all spiritual blessings in heavenly places in Christ, and I stand holy and without blame before Him in love. [**Ephesians 1:3, 4**]

~ Lesson 3 ~
Pursue, Smite, and Consume

Joshua 10:19-20 And stay ye not, but pursue after your enemies, and smite the hindmost of them; *suffer* them not to enter into their cities: for the Lord your God hath delivered them into your hand. And it came to pass, when Joshua and the children of Israel had made an end of slaying them with a very great slaughter, till they were consumed, that the rest which remained of them entered into fenced cities.

⟹The calling of leadership is to meet the enemy with the word of God, binding the strongmen so that the enemy army flees in confusion. The army of God then joins in the chase and must not stop until the enemy is utterly destroyed.

❖ Gideon and 300 leaders split the ranks and caused the enemy to turn and run. Then all the people joined in the pursuit.

Judges 7:22-23 And the three hundred blew the trumpets, and the LORD set every man's sword against his fellow, even throughout the host: and the host fled to Bethshittah in Zererath, and to the border of Abelmeholah, unto Tabbath. And the man of Israel gathered themselves together out of Naphtali and out of Asher, and out of Manasseh, and pursued after the Midianites.
James 4:7 Submit yourselves therefore to God. Resist the devil, and he will flee from you.

⟹We must not stop short of total destruction and spoiling (or wasting of) the enemy.

1 John 3:8 He that committeth sin is of the devil; for the devil sinneth from the beginning. For this purpose the Son of God was manifested, that he might destroy the works of the devil.

❖ King Saul lost his place of rulership because he rationalized instead of obeying God.

1 Samuel 15:9-11 But Saul and the people spared Agog, and the best of the sheep, and the lambs, and all that was good, and would not utterly destroy them: but everything that was vile and refuse, that they destroyed utterly. Then came the word of the LORD unto Samuel, saying, It repenteth me that I have set up Saul to be king: for he is turned back from following me, and hath not performed my commandments. And it grieved Samuel; and he cried unto the Lord all night.

❖ Elisha rebuked Joash, king of Israel because he stopped short.

2 Kings 13:18-19 And he said, Take the arrows. And he took them. And he said unto the king of Israel, Smite upon the ground. And he smote thrice, and stayed. And the man of God was wroth with him, and said, Thou shouldest have smitten five or six times; then hadst thou smitten Syria till thou hadst consumed it: whereas now thou shalt smite Syria but thrice.

⟹After a stone from David's slingshot (a lively stone) bound the strongman, Goliath, the men of Israel and Judah arose, shouted and pursued to the gates of ***Ekron***.

1 Samuel 17:50-52 So David prevailed over the Philistine with a sling and with a stone, and smote the Philistine, and slew him; but there was no sword in the hand of David. Therefore David ran, and stood upon the Philistine, and took his sword, and drew it out of the sheath thereof, and slew him, and cut off

his head therewith. And when the Philistines saw their champion was dead, they fled. And the men of Israel and of Judah arose, and shouted, and pursued the Philistines, until thou some to the valley, and to the gates of Ekron. And the
wounded of the Philistines fell down by the way to Shaaraim, even unto Gath, and unto Ekron.

Definition: *Ekron* (Hebrew) – '*Eqrown* (ek-rone'); from *'aqar*; eradication; Ekron, a place in Palestine – *'aqar* (aw-kar'); a primitive root; to pluck up (especially by the roots); specifically, to hamstring; figuratively, to exterminate: dig down hough, pluck up, root up.

❖ Israel and Judah are the mighty weapons of pursuit.

Definition: *Israel – Yisra'el* (yis-raw-ale'); from *sarah*; he will rule as God; Jisrael, a symbolical name of Jacob; also (typically) of his posterity.
– *sarah* (saw-raw'); a primitive root; to prevail; have power (as a prince).

Definition: *Judah – yadah* (yaw-dau~); a primitive root; literally, to use (ie. hold out) the hand; physically, to throw (a stone, an arrow) at or away; especially to revere or worship (with extended hands); intensively, to bemoan (by wringing the hands): cast (out), (make) confess (-ion), praise, shoot, (give) thank (-ful, -s, -sgiving).

❖ The authority of God's word gives princely power to the church, in agreement with the Spirit revealed will of God, to rule as God on earth

Matthew 18:20 For where two or three are gathered together in my name, there am I in the midst of them.

❖ "In my name" means under the authority of the new covenant.

❖ To "throw a stone" or "shoot an arrow" is to release God's word toward the enemy. To stand with hands extended in worship toward God is a sign of total release to the Almighty sovereign God.

Psalms 18:13-14 The Lord also thundered in the heavens, and the Highest gave his voice; hail stones and coals of fire. Yea, he sent out his arrows, and scattered them; and he shot out lightnings, and discomfited them.

Zechariah 9:14-15 And the Lord shall be seen over them, and his arrow shall go forth as the lightning; and the Lord GOD shall blow the trumpet, and shall go with whirlwinds of the south. The Lord of hosts shall defend them; and they shall devour, and subdue with sling stones; and they shall drink, and make a noise as through wine; and they shall be filled like bowls, and as the comers of the altar.

⟹Our goal is rest in Christ Jesus -- the knowledge that the weapons have been launched and that the direction and destructive power is in total control of the Spirit of God.

❖ The positions of meekness and rest are different expressions of the same thing.

Hebrews 4:1 Let us therefore fear, lest a promise being left us of entering into his rest, any of you should seem to come short of it.

Psalms 149:4-9 For the Lord taketh pleasure in his people: he will beautify the meek with salvation. Let the saints be joyful in glory: let them sing aloud upon their beds. Let the high praises of God be in their mouth, and a two edged sword in their hand; To execute vengeance upon the heathen, and punishments upon the people; To bind their kings with chains, and their nobles with fetters of iron; To execute upon them the judgment written: this honor have all his saints. Praise ye the Lord.

~ Lesson 4 ~
The Triumphant Walk

Joshua 10:24 And it came to pass, when they brought out those kings unto Joshua, that Joshua called for all the men of Israel, and said unto the captains of the men of war which went with him, Come near, put your feet upon the necks of these kings. And they came near, and put their feet upon the necks of them.

⟹Although with God there is no respecting of persons, he does allow leaders to experience things of authority first.

1 Corinthians 12:28 And God hath set some in the church, first apostles, secondarily prophets, thirdly teachers, after that miracles, then gifts of healings, helps, governments, diversities of tongues.

❖ Captains of the men of war are those who lead in spiritual warfare.

❖ If a church is going to have victory, the leaders must first come near for the revelation of dominion over the enemy.

James 4:8 Draw nigh to God, and he will draw nigh to you. Cleanse your hands, ye sinners; and purify your hearts, ye double minded.

❖ A public display of triumph over Satan and demons is to be seen by the enemy army and also by the army of God.

Colossians 2:15 And having spoiled principalities and powers, he made a shew of them openly, triumphing over them in it.

❖ God magnifies his leaders through signs and wonders.

Definition: *Magnify* – *megaluno* (meg-al-oo'-no); to make (or declare) great, ie. increase or (figuratively) extol: enlarge, magnify, shew great.

❖ It is not the magnification of the person but Christ being enlarged in a flesh and blood body.

Philippians 1:20 According to my earnest expectation and my hope, that in nothing I shall be ashamed, but that with all boldness, as always, so now also Christ shall be magnified in my body, whether it be by life, or by death.

Joshua 3:7 And the LORD said unto Joshua, This day will I begin to magnify thee in the sight of all Israel, that they may know that, as I was with Moses, so I will be with thee.

Acts 5:12-13 And by the hands of the apostles were many signs and wonders wrought among the people; (and they were all with one accord in Solomon's porch). And of the rest durst no man join himself to them: but the people magnified them.

2 Corinthians 12:12 Truly the signs of an apostle were wrought among you in all patience, in signs, and wonders, and mighty deeds.

Numbers 17:8 And it came to pass, that on the morrow Moses went into the tabernacle of the witness; and, behold, the rod of Aaron for the house of Levi was budded, and brought forth buds, and bloomed blossoms, and yielded almonds.

2 Corinthians 2:14 Now thanks be unto God, which always causeth us to triumph in Christ, and maketh manifest the savour of his knowledge by us in every place.

- ❖ **Leaders demonstrate the power so others can follow with faith in the power of God.**

1 Corinthians 2:4-5 And my speech and my preaching was not with enticing words of man's wisdom, but in demonstration of the Spirit and of power; That your faith should not stand in the wisdom of men, but in the power of God.

⇒The seventy are sent out.

- ❖ The gospel of the kingdom includes the healing of the sick and the demonstration of authority over devils.

Luke 10:9 And heal the sick that are therein, and say unto them, The kingdom of God is come nigh unto you.

- ❖ The Father chose to make Jesus "famous" in this manner.

Matthew 4:23-24 And Jesus went about all Galilee, teaching in their synagogues, and preaching the gospel of the kingdom, and healing all manner of sickness and all manner of disease among people. And his fame went throughout all Syria: and they brought unto him all sick people that were taken with divers diseases and torments, and those which were possessed with devils, and those which were lunatick, and those that had the palsy; and he healed them.

- ❖ When Jesus is being manifested through us, it is not a "heavy trip" but a joyful experience.

Luke 10:17 And the seventy returned again with joy, saying, Lord, even the devils are subject unto us through thy name.

- ❖ Jesus is saying, "See, I have told you that Satan no longer reigns over you."

Luke 10:18 And he said unto them, I beheld Satan as lightning fall from heaven.

- ❖ This is called "the power to walk over devils" ministry

Luke 10:19 Behold, I give unto you power to tread on serpents and scorpions, and over all the power of the enemy; and nothing shall by any means hurt you.
Joshua 1:3 Every place that the sole of your foot shall tread upon, that have I given unto you, as I said unto Moses.

- ❖ Jesus indicates that anyone whose name is written in heaven has this authority.

Luke 10:20 Not withstanding in this rejoice not, that the spirits are subject unto you; but rather rejoice, because your names are written in heaven.

- ❖ Jesus gives a visual demonstration of "treading".

Luke 10:21 In that hour Jesus rejoiced in spirit, and said, I thank thee, O Father, Lord of heaven and earth, that thou hast hid these things from the wise and prudent, and has revealed them unto babes: even so, Father, for so it seemed good in thy sight.

Definition: *Rejoiced – agalliao* (ag-al-lee-ah'-o); from *agan* (much) and 242; properly, to jump for joy, ie. exult; be (exceeding) glad, with exceeding joy, rejoice (greatly).

❖ Treading the winepress, shouting and rejoicing:

Jeremiah 48:33 And joy and gladness is taken from the plentiful field, and from the land of Moab; and I have caused wine to fail from the winepresses; none shall tread with shouting; their shouting shall be no shouting.

⇒All things are under the feet of the Captain of our salvation.

Hebrews 2:8-10 Thou hast put all things in subjection under his feet. For in that he put all in subjection under him, he left nothing that is not put under him. But now we see not yet all things put under him. But we see Jesus, who was made a little lower than the angels for the suffering of death, crowned with glory and honour; that he by the grace of God should taste death for every man. For it became him, for whom are all things, and by whom are all things, in bringing many sons unto glory, to make the captain of their salvation perfect through sufferings.

❖ What has happened to the body spiritually has not been fully manifested in the natural, yet it is possible through faith.

Ephesians 1:20-23 Which he wrought in Christ, when he raised him from the dead, and set him at his own right hand in the heavenly places. Far above all principality, and power, and might, and dominion, and every name that is named, not only in this world, but also in that which is to come: And hath put all things under his feet, and gave him to be the head over all things to the church, which is his body, the fullness of him that filleth all in all.

❖ The last enemy to be put under his feet is natural and spiritual death.

1 Corinthians 15:25-26 For he must reign, till he hath put all enemies under his feet. The last enemy that shall be destroyed is death.

❖ Satan has no power of death over the believer.

1 Corinthians 15:55-57 O death, where is thy sting? O grave, where is thy victory? The sting of death is sin; and the strength of sin is the law. But thanks be to God, which giveth us the victory through our Lord Jesus Christ.

❖ Jesus destroyed the devil who had the power of death.

Hebrews 2:14-15 Forasmuch then as the children are partakers of flesh and blood, he also himself likewise took part of the same; that through death he might destroy him that had the power of death, that is the devil; And deliver them who through fear of death were all their lifetime subject to bondage.

❖ The church must be free of the fear of death in order to be used to make a public example of Satan's powerless position over the body of Christ.

Matthew 10:27-28 What I tell you in darkness, that speak ye in light; and what ye hear in the ear, that preach ye upon the housetops. And fear not them which kill the body, and are not able to kill the soul; but rather fear him which is able to destroy both soul and body in hell.

⟹World powers must bow to the authority of the name of Jesus Christ.

Isaiah 60:11-14 Therefore thy gates shall be open continually; they shall not be shut day nor night; that men may bring unto thee the forces of the Gentiles, and that their kings may be brought. For the nation and kingdom that will not serve thee shall perish; yea, those nations shall be utterly wasted. The glory of Lebanon shall come unto thee, the fir tree, the pine tree, and the box together, to beautify the place of my sanctuary; and I will make the place of my feet glorious. The sons also of them that afflicted thee shall come bending unto thee; and all they that despised thee shall bow themselves down at the soles of thy feet; and they shall call thee, The city of the LORD, The Zion of the Holy One of Israel.

⟹**There is NO higher level of authority than the NAME of Jesus.**

Philippians 2:9-11 Wherefore God also hath slightly exalted him, and given him a name which is above every name; That at the name of Jesus every knee should bow, of things in heaven, and things in earth, and things under the earth; And that every tongue should confess that Jesus Christ is Lord, to the glory of God the Father.

~ Lesson 5 ~
The Fight of Faith

Joshua 10:25 And Joshua said unto them, Fear not, nor be dismayed, be strong and of good courage: for thus shall the Lord do to all your enemies against whom ye fight.

⟹Three enemies of the mind which must be fought:
- ❖ Fear
- ❖ Dismay

Definition: *dismayed* – **chathath** (khaw-thath'); a primitive root; properly, to prostrate; hence, to beak down, either (literally) by violence, or (figuratively) by confusion and fear: abolish, affright, be (make) afraid, amaze, beat down, discourage, (cause to) dismay, go down, scare, terrify.

- ❖ Passivity

Webster's Dictionary definition: Offering no resistance; not reacting to external influence; lacking initiative or drive.

⟹The "fight of faith" is the condition to receiving the promises of God.

1 Timothy 6:12 *Fight* the good fight of faith, lay hold on eternal life, whereunto thou art also called, and hast professed a good profession before many witnesses.

Definition: *fight* – **agonizomai** (ag-o-nid'-zom-ahee); to struggle, literally (to compete for a prize), figuratively (to contend with an adversary), or genitive case (to endeavor to accomplish something; fight, labor fervently, strive.
- ❖ To "fight" is a spiritual labor to accomplish something. To be attacked by fear, etc. is as simple as getting tired. The answer is to fight DAILY the fight of faith in order to enter into spiritual rest.

Hebrews 4:11 Let us labour therefore to enter into that rest, lest any man fall after the same example of unbelief.

Hebrews 11:33-34 Who through faith subdued kingdoms, wrought righteousness, obtained promises, stopped the mouths of lions, Quenched the violence of fire, escaped the edge of the sword, out of weakness were made strong, waxed valiant in fight, turned to flight the armies of the aliens.

2 Corinthians 10:5 Casting down imaginations, and every high thing that exalteth itself against the knowledge of God, and bringing into captivity every thought to the obedience of Christ.

- ❖ Our faith is based on the Truth that Jesus has fought our battles for us and has destroyed the devil.

Hebrews 2:14 Forasmuch then as the children are partakers of flesh and blood, he also himself likewise took part of the same; that through death he might destroy him that had the power of death, that is, the devil.

Psalms 56:4 In God I will praise his word, in God I have put my trust. I will not fear what flesh can do unto me. Praising His Word is the same as worshipping in Spirit and in Truth.

John 4:23 But the hour cometh, and now is, when the true worshippers shall worship the Father in spirit and in truth: for the Father seeketh such to worship him.

⟹Leaders must exhort the people to be strong in the Lord and to "fear not". [**Ephesians 6:10**]

Isaiah 35:4-6 Say to them that are of a fearful heart, Be strong, fear not: behold, your God will come with vengeance, even God with a recompense; he will come and save you. Then the eyes of the blind shall be opened, and the ears of the deaf shall be unstopped. Then shall the lame man leap as an hart, and the tongue of the dumb sing: for in the wilderness shall waters break out, and streams in the desert.

❖ Priests

Deuteronomy 20:2-4 And it shall be, when ye are come nigh unto the battle, that the priest shall approach and speak unto the people, And shall say unto them, Hear, O Israel, ye approach this day unto battle against your enemies: let not your hearts faint, fear not, and do not tremble, neither be ye terrified because of them; For the LORD your God is he that goeth with you, to fight for you against your enemies, to save you.

❖ Jesus

Matthew 8:26 And he saith unto them, Why are ye fearful, O ye of little faith? Then he arose, and rebuked the winds and the sea; and there was a great calm.

Matthew 14:26-27 And when the disciples saw him walking on the sea, they were troubled, saying, It is a spirit; and they cried out for fear. But straightway Jesus spake unto them, saying, Be of good cheer; it is I; be not afraid.

Matthew 17:7 And Jesus came and touched them, and said, Arise, and be not afraid.

Matthew 28:10 Then said Jesus unto them, Be not afraid: go tell my brethren that they go into Galilee, and there shall they see me.

Mark 5:35-36 While he yet spake, there came from the ruler of the synagogue's house certain which said, Thy daughter is dead: why troublest thou the Master any further? As soon as Jesus heard the word that was spoken, he saith unto the ruler of the synagogue, Be not afraid, only believe.

John 14:27 Peace I leave with you, my peace I give unto you: not as the world giveth, give I unto you. Let not your heart be troubled, neither let it be afraid.

⟹Fear is contagious and <u>cannot</u> be tolerated in the army of God.

Deuteronomy 20:8 And the officers shall speak further unto the people, and they shall say, What man is there that is fearful and fainthearted? Let him go and return unto his house, lest his brethren's heart faint as well as his heart.

Judges 7:3 Now therefore go to proclaim in the ears of the people, saying, Whosoever is fearful and afraid, let him return and depart eagerly from Mount Gilead. And there returned of the people twenty and two thousand; and there remained ten thousand.

❖ Do not speak in fear. To have you do so is the united effort of Satan's army.

Isaiah 8:12 Say ye not, A confederacy, to all them to whom this people shall say, A confederacy; neither fear ye their fear, not be afraid.

❖ Remember-- the Lord of Hosts means an innumerable army of men and angels!

Isaiah 8:13 Sanctify the LORD of hosts himself; and let him be your fear, and let him be your dread.

❖ The enemy fears and dreads the Lord of Hosts who surrounds the righteous.

2 Kings 6:16-17 And he answered, Fear not; for they that be with us are more than they that be with them. And Elisha prayed, and said, LORD, I pray thee, open his eyes, that he may see. And the LORD opened the eyes of the young man; and he saw; and, behold, the mountain was full of horses and chariots of pre round about Elisha.

⇒Make a decision for the Lord and confess it before the attack:

Psalms 27:3 Though an host should encamp against me, my heart shall not fear: though war should rise against me, in this will I be confident.
Psalms 46:2 Therefore will not we fear, though the earth be removed, and though the mountains be carried into the midst of the sea.
Psalms 118:6 The LORD is on my side; I will not fear. What can man do unto me?

⇒Do not fear to take (to accept, to receive) what God has given.

Luke 12:32 Fear not, little flock; for it is your Father's good pleasure to give you the kingdom.

❖ The 'violent' take it!
Matthew 11:12 And **from the days of John** the Baptist until now the kingdom of heaven suffereth violence, and the violent take it by force.

❖ There is a spiritual 'violence' which is about self-sacrificing love.
1 John 4:18 There is no fear in love; but perfect love casteth out fear because fear hath torment. He that feareth is not made perfect in love.

❖ Mature love is a confession that we, by faith, are already dead.
Colossians 3:3 For ye are dead, and your life is hid with Christ in God.
Matthew 16:25 For whosoever will save his life shall lose it: and whosoever will lose his life for my sake shall find it.
Luke 12:4 And I say unto you my friends, Be not afraid of them that kill the body, and after that have no more that they can do.

❖ Lay hold according to our confession. [**1 Timothy 6:12b**]

❖ Get a wrestler's grip on truth, in faith and love.

2 Timothy 1:13 Hold fast the form of sound words, which thou hast heard of me, in faith and love which is in Christ Jesus.
1 Timothy 6:19 Laying up in store for themselves a good foundation against the time to come, that they may lay hold on eternal life.

❖ Be well trained in order to **"hit the mark"**.
1 Corinthians 9:26 I therefore so run, not as uncertainly; so fight I, not as one that beateth the air.

❖ The War Horse
Job 39:19-25 Hast thou given the horse strength? hast thou clothed his neck with thunder? Canst thou make him afraid as a grasshopper? the glory of his nostrils is terrible He paweth in the valley, and rejoiceth in his strength: he goeth on to meet the armed men. He mocketh at fear, and is not affrighted;

neither turneth he back from the sword The quiver rattleth against him, the glittering spear and the shield. He swalloweth the ground with fierceness and rage: neither believeth he that it is the sound of the trumpet. He saith among the trumpets, Ha, ha; and he smelleth the battle afar off, the thunder of the captains, and the shouting.

Zechariah 10:3-5 Mine anger was kindled against the shepherds, and I punished the goats: for the LORD of hosts hath visited his flock the house of Judah, and hath made them as his goodly horse in the battle Out of him came forth the corner, out of him the nail, out of him the batte bow, out of him every oppressor together. And they shall be as mighty men, which tread down their enemies in the mire of the streets in the battle: and they shall fight, because the LORD is with them, and the riders on horses shall be confounded.

❖ Decide to finish what we begin.
2 Timothy 4:7 I have fought a good fight, I have finished my course, I have kept the faith.

~ Lesson 6 ~
The Cross and the Grave

Joshua 10:26 And afterward Joshua smote them, and slew them, and hanged them on five trees; and they were hanging upon the trees until the evening.

⟹Joshua hanging the kings on trees is a type of the cross where Jesus took the curse of sin.

❖ He was despised and mocked as a wicked king.

Matthew 27:29 And when they had platted a crown of thorns, they put it upon his head, and a reed in his right hand: and they bowed the knee before him, and mocked him, saying, Hail, King of the Jews!
Matthew 27:42 He saved others; himself he cannot save. If he be the King of Israel, let him now come down from the cross, and we will believe him.
Isaiah 53:9,12 And he made his grave with the wicked, and with the rich in his death; because he had done no violence, neither was any deceit in his mouth. Therefore will I divide him a portion with the great, and he shall divide the spoil with the strong; because he hath poured out his soul unto death: and he was numbered with the transgressors; and he bare the sin of many, and made intercession for the transgressors.

❖ All of the spiritual rulers of the principalities of wickedness and darkness attached to the body and mind of Jesus at the cross and were covered by His precious Blood.

Psalms 22:16 For dogs have compassed me: the assembly of the wicked have inclosed me: they pierced my hands and my feet.
Galatians 3:13 Christ hath redeemed us from the curse of the law, being made a curse for us: for it is written, Cursed is every one that hangeth on *a* tree.
Acts 5:30 Thy God of our fathers raised up Jesus, whom ye slew and hanged on a tree.
2 Corinthians 5:21 For he hath made him to be sin for us, who knew no sin; that we might be made the righteousness of God in him.
John 3:14-15 And as Moses lifted up the serpent in the wilderness, even so must the Son of man be lifted up:
That whosoever believeth in him should not perish, but have eternal life.

❖ Because of the demonic curses of mankind, God, for but a moment, turned his face away from Jesus.

Isaiah 54:7-8 For a small moment have I forsaken thee; but with great mercies will I gather thee. In a little wrath I hid my face from thee for a moment; but with everlasting kindness will I have mercy on thee, saith the LORD thy Redeemer.
Hebrews 8:12 For I will be merciful and their unrighteousness and their sins and their iniquities will I remember no more.

❖ People today still turn their faces away because they have no revelation of our loving King and Redeemer.

Isaiah 53:3 He is despised and rejected of men; a man of sorrows, and acquainted with grief: and we hid as it were our faces from him; he was despised, and we esteemed him not.

Revelation 20:11 And I saw a great white throne, and him that sat on it, from whose face the earth and the heaven fled away; and there was found no place for them.

Psalms 27:8 When thou saidst, Seek ye my face; my heart said unto thee, Thy face, LORD, will I seek.

⟹A type of "the grave", Hades, or spiritual death…

Joshua 10:27 And it came to pass at the time of the going down of the sun, that Joshua commanded, and they took them down off the trees, and cast them into the cave wherein they had been hid, and laid great stones in the cave's mouth, which remain until this very day.

❖ Jesus was hastily taken down from the cross and buried at sundown.
John 19:31 The Jews therefore, because it *was* the preparation that the bodies should not remain upon the cross on the sabbath day (for that sabbath day was an high day) besought Pilate that their legs might be broken, and that they might be taken away.

❖ A great stone was laid on the door.
Matthew 27:60 And laid it in his own new tomb, which he had hewn out in the rock: and he rolled a great stone to the door of the sepulchre, and departed.

❖ The chief priests and pharisees sealed the tomb.
Matthew 27:66 So they went, and made the sepulchre sure, sealing the stone and setting a watch.

❖ The angel of the Lord broke the seal and rolled the stone away.
Matthew 28:2 And, behold, there was a great earthquake: for the angel of the Lord descended from heaven, and came and rolled back the stone from the door, and sat upon it.

❖ Angels still assist in removing the binding stones of mountains in our lives today.
Hebrews 1:13-14 But to which of the angels said he at any time, Sit on my right hand, until I make thine enemies my footstool? Are they not all ministering spirits, sent forth to minister for them who shall be heirs of salvation?

❖ Jesus left all his bindings in the tomb when he arose.
Luke 24:12 Then arose Peter, and ran unto the sepulchre; and stooping down, he beheld the lined clothes laid by themselves, and departed, wondering in himself at that which was come to pass.

Colossians 2:12-15 Buried with him in baptism, wherein also ye are risen with him through the faith of the operation of God, who hath raised him from the dead. And you, being dead in your sins and the uncircumcision of your flesh, hath he quickened together with him, having forgiven you all trespasses; Blotting out the handwriting of ordinances that was against us, which was contrary to us, and took it out of the way, nailing it to his cross; And having spoiled principalities and powers, he made a shew of them openly, triumphing over them in it.

❖ Jesus sealed the rulers of darkness and spiritual wickedness, and also gave his "stamp of approval" to His church by giving the gift of the Holy Spirit.

Ephesians 4:8-10 Wherefore he saith, When he ascended up on high, he led captivity captive, and gave gifts unto men. (Now that he ascended, what is it but that he also descended first into the lower parts of the earth? He that descended is the same also that ascended up far above all heavens, that he might fill all things.)

⟹It must be noted here that the cave of Makkedah is not a type of the true spiritual church, but a place of institutional religious bondage.

❖ Herding and branding
Definition: *Makkedah* – *Maqqedah* (mak-kay-daw); from the same as *naqod* in the denominative sense of herding; fold; Makkedah, a place in Palestine.
– *naqod* (naw-kode'); from an unused root meaning to mark (by puncturing or branding); spotted: speckled.

❖ Synagogue of Satan
Revelation 2:9 I know thy works, and tribulation, and poverty, (but thou art rich) and I know the blasphemy of them which say they are Jews, and are not, but are the synagogue of Satan.

❖ The two-fold child of hell
Matthew 23:15 Woe unto you, scribes and Pharisees, hypocrites! for ye compass sea and land to make one proselyte, and when he is made, ye make him two-fold more the child of hell than yourselves.

❖ The latter end is worse than the beginning:
2 Peter 2:19-20 While they promise them liberty, they themselves are the servants of corruption: for of whom a man is overcome, of the same is he brought in bondage.
For if after they have escaped the pollutions of the world through the knowledge of the Lord and Saviour Jesus Christ, they are again entangled therein, and overcome, the latter end is worse with them than the beginning.

❖ Religious bondage is a subtle counterfeit for the seal of the Holy Spirit.
Definition: *bondage* – *katadouloo* (kat-ad-oo-lo'-o); to enslave utterly: bring into bondage.
⟹Seal
Definition: *sphragizo* (sirag-id'-zo); to stamp (with a signet or private mark) for security or preservation (literally or figuratively); by implication, to keep secret, to attest: (set a, set to) seal up, stop.

❖ Jesus is sealed with the Spirit:
John 6:27 Labour not for the meat which perisheth, but for that meat which endureth unto everlasting life, which the Son of man shall give unto you: for him hath God the Father sealed.
Matthew 3:16-17 And Jesus, when he was baptized, went up straightway out of the water: and, lo, the heavens were opened unto him, and he saw the Spirit of God descending like a dove, and lighting upon him: And low a voice from heaven, saying, This is my beloved Son, in whom I am well pleased.

❖ Being sealed with the anointing:
2 Corinthians 1:21-22 Now he which establisheth us with you in Christ, and hath anointed us, is God; Who hath also sealed us, and given the earnest of the Spirit in our hearts.

❖ Being sealed after believing:
Ephesians 1:13 In whom ye also trusted, after that ye heard the word of truth, the gospel of your salvation: in whom also after that ye believed, ye were sealed with that Holy Spirit of promise.

❖ Being sealed until the day of redemption:
Ephesians 4:30 And grieve not the Holy Spirit of God, whereby ye are sealed unto the day of redemption.

❖ There is protection under the seal:
Revelation 9:4 And it was commanded them that they should not hurt the grass of the earth, neither any green thing, neither any tree; but only those men which have not the seal of God in their foreheads.

❖ The "seal" is Holy Spirit living:
2 Timothy 2:19 Nevertheless the foundation of God standeth sure, having this seal, The Lord knoweth them that are his. And, let everyone that nameth the name of Christ depart from iniquity.

❖ The rock sealed by man is a type of the gates of hell or the grave which could not prevail
Revelation 1:18 I am he that liveth, and was dead; and, behold, I am alive for evermore, Amen; and have the keys of hell and of death.

Matthew 16:18-19 And I tell you that you are Peter, and on this rock I will build my church, and the gates of Hades will not overcome it. I will give you the keys of the kingdom of heaven; whatever you bind on earth will be bound in heaven, and whatever you loose on earth will be loosed in heaven (NIV)

❖ *Hell* and *the grave* are used synonymously:
Definition: *haides* (hah'-dace); properly, unseen, ie. "Hades" or the place (state) of departed souls; grave, hell.

❖ Hades is translated *hell* 10 times in the New Testament:
Matthew 11:23; 16:18; Revelation 1:18; Luke 10:15; 16:23; Revelation 6:8; Acts 2:27, 31; Revelation 20:13, 14

❖ Example of how *hell* and *the grave* are used synonymously:
Acts 2:27 – **NIV**-Because you will not abandon me to the grave, nor will you let your Holy One see decay.
Acts 2:27 – **KJV**-Because thou wilt not leave my soul in hell, neither wilt thou suffer thine Holy One to see corruption.

❖ Satanic rulers of darkness are bound in Hades now but shall be bound eternally in the everlasting hell fire.

~ Lesson 7 ~
Jesus in the Midst

Genesis 15:6 And he believed in the Lord; and he counted it to him for righteousness.

$\Rightarrow$ The wedding gift of righteousness:

Revelation 19:7-8 Let us be glad and rejoice, and give honour to him: for the marriage of the Lamb is come, and his wife hath made herself ready. And to her was granted that she should be arrayed in fine linen, clean and white: for the fine linen is the righteousness of saints.
Isaiah 61:10 I will greatly rejoice in the Lord, my soul shall be joyful in my God; for he hath clothed me with the garments of salvation, he hath covered me with the robe of righteousness, as a bridegroom decketh himself with ornaments, and as a bride adorneth herself with her jewels.

❖ Righteousness is given but must be worn and displayed in order to glorify the Master.
Ephesians 4:22-23 That ye put off concerning the former conversation the old man, which is corrupt according to the deceitful lusts; And be renewed in the spirit of your mind.

❖ David was given the royal family robe because he cut the covenant with Jonathan, the son, and received acceptance of Saul, the father, and all the people.
1 Samuel 18:1-5 And it came to pass, when he had made an end of speaking unto Saul. that the soul of Jonathan was knit with the soul of David, and Jonathan loved him as his own soul. And Saul took him that day, and would let him go no more home to his father s house. Then Jonathan and David made a covenant, because he loved him as his own soul. And Jonathan stripped himself of the robe that was upon him and gave it to David, and his garments, even to his sword and to his bow and to his girdle. And David went out whithersoever Saul sent him, and behaved himself wisely: and Saul set him over the men of war, and he was accepted in the sight of all the people and also in the sight of Saul's servants.

$\Rightarrow$ How shall I know?

Genesis 15:7-8 And he said unto him, I am the Lord that brought thee out of Ur of the Chaldees, to give thee this land to inherit it. And he said, Lord God, whereby shall I know that I shall inherit it?

❖ Abram is asking for a higher level of revelation than being counted righteous through faith.

❖ To believe in the Lord is one thing. To know we will inherit is another.
Hebrews 8:10-11 For this is a covenant that I will make with the house of Israel *after* those days, saith the Lord; I will put my laws into their mind, and write them in their hearts: and I will be to them a God, and they shall be to me a people: And they shall not teach every man his neighbor, and every, man his brother, saying, Know the Lord: for all shall know me, from the least to the greatest.

$\Rightarrow$ From Mt. Lebanon to Mt. Amana:

❖ Righteousness covering to sure knowing:
Song of Songs 4: 7-9 Thou art all fair, my love; there is no spot in thee. Come with me from Lebanon, my spouse, with me from Lebanon: look from the top of Amana, from the top of Shenir and Hermon,

from the lions' dens, from the mountains of the leopards. Thou hast ravished my heart, my sister, my spouse; thou hast ravished my heart with one of thine eyes, with one chain of thy neck.

♦ Lebanon (Righteous Covering):
Definition: *Lebanown* (leb-aw-nohn'); (the) - white mountain (from its snow); Lebanon, a mountain range in Palestine.

♦ Amana (Sure Covenant):
Definition: *'amanah* (am-aw-naw?); something fixed, i.e. a covenant, an allowance: certain portion, sure.

❖ In Hebrew custom, the only way one could know for sure he could trust another was to cut a blood covenant.
Hebrews 6:13-17 For when God made promise to Abraham, because he could swear by no greater, he sware by himself, Saying, Surely blessing I will bless thee, and multiplying l will multiply thee. And so, after he had patiently endured, he obtained the promise. For men verily swear by the greater: and an oath for confirmation is to them an end of all strife. Wherein God, willing more abundantly to shew unto the heirs of promise the immutability of his counsel, confirmed it by an oath.

❖ This oath ended all strife and questions between men. How much more abundant and permanent is God's covenant?!
Genesis 15:9-10 And he said unto him, Take me an heifer of three years old, and a she goat of three years old, and a ram of three years old, and a turtledove, and a young pigeon. And he took unto him all these, and divided them in the midst, and laid each piece one against another: but the birds divided he not.

❖ This was a well-known practice to any Jewish believer of that day and time.
Jeremiah 34:18-19 And I will give the men that have transgressed my covenant, which have not performed the words of the covenant which they had made before me, when they cut the calf in twain, and passed between the parts thereof, The princes of Judah and the princes of Jerusalem, the eunuchs, and the priests, and all the people of the land, which passed between the parts of the calf.

❖ God is saying to Abram that the only sure way to know if he could trust him was to cut a covenant. The only sure way to know now, under the new covenant, is to present our bodies as a living sacrifice.
❖
Romans 12:1-2 I beseech you therefore, brethren, by the mercies of God, that ye present your bodies a living sacrifice, holy, acceptable unto God, which is your reasonable service. 2 And be not conformed to this world: but be ye transformed by the renewing of your mind, that ye may prove what is that good and acceptable and perfect will of God.

⟹ The fowls are a type of the devil who tries to steal the truth of the sacrifice by blood out of our prayers.

Genesis 15:11 And when the fowls came down upon the carcasses, Abram drove them away.
Mark 4:4 And it came to pass, as he sowed, some fell by the way side and the fowls of the air came and devoured it up.

❖ It is the believer's responsibility to protect the blood sacrifice and cause the fowls to flee.
James 4:7-8 Submit **yourselves therefore** to God. Resist the devil and he will flee from you. Draw nigh to God and he will draw nigh to you. Cleanse your hands, ye sinners; and purify your hearts, ye double minded.

1 Peter 5:8-9 Be sober, be vigilant; because your adversary, the devil, as a roaring lion walketh about seeking whom he may devour; Whom resist steadfast in the faith, knowing that the same afflictions are accomplished in your brethren that are in the world.

❖ Resist through faith and the testimony of the Blood.
Revelation 12:11 And they overcame him by the blood of the Lamb and by the word of their testimony; and they loved not their lives unto the death.

❖ When the devil accuses, our plea is that we come with the Blood of Christ.
Hebrews 9:7 But into the second went the high priest alone once every year, not without blood, which he offered for himself and for the errors of the people.

❖ Through the Blood our conscience is purged.
Hebrews 9:14 How much more shall the blood of Christ, who through the eternal Spirit offered himself without spot to God, purge your conscience from dead works to serve the living God?

❖ All things are redeemed by the Blood:
Hebrews 9:22 And almost all things are by the law purged with blood; and without shedding of blood is no remission.

❖ Jesus, the Atonement:
Leviticus 17:11 For the life of the flesh is in the blood: and I have given h to you upon the attar to make an atonement for your souls: for it is the blood that maketh an atonement for the soul.

❖ Redeemed from the curse:
Galatians 3:13-14 Christ hath redeemed us from the curse of the law, being made a curse for us: for it is written, Cursed is every one that hangeth on a tree: That the blessing of Abraham might come on the Gentiles through Jesus Christ; that we might receive the promise of the Spirit through faith.

❖ To any curse that is offered, our answer must be "the Blood".
Deuteronomy 28:61-62 Also every sickness and every plague which is not written in the book of this law, them will the LORD bring upon thee until thou be destroyed. And ye shall be left few in number, whereas ye were as the stars of heaven for multitude; because thou wouldest not obey the voice of the LORD thy God.

❖ Our plea before the accuser is neither innocence nor guilt but rather blamelessness because of the Blood of Jesus Christ.

1 Thessalonians 5:23 And the very God of peace sanctify you wholly; and I pray God your whole spirit and soul and body be preserved blameless unto the coming of our Lord Jesus Christ.

⇒Abram was not allowed to perform in this covenant.

Genesis 15:12 And when the sun was going down a deep sleep fell upon Abram; and, lo, an horror of great darkness fell upon him.

❖ Religious zeal will not bring one into the sure covenant.

Romans 10:2-3 For I bear them record that they have a zeal of God but not according to knowledge. For they being ignorant of God's righteousness and going about to establish their own righteousness have not submitted themselves unto the righteousness of God.

❖ Faith must be in the performance of the Lord.

Romans 4:20-21 He staggered not at the promise of God through unbelief; but was strong in faith, giving glory to God; And being fully persuaded that, what he had promised, he was able also to perform.

❖ Jesus came to perform the covenant for us.

Luke 1:71-75 That we should be saved from our enemies and from the hand of all that hate us; To perform the mercy promised to our fathers and to remember His holy covenant; The oath which he sware to our father Abraham, that he would grant unto us that we, being delivered out of the hand of our enemies might serve him without fear, In holiness and righteousness before him, all the days of our life.

❖ He swore that we are delivered from the hands of our enemies and have been given power to serve Him without fear, in holiness and righteousness, 365 days of the year, regardless of circumstance.

⟹Imputed righteousness (to count, to credit):

❖ NIV translation uses "credited righteousness".

Romans 4:7-11 Blessed are they whose transgressions are forgiven, whose sins are covered. Blessed is the man whose sin the Lord will never count against him. Is this blessedness only for the circumcised, or also for the uncircumcised? We have been saying that Abraham's faith was credited to him as righteousness. Under what circumstances was it credited? Was it after he was circumcised, or before? It was not after, but before! And he received the sign of circumcision, a seal of the righteousness that he had by faith while he was still uncircumcised. So then, he is the father of all who believe but have not been circumcised, in order that righteousness might be credited to them. (NIV)

❖ Righteousness came before the cutting of the covenant; therefore, the born again experience does not bring us into covenant fruitfulness but, by presenting our bodies to the sword of the Spirit, we can know for certain what the will of God is.

Romans 12:1-2 I beseech you therefore, brethren, by the mercies of God, that ye present your bodies a living sacrifice, holy, acceptable to God, which is your reasonable service. And be not conformed to this world: but be ye transformed by the renewing of your mind, that ye may prove what is that good and acceptable and perfect will of God.

❖ The Great Bookkeeper:

Romans 4:22-24 And therefore it was imputed to him for righteousness. Now it was not written for his sake alone that it was imputed to him; But for us also, to whom it shall be imputed, if we believe on him that raised up Jesus our Lord from the dead.

Romans 5:17-18 For if by one man's offense death reigned by one, much more they which receive abundance of grace and of the gift of righteousness shall reign in life by one Jesus Christ. Therefore, as by the offense of one judgment came upon all men to condemnation, even so by the righteousness of one the free gift came upon all men unto justification of life.

>> The Second Experience>>

⇒The baptism of the Holy Ghost and fire is a second experience which helps us to know through signs, wonders and miracles:

Genesis 15:17 And it came to pass that, when the sun went down and it was dark, behold, a smoking furnace and a burning lamp that passed between those pieces.
John 8:56 Your father Abraham rejoiced to see my day: and he saw it and was glad.

Definition: *rejoice/exult – agalliao* (ag-al-lee-ah'-o); jump for joy, i.e. exult: be (exceeding) glad, with exceeding joy, rejoice (greatly).

❖ Abram saw Jesus walking through death on his behalf. He performed the blood covenant perfectly through the power of the Holy Spirit.

❖ The virgin Mary asked the same question Abram asked. How shall this be?
Luke 1:34-35 They said Mary unto the angel, How shall this be, seeing I know not a man? And the angel answered and said unto her, The Holy Ghost shall come upon thee and the power of the Highest shall overshadow thee: therefore also that holy thing which shall be born of thee shall be called the Son of God.

❖ The answer is that the "Holy Ghost will come upon thee."

❖ "I know no man" as used here means "I have no seed planting experience."

❖ The Holy Ghost will overshadow you and spiritual seed will be implanted by the power of God.

⇒**Darkness is a type of not knowing**; the smoking furnace is the refinement which comes through the baptism of fire; and the burning lamp is revelation through the various gifts of the Holy Spirit.

❖ When fire falls on the blood-covered flesh, we move from believing on the Lord to <u>knowing</u> we have the inheritance.

❖ A wilderness experience in between darkness and knowing:
Joel 2:2-5 A day of darkness and of gloominess, a day of clouds and of thick darkness! as the morning spread upon the mountains; a great people and a strong; there hath not been ever the like, neither shall be any more after it, even to the years *of* many generations. A fire devoureth before them; and behind them a flame burneth: the land is as the garden of Eden before them and behind them a desolate wilderness; yea, and nothing shall escape them. The appearance of them is as the appearance of horses; and as horsemen, so shall they run. Like the noise of chariots on the tops of mountains shall they leap, like the noise of a flame of fire that devoureth the stubble, as a strong people set in battle array.

Acts 2:3-4 And there appeared unto them cloven tongues like as of fire, and it sat upon each of them. And they were filled with the Holy Ghost and began to speak with other tongues as the Spirit gave them utterance.

❖ The burning of the bindings of babyhood:
Matthew 3:11-12 I indeed baptize you with water unto repentance: but he that cometh after me is mightier than I, whose shoes I am not worthy to bear: he shall baptize you with the Holy Ghost and with fire: Whose fan is in his hand and he will throughly purge his floor and gather his wheat into the garner; but he will bum up the chaff with unquenchable fire.

❖ Precious faith is a knowing which comes through the trial of fire.
1 Peter 1:6-7 Wherein ye greatly rejoice, though now for a season, if need be, ye are in heaviness through manifold temptations: That the trial of your faith, being much more previous than of gold that perisheth, though it be tried with fire, might be found unto praise and honour and glory at the appearing of Jesus Christ.

❖ Jesus is coming for a bride who has been purged from all retreat or apostasy.
Isaiah 1:25-26 And I will turn my hand upon thee, and purely purge away thy *dross* and take away all thy tin: And I will restore thy judges as at the first, and thy counselors us at the beginning: afterward thou shalt be called The City of Righteousness, the faithful city.

Definition: *dross – cuwg* (soog); a primitive root; properly, to flinch, i.e. (by implication) to go back, literally (to retreat) or figuratively (apostatize): backslider, drive, go back, turn (away, back).

❖ Purified gold and silver:
Malachi 3:2-3 But who may abide the day of his coming? and who shall stand when he appeareth for he is like a refiner's fire, and like fullers' soap: And he shall sit as a refiner and purifier of silver: and he shall purify the sons of Levi, and purge them as gold and silver, that they may offer unto the LORD an offering in righteousness.

⟹Hebrew children refused to retreat and were promoted from children to sons of God by meeting the Son of God in the fiery furnace.

❖ A test of the enemy could not destroy them but, instead, loosed them.
Daniel 3:25-30 He answered and said, Lo, I see four men loose, walking in the midst of the fire, and they have no hurt; and the form of the fourth is like the Son of God. Then Nebuchadnezzar came near to the mouth of the burning fiery furnace and spake, and said, Shadrach, Meshach and Abednego, ye servants of the most high God, come forth and come hither. Then Shadrach, Meshach and Abednego came forth of the midst of the fire. And the princes, governors and captains, and the king's counselors. being gathered together, saw these men, upon whose bodies the fire had no power, nor was an hair of their head singed, neither were their coats changed, nor the smell of fire had passed on them. Then Nebuchadnezzar spake, and said, Blessed be the God of Shadrach, Meshach and Abednego, who hath sent his angel and delivered his servants that trusted in him and have changed the king's word and yielded their bodies that they might not serve nor worship any god except their own God. Therefore I make a decree, That every people, nation and language which speak anything amiss against the God of Shadrach, Meshach and Abednego, shall be cut in pieces and their houses shall be made a dunghill: because there is no other God that can

deliver after this sort. Then the king promoted Shadrach, Meshach and Abednego in the province of Babylon.

Isaiah 43:2 When thou passest through the waters, I will be with thee; and through the rivers, they shall not overflow thee: when thou walkest through the fire, thou shalt not be burned; neither shall the flame kindle upon thee.

⟹The burning bush:

❖ Trees of righteousness will not be consumed by fiery trials. [**Isaiah 61:3**]
Exodus 3:2 And the angel of the Lord appeared unto him in a flame of fire out of the midst of a bush: and he looked, and behold, the bush burned with fire and the bush was not consumed.

❖ Holy ground is the place of covenant
Exodus 3:5-6 And he said, Draw not nigh hither: put off thy shoes from off thy feet, for the place whereon thou standest is holy ground. Moreover he said, I am the God of thy father, the God of Abraham, the God of Isaac, and the God of Jacob. And Moses hid his face; for he was afraid to look upon God.

⟹Gideon wanted to know.

❖ Asked for a sign:
Judges 6:17 And he said unto him, If now I have found grace in thy sight, then shew me a sign that thou talkest with me.

❖ Fire-consumed flesh:
Judges 6:21 Then the angel of the Lord put forth the end of the staff that was in his hand and touched the flesh and the unleavened cakes; and there rose up fire out of the rock and consumed the flesh and the unleavened cakes. Then the angel of the Lord departed out of his sight.

⟹When Elijah prayed in the name of the covenant God of Abraham and Isaac, fire fell so that the people might know.

1 Kings 18:36-40 And it came to pass at the time of the offering of the evening sacrifice that Elijah, the prophet, came near and said, LORD God of Abraham, Isaac and of Israel, let it be known this day that thou art God in Israel and that I am thy servant and that I have done all these things at thy word. Hear me, O LORD, hear me, that this people may know that thou art the LORD God, and that thou hast turned their heart back again. Then the fire of the LORD fell and consumed the burnt sacrifice and the wood and the stones and the dust and licked up the water that was in the trench. And when all the people saw it, they fell on their faces: and they said, the LORD, he is the God; the LORD, he is the God. And Elijah said unto them, Take the prophets of Baal; let not one of them escape. And they took them: and Elijah brought them down to the brook Kishon and slew them there.

⟹The consuming fire is the "mediator":

Hebrews 12:18 For ye are not come unto the mount that might be touched and that burned with fire, nor unto blackness and darkness and tempest.

Hebrews 12:22-24 But ye are come unto Mount Sion and unto the city of the living God, the heavenly Jerusalem, and to an innumerable company of angels, To the general assembly and church of the firstborn, which are written in heaven, and to God the Judge of all, and to the spirits of just men made perfect, And to Jesus the mediator of the new covenant and to the blood of sprinkling that speaketh better things than that of Abel.

Hebrews 12:29 For our God is a consuming fire.

~ Lesson 8 ~
Intercessory Prayer

Genesis 18:16-19 And the men rose up from thence and looked toward Sodom: and Abraham went with them to bring them on the way. And the Lord said, Shall l hide from Abraham that thing which I do; Seeing that Abraham shall surely become a great and mighty nation and all the nations Of the earth shall be blessed in him?

⇒One part of the covenant promise is that God will be our friend and will not hide from us.

❖ Because of their covenant, God could not destroy Sodom before he told righteous Abraham.
Amos 3:7 Surely the Lord God will do nothing but he revealeth his secret unto his servants, the prophets.

❖ All the prophets knew it was time for Elijah to be taken, however, the fact that they searched for him later seems to indicate that they were weaker than Elisha.
2 Kings 2:5 And the sons of the prophets that were at Jericho came to Elisha and said unto him, Knowest thou that the Lord will take away thy master from thy head to day? And he answered, Yea, I know it; hold ye your peace.

❖ The new covenant is better than the old in that all shall prophesy the same thing. Under the old covenant, there seemed to be only one prophet ministering per time period.
Acts 2:17-18 And it shall come to pass in the last days, saith God, I will pour out of m, Spirit upon all flesh: and your sons and your daughters shall prophesy and your young men shall see visions and your old men shall dream dreams. And on my servants and on my handmaidens I will pour out in those days of my Spirit; and they shall prophesy.

⇒Abraham was known as God's friend and was trusted by God.

Genesis 18:19 For I know him, that he will command his children and his household after him, and they shall keep the way of the Lord, to do justice and judgment; that the Lord may bring upon Abraham that which he hath spoken of him.

❖ To know God is not something which can be taught but must be revealed.
Hebrews 8:10-11 For this is the covenant that I will make with the house of Israel after those days, saith the Lord; I will put my laws into their mind and write them in their hearts: and I will be to them a God and they shall be to me a people: And they shall not teach every man his neighbor and every man his brother, saying, Know the Lord: for all shall know me, from the least to the greatest.

❖ One can know Jesus only by taking up the cross and following in His footsteps.
Philippians 3:10 That I may *know* him and the power of his resurrection and the fellowship of his sufferings being made conformable unto his death.

Definition: *know* – *ginosko* (ghin-oce'-ko); a prolonged form of a primary verb; to "know" (absolutely); allow, be aware (of), feel, (have) know (-ledge), perceived, be resolved, can speak, be sure, understand.

❖ **Abraham was called the friend of God because of his exercise of faith.**

James 2:23 And the scripture was fulfilled which saith, Abraham believed God, and it was imputed unto him for righteousness: and he was called the Friend of God.

❖ More than a casual acquaintance:
Definition: *friend – philos* (fee'-los); properly, dear, i.e. a friend; actively, fond, i.e. friendly (still as a noun, an associate, neighbor, etc.): friend.

❖ God sticks close to us as we show ourselves friendly to him through obedience.
Proverbs 18:24 A man that hath friends must shew himself friendly: and there is a friend that sticketh closer than a brother.

❖ Friendship, in the eyes of the Lord, is obedience to the revelation of the spirit of Truth.
John 14:21 He that hath my commandments and keepeth them, he it is that loveth me: and he that loveth me shall be loved of my Father, and I will love him and will *manifest* myself to him.

Definition: *manifest – emphanizo* (em-fan-id'-zo); to exhibit (in person) or disclose (by words); signify; appear, declare (plainly), inform, (will) manifest, shew.

❖ A friend enjoys a higher position than that of a servant.
John 15:15 Henceforth I call you not servants; for the servant knoweth not what his lord doeth: but I have called you friends; for all things that I have heard of my Father I have made known unto you.

❖ It was evident that Peter and John were close friends with Jesus because of the boldness they displayed with Him.
Acts 4:13 Now when they saw the boldness of Peter and John, and perceived that they were unlearned and ignorant men, they marveled; and they took knowledge of them that they had been with Jesus.

❖ To be shown things to come is a friendship gesture from the Father, Son and Holy Spirit.
John 16:13 Howbeit when he, the Spirit of truth is come, he will guide you into all truth: for he shall not speak of himself; but whatsoever he shall hear, that shall be speak: and he will shew you things to come.

❖ No need to try to predict times and seasons with the natural mind.
1 Thessalonians 5:1-3 But of the times and the seasons, brethren, ye have no need that I write unto you. For yourselves know perfectly that the day of the Lord so cometh as a thief in the night. For when they shall say, Peace and safety; then sudden destruction cometh upon them, as travail upon a woman with child; and they shall not escape.

❖ Friends of God are awake and walking in the Light.
1 Thessalonians 5:4-6 But ye, brethren, are not in darkness, that day should overtake you as a thief. Ye are all the children of light, and the children of the day: we are not of the night, nor of darkness. Therefore let us not sleep, as do others; but let us watch and be sober.

❖ Even though the way of escape has been provided, some could miss it through being spiritually asleep.

⇒Abraham, the intercessor

Genesis 18:20-25 And the Lord said, Because the cry of Sodom and Gomorrah is great, and because their sin is very grievous; I will go down now, and see whether they have done altogether according to the cry of it, which his come unto me; and if not, I will know. And the men turned their faces from thence, and went toward Sodom: but Abraham stood yet before the Lord. And Abraham drew near, and said, Wilt thou also destroy the righteous with the wicked? Peradventure there be fifty righteous within the city: wilt thou also destroy: and not spare the place for the fifty righteous that are therein? That be far from thee to do *after* this manner, to slay the righteous with the wicked: and that the righteous should be as the wicked, that be far from thee: Shall not the Judge of all the earth do right?

  ❖ When the Lord said, "I know him", He knew that Abraham would intercede according to the covenant for the righteous.
  ❖ Intercession is **NOT** "woman's work".

Ezekiel 22:30 And I sought for a man among them that should make up the hedge and stand in the gap before me for the land that I should not destroy it: but I found none.

1 Timothy 2:8 I will therefore that men pray everywhere, lifting up holy hands, without wrath and doubting.

  ❖ Without the intercession of Simeon and Anna, Jesus could not have been born.
Luke 2:25-26 And, behold, there was a man in Jerusalem, whose name was Simeon; and the same man was just and devout, waiting for the consolation of Israel: and the Holy Ghost was upon him. And it was revealed unto him by the Holy Ghost that he should not see death before he had seen the Lord's Christ.

Luke 2:36-37 And there was one Anna, a prophetess, the daughter of Phanuel, of the tribe of Aser: she was of a great age, and had lived with an husband seven years from her virginity; And she was a widow of about fourscore and four years, which departed not from the temple but served God with fastings and prayers night and day.

  ❖ Moses spoke face-to-face with God.
Exodus 33:11 And the Lord spake unto Moses face to face, as a man speaketh unto his friend. And he turned again into the camp: but his servant Joshua, the son of Nun, a young man, departed not out of the tabernacle.

  ❖ Moses did not intercede on the basis of right or wrong actions of the children of Israel but he pleaded by the blood covenant.
Exodus 32:9-14 And the Lord said unto Moses, I have seen this people, and, behold, it is a stiff necked people: Now therefore let me alone, that my wrath may wax hot against them and that I may consume them: and I will make of thee a great nation. And Moses besought the Lord his God, and said, Lord, why doth thy wrath wax hot against thy people, which thou hast brought forth out of the land of Egypt with great power, and with a mighty hand? Wherefore should the Egyptians speak, and say, For mischief did he bring them out, to slay them in the mountains, and to consume them from the face of the earth? Turn from thy fierce wrath, and repent of this evil against thy people. Remember Abraham, Isaac, and Israel, thy servants, to whom thou swarest by thine own self, and saidst unto them, I will multiply your seed as

the stars of heaven, and all this land that l have spoken of will l give unto your seed, and they shall inherit it forever. And the Lord repented of the evil which he thought to do unto his people.

Exodus 32:31-32 And Moses returned unto the LORD, and said, Oh, this people have sinned a great sin, and have made them gods of gold. Yet now, if thou wilt forgive their sin --; and if not, blot me, I pray thee, out of thy book which thou hast written.

❖ The intercession of Jesus.
Isaiah 53:12 Therefore will l divide him a portion with the great and he shall divide the spoil with the strong; because he hath poured out his soul unto death: and he was numbered with the transgressors; and he bare the sin of many and made *intercession* for the transgressors.

Definition: *intercession – paga'* (paw-gah'); a primitive root; to impinge, by accident or violence, or (figuratively) by importunity; come (betwixt), cause to entreat, fall (upon), make intercession, intercessor, entreat, lay, light [upon], meet (together), pray, reach, run.

❖ To light upon (*paga*)
Genesis 28:11-14 And he lighted upon a certain place, and tarried there all night, because the sun was set; and he took of the stones of that place, and put them for his pillows, and lay down in that place to sleep. And he dreamed, and behold a ladder set up on the earth, and the top of it reached to heaven: and behold the angels of God ascending and descending on it. And, behold, the Lord stood above it, and said, l am the Lord God of Abraham thy father, and the God of Isaac: the land whereon thou liest, to thee will l give it, and to thy seed; And thy seed shall be as the dust of the earth, and thou shalt spread abroad to the west, and to the east, and to the north, and to the south: and in thee and in thy seed shall all the families of the earth be blessed.

❖ To fall upon and violently attach an enemy at the command of the king (*paga*)
1 Samuel 22:18 And the king said to Doeg, Turn thou and fall upon the priests. And Doeg, the Edomite, turned and he fell upon the priests and slew on that day fourscore and five persons that did wear a linen ephod.
Matthew 11:12 And from the days of John the Baptist until now, the kingdom of heaven suffereth violence and the violent take it by force.

❖ To reach a boundary (*paga*)
Joshua 19:11 And their border went up toward the sea, and Maralah, and reached to Dabbasheth, and reached to the river that is before Jokneam.

❖ The Holy Spirit causes us to know what to pray when we pray in tongues.
Romans 8:26-28 Likewise the Spirit also helpeth our infirmities: for we know not what we should pray for as we ought: but the Spirit itself maketh intercession for us with groanings which cannot be uttered. And he that searcheth the hearts knoweth what is the mind of the Spirit, because he maketh *intercession* for the saints according to the will of God. And we know that all things work together for good to them that love God, to them who are the called according to his purpose.

Definition: *intercession – huperentugchano* (hoop-er-en-toong-than -o); from *huper* and *entugchano*; to intercede on behalf of; make intercession for.
– *huper* (hoop-er'); a primary preposition; "over", i.e. (with the genitive case) of place, above, beyond, across, or causal, for the sake of, instead, regarding; with the accusative case superior to, more than;

(exceeding, abundantly) above, in (on) behalf of, beyond, by, very chiefest, concerning, exceeding (above, -ly), for, very highly, more (than), of, over, on the part of, for sake of, instead, than, to (-ward), very. In comparison, it retains many of the above applications.

– *entugchano* (en-toong-khan'-o); from 1722 and 5177; to chance upon, i.e. (by implication) confer with; by extension to entreat (in favor or against): KJV -- deal with, make intercession. (DIC)

1 Timothy 2:1 I exhort therefore, that, first of all, supplications, prayers, intercessions, and giving of thanks, be made for all men.

❖ He ever lives to intercede.

Hebrews 7:25 Wherefore he is able also to save them to the uttermost that come unto God by him, seeing he ever liveth to make intercession for them.

❖ This dealing was for the sake of communing.

Genesis 18:31-33 And he said, Behold now, I have taken upon me to speak unto the Lord: Peradventure there shall be twenty found there. And he said, I will not destroy it for twenty's sake. And he said, Oh let not the Lord be angry, and I will speak yet but this once: Peradventure ten shall be found there. And he said, I will not destroy it for ten's sake. And the LORD went his way, as soon as he had left communing with Abraham: and Abraham returned unto his place.

⟹Escape is provided in the covenant.

❖ They were encouraged to hasten to escape.

Genesis 19:15-17 And when the morning arose, then the angels hastened Lot, saying, Arise, take thy wife, and thy two daughters, which are here; lest thou be consumed in the iniquity of the city. And while he lingered, the men laid hold upon his hand, and upon the hand of his wife, and upon the hand of his two daughters; the LORD being merciful unto him: and they brought him forth, and set him without the city. And it came to pass, when they had brought them forth abroad, that he said, Escape for thy life; look not behind thee, neither stay thou in all the plain; escape to the mountain, lest thou be consumed.

❖ The Lord knows to deliver each one of his children.

2 Peter 2:9 The Lord knoweth how to deliver the Godly out of temptations, and to reserve the unjust unto the day of judgment to be punished.

❖ For each temptation there has been a way of escape provided.

1 Corinthians 10:13 There hath no temptation taken you but such as is common to man: but God is faithful, who will not *suffer* you to be tempted above that ye are able; but will with the temptation also make a way to escape, that ye may be able to bear it.

❖ Give more earnest heed and do not let the way of escape slip away.

Hebrews 2:1-3 Therefore we ought to give the more earnest heed to the things which we have heard, lest at any time we should let them slip. For if the word spoken by angels was steadfast, and every transgression and disobedience received a just recompense of reward; How shall we escape, if we neglect so great salvation; which at the first began to be spoken by the Lord, and was confirmed unto us by them that heard him.

❖ The Lord could be waiting on you today.

Genesis 19:22 Haste thee, escape thither; for I cannot do anything till thou become thither. Therefore the name of the city was called Zoar.

Revelation 7:3 Saying, Hurt not the earth, neither the sea, nor the trees, till we have seated the servants of our God in their foreheads.

⇒Lot's wife delayed and was lost.

Genesis 19:23-26 The sun was risen upon the earth when Lot entered into Zoar. Then the LORD rained upon Sodom and upon Gomorrah brimstone and fire from the LORD out of heaven; And he overthrew those cities, and all the plain, and all the inhabitants of the cities, and that which grew upon the ground. But his wife looked back from behind him, and she became a pillar of salt.

❖ Sisters of Sodom:

Ezekiel 16:49 Behold, this was the iniquity of thy sister Sodom, pride, fullness of bread, and abundance of idleness was in her and in her daughters, neither did she strengthen the hand of the poor and needy.

❖ Pride, fullness of bread, abundance of idleness and laziness in the performance of righteousness.

❖ Lot's wife is a type of the sisters of Sodom.

❖ "Remember Lot's wife."

Luke 17:28-33 Likewise also as it was in the days of Lot; they did eat, they drank, they bought, they sold, they planted, they builded; But the same day that Lot went out of Sodom it rained fire and brimstone from heaven, and destroyed them all. Even thus shall it be in the day when the Son of man is revealed. In that day, he which shall be upon the housetop, and his stuff in the house, let him not come down to take it away: and he that is in the field, let him likewise not return back. Remember Lot's wife. Whosoever shall seek to save his life shall lose it; and whosoever shall lose his life shall preserve it.

❖ Covenant promises are not for the lazy.

Hebrews 6:12 That ye be not *slothful*, but followers of them who through faith and patience inherit the promises.

Definition: *slothful – nothros* (no-thros?); sluggish, lazy or stupid; dull, slothful.

❖ A worldly **'hang over'**:

Luke 21:34-36 And take heed to yourselves, lest at any time your hearts be overcharged with *surfeiting*, and drunkenness, and cares of this life, and so that day come upon you unawares. For as a snare shall it come on all them that dwell on the face of the whole earth. Watch ye therefore, and pray always, that ye may be accounted worthy to escape all these things that shall come to pass, and to stand before the Son of man.

Definition: *surfeiting – kraipale* (krahee-pal'-ay); properly, a headache (as a seizure of pain) from drunkenness, i.e. (by implication) a debauch.

❖ The Lord pleads with all.

Isaiah 66:16 For by pure and by his sword will the Lord plead with all perish: and the slain of the Lord shall be many.

❖ After this, the gospel of the Kingdom will be preached to all nations.

Isaiah 66:19 And I will set a sign among them, and I will send those that escape of them unto the nations, to Tarshish, Pul, and Lud, that draw the bow, to Tubal, and Javan. to the isles afar *off,* that have not heard my fame, neither have seen my glory; and they shall declare my glory among the Gentiles.

Matthew 24:14-16 And this gospel of the kingdom shall be preached in all the world for a witness unto all nations; and then shall !he end come. When ye therefore shall see the abomination of desolation, spoken of by Daniel the prophet, stand in the holy place, (whoso readeth, let him understand:) Then let them which be in Judaea flee into the mountains:

⟹Righteousness was given to Lot for the sake of the covenant between Abraham and God.

Genesis 19:29 And it came to pass, when God destroyed the cities of the plain, that God remembered Abraham, and sent Lot out of the midst of the overthrow, when he overthrew the cities in the which Lot dwelt.

❖ Because of the covenant cut between Jonathan and David, the king (David) searched out Jonathan's seed in order to bless them.

2 Samuel 9:1 And David said, ls there yet any that is left of the house of Saul, that I may show him kindness for Jonathan's sake?

❖ The promise is always to one's "seed" and one's "seed's seed".

1 Samuel 20:14-17 And thou shalt not only while yet I live show me the kindness of the Lord, that I die not: But also thou shalt not cut *off* thy kindness from my house for ever: no, not when-the Lord hath cut off the enemies of David every one from the face of the earth. So Jonathan made a covenant with the house of David, saying, Let the Lord even require it at the hand of David's enemies. And Jonathan caused David to swear again, because he loved him: for he loved him as he loved his own soul.

❖ Because Jesus has given us His name, we are forgiven. The Father is sending the Holy Spirit to plead with the heirs of salvation to receive the mercy which is extended.

Ephesians 4:32 And be ye kind one to another, tenderhearted, forgiving one another, even us God for Christ's sake hath forgiven you.

2 Corinthians 5:21 For he hath made him to be sin for us, who knew no sin; that we might be made the righteousness of God in him.

John 3:14-15 And as Moses lifted up the serpent in the wilderness, even so must the Son of man be lifted up:That whosoever believeth in him should not perish, but have eternal life.

Hebrews 12:1-2 Wherefore seeing we also are compassed about with so great a cloud of witnesses, let us lay aside every weight, and the sin which doth so easily beset us, and let us run with patience the race that is set before us, Looking unto Jesus the author and finisher of our faith; who for the joy that was set before him endured the cross, despising the shame, and is set down at the right hand of the throne of God.

~ Lesson 9 ~
Warfare Through Intercessory Prayer

⇒ In intercessory prayer, the one praying commands the devil to stop his activity so that the will of God can be fulfilled.

⇒ Satan stands against God's promises and binds people today. He binds the demonic powers like alcohol, depression, and anger which are holding a person in bondage.

⇒ During intercessory prayer we will pray in our **prayer language** most of the time.

An intercessor is someone who pulls two that have been separated back together again. For better understanding imagine four different persons: GOD, MAN, DEVIL, and the INTERCESSOR. The devil has his arms around the man and is pulling him away from God. Though the man tries to reach out for God, he is unable to reach Him because the man is bound by the devil. The intercessor first breaks the bonds of the devil (breaking the hold around the man's waist) and then joins the man with God (representing his will joining God's will).

Matthew 9:35, 36 show us that the basis for Jesus' ministry was love and compassion for all mankind. It never said that He took pity on someone. Likewise the basis for intercessor prayer is love and compassion. Compassion goes further than pity. Both express sorrow for the suffering of others; however, compassion acts to do something about it spiritually.

Steps of Intercessory Prayer

➢ **Go Through the Gates:** In the Bible the gate stands for authority. It is at the city gates where the authority of the city sat and ruled. Satan is the father of all unbelievers and the authority over everything on earth. When we pray a prayer of intercession, we go past the authority holding the person from coming to the Lord. "…And the gates of hell shall not prevail against (the church)" – [**Matthew 16:18**]

➢ **Prepare the Way of the People; Cast (Build) up the Highway:** In a prayer of intercession we prepare the way for the people to come to God through salvation by building up a highway in the spirit. We plow the 'hard ground' by praying in tongues. We 'build the highway' by speaking the promises of salvation found in the Bible [**Acts 16:31; 2 Peter 3:9**] "The voice of him that crieth in the wilderness, Prepare ye the way of the Lord, make straight in the desert a highway for our God." – [**Isaiah 40:3**]

➢ **Gather (Cast) Out the Stones:** We pray the hindrances from the person's life that would keep them from coming to the Lord like fear, unbelief, unworthiness, and false doctrine.

➢ **Lift up a Standard:** Teach them God's word

Intercessory prayer is a prayer of persistence.

Luke 11:5-13 is a Biblical example of the prayer of intercession. We find in verse 9 that if we ask we will receive. Therefore, keep on asking, seeking, and knocking. It is not just a prayer of petition because this kind of praying involves another's will who has been deceived by and bound by Satan and strongholds have built up as a result.

Persistence is a strong, shameless stand on the word of God.

We will not look at the circumstances or what the person is doing. We will look at God's promises instead and believe them no matter what it looks like. We are going to continue to persist against the gates of hell until the answer comes. And we will take authority over the spiritual forces that are controlling the person's life.

NOTES

Chapter 5
The Emotional Strongman

Take every thought captive to obey Christ.
[2 Corinthians 10:5]

Do **NOT** let your emotions rule you; instead, allow the Spirit of God to rise up within you.

Ephesians 6:17 instructs us to put on the whole armor of God and to *"take the helmet of salvation and the sword of the Spirit, which is the word of God."* When a soldier suited up for battle, the helmet was the last piece of armor to go on. It was the final act of readiness in preparation for combat. A helmet was vital for survival because it protected the brain, the command station for the rest of the body. If the head were badly damaged, the rest of the armor would be of little use.

The assurance of salvation is our impenetrable defense against anything the enemy throws at us. Jesus said, "Do not be afraid of those who kill the body but cannot kill the soul. Rather, be afraid of the **one** who can destroy both soul and body in hell" [**Matthew 10:28**]. The idea in this verse is that, as we prepare for Satan's attacks, we must grab that helmet and buckle it on tightly. Salvation is not limited to a one-time act of the past or even a future hope. God's salvation is an ongoing, eternal state that His children enjoy in the present. It is daily protection and deliverance from our sin nature and Satan's schemes.

Because of the power of the cross, our enemy no longer has any hold on us [**Romans 6:10; 8:2; 1 Corinthians 1:18**]. He knows that, but he also knows that most of God's children do not know that—or, at least, they do not live as if they know. We must learn to keep our helmets buckled so that his fiery missiles do not lodge in our thoughts and set us on fire. Through this helmet of salvation, we can "destroy arguments and every lofty opinion raised against the knowledge of God, and **take every thought captive to obey Christ**" [**2 Corinthians 10:5**].

❖ **Renew our minds.** *Our minds are battlefields.* The outcomes of those battles determine the course of our lives. **Romans 12:1, 2** instructs us to renew our minds by allowing the truth of God's Word to wipe out anything contrary to it. Old ideas, opinions, and worldviews must be replaced. We must allow God's truth to continually wash away the world's filth, lies, and confusion from our minds and adopt God's perspective.

❖ **Reject doubts that arise from circumstances.** Human beings are sensory creatures. What we cannot fathom with our five senses, we tend to disregard. If we allow them to, circumstances may convince us that God does not really love us or that His Word is not true. It is impossible to have faith and doubt at the same time. God rewards our faith. With the helmet of salvation firmly in place, we can choose to believe what appears impossible [**Hebrews 11:6; 1 Peter 1:8, 9**].

❖ **Keep an eternal perspective**. When life crashes in around us, we must remember to look up. Our salvation is the most precious gift we have received. Keeping our eyes on that can help us weather life's storms. We can choose to live our lives by the motto "If it doesn't have eternal significance, it's not important." [**Matthew 6:20; 1 Corinthians 3:11-13**]

❖ **Remember that victory is already accomplished.** When we consider ourselves "dead to sin but alive to God" [Romans 6:11], we eliminate many of the opportunities Satan uses to entrap us. When choosing sin is no longer an option for us because we recognize ourselves to be 'new creatures' [**2 Corinthians 5:17; 1 John 3:9**], we effectively cut off many avenues of failure.

❖ **Find all our hope in Him.** [**Psalm 73:25**] says, "Whom have I in heaven but You? Besides You, I desire nothing on earth." Our helmet is most effective when we treasure what it represents. The salvation Jesus purchased for us cannot share the place of importance in our hearts with earthly things. When pleasing the Lord is our supreme delight, we eliminate many of Satan's lures and render his evil suggestions powerless.

As we wear the helmet of salvation everyday, our minds become more insulated AGAINST the suggestions of emotions, desires, and traps the enemy lays for us.

We choose to guard our minds from excessive worldly influence and instead think on things that honor Christ [**Philippians 4:8**]. In doing so, we wear our salvation as a protective helmet that will "guard our hearts and minds in Christ Jesus" [**Philippians 4:7; Isaiah 26:3; 1 Peter 1:5**]

~ Lesson 1 ~
Exposing the Names of the Different Emotional Strongmen

Emotions are quite natural and everybody has them. I am not saying that just because we are emotional we are under the control of spiritual strongmen. Neither am I saying that if someone suffers from an emotional or mental illness, they are demon possessed.

My own father was an epileptic for well over forty years of his life. I have had friends and associates in the ministry who were epileptics as well as patients I saw while working in the medical field. Evil spirits did not control them. However, I have seen many people who, when the unclean spirits were cast out of them, no longer suffered from seizures.

Everyone who suffers from emotional problems is not necessarily demon possessed. On the other hand, everyone who is demon possessed suffers from emotional problems. For example, we see this in the young boy who was brought by his father to Jesus because the disciples could not help the boy. Then there is the demoniac of the Gadarenes who lived among the graves.

Sometimes damaged emotions can bring on mental illness. It's obvious that there are strongmen who work behind and through damaged emotions. There is **Aclahayr**, *the spirit behind mental illness*, who seeks to enslave the minds of men and bring them to ruin. The **Aeshma** *spirit works through wrath, anger, rages, and fury*. He drives men to cause great harm, destruction and even murder.

Deception, Lies, Accusations, Broken Relationships, Marriages

Agathodemon is a very *powerful spirit of deception and lies*. He perverts the truth and ruins lives through slander, false accusations and defamation of character. He leaves behind him a vast tract of broken relationships, marriages, friendships and partnerships – forever destroyed because of his deception.

The powerful spirit of revenge is called **Afrit**. He causes people to seek not justice for an act done to them, but for revenge. He cries out "an eye for an eye, a tooth for a tooth, and a life for a life." He deafens you to the words of Jesus: "If your brother strikes you on one cheek, turn to him the other." *He stops man from hearing the Lord proclaim: "Revenge is Mine."* He keeps plaguing the mind of man until he cries out "blood for blood." He is not satisfied until he extracts his pound of flesh for the acts done against him. **Afrit** works well with other strongmen known as **Alastor** and **Danglathas**, which are *spirits of murder*.

Afrit has an evil twin who is also a terrible spirit of revenge, called **Arioch**.

Agares is the *spirit of fake courage* who works extremely well with **Agramon**, the **spirit of fear**, and **Inguma**, a *Baskian spirit of fear*. This spirit works to rob man of any peace, joy, or confidence he may have in God, his fellowman of himself.

Strongmen of Perversions

There are spirits like: **Aka Manah**, a *spirit behind perverted minds and deeds*; **Ashtaroth**, *spirit of lust and seduction* and a leader of the **Incubus** and **Succubus**. **Alu-Demon** is a night spirit that works when men are asleep. **Jaldabaoth** is the *strongman of lust*. **Ornias** is the *strongman of homosexuality* and

Dantalion is a *spirit of bisexualism.* **Ezuli** is a *spirit of fornication and adultery.* **Philatanus** is a very powerful *strongman behind sodomy and pedophile acts*, while **Proserpine** is a *spirit of sodomy* and **Druj** is a **spirit of perversion and corruption.**

The strongmen behind the acts of evil are **Akatash**, and the Hebrew snake spirit of evil and stubbornness is **Aspis**, while **Az** is the strongman behind evil desires.

A tormenting spirit keeps a person
from feeling forgiven and accepted by God.

Aku Aku is the *spirit that causes the mind to be troubled and extremely aggravated.* He renders the mind unable to be at peace, to feel joy, happiness or love. **Ammit** is the *spirit of spiritual torment.* This tormenting spirit keeps a person from feeling forgiven and accepted by God. They feel constantly inadequate to be loved and redeemed from their past. They struggle with the concept that they have committed the unpardonable sin.

Ammit works well with **Angra Mainyu**, the s*pirit of pain, torment and suffering.* **Aka Manah** and **Ammit** will often join forces together with **Alperer**, a *strongman who specializes in tormenting and troubling the minds of lonely women.* **Alperer** will open the door for another spirit called **Hunza** who *specializes in tormenting women.* **Chil Gazi** is an ***incubus*** who *seduces women sexually and eventually leads them to perform suicides.*

Destruction, Chaos, Hate, Violence, Slander, Accusation, Discord, Strife, Poverty

There are also *spirits of destruction and chaos* like **Azathoth** and **Joetun**. In fact **Joetun** is a *GIANT spirit of destruction and chaos.* **Ardat-Lile** is a *strongman specializing in **family** destruction and chaos.* **Apasmara** is the *spirit of mindlessness and confusion.* **Bael** is the *Hebrew strongman of shrewdness and deception.* **Caym** is the *spirit behind vain logic and puns.*

Indra is the *Iranian spirit of hate and violence.* He hates the truth and works with **Jezebeth**, the *spirit of falsehood and lies*, and also **Malphas**, *the spirit of deception and lies.* There are several other lying spirits like **Murmur**, the *master spirit of lies, deceit, slander, falsehood and accusations.*

He works with **Pyro**, the *spirit of falsehood*, and **Samael**, the *Hebrew fallen watcher* who is the *leader of the spirits of slander and accusation and is a major seducer.* Then there are the vastly powerful *spirits of hos*tility like **Mastema**, and the equally powerful *spirit of war, discord, quarrels, strife and poverty* – the strongman **Pruflas**. **Busas**, *the spirit of poverty*, works not only on the materialist but also very much so in the area of the mind and the spirit of man.

Another strongman who also assaults us is **Gresil**, or **Gressil**, the *spirit of procrastination and laziness.* Then there are the very powerful *principalities of drunkenness, jealousy and envy* called **Daevas**, with its Hebrew counterpart, **Sonneillon**, *the spirit of hate*, **Succorbenoth**, *another spirit of hate*, and **Uphir**, *the spirit of pharmaceutical drug abuse and addiction.* **Daevas**, *the spirit of drunkenness*, and **Uphir** the *strongman of drug addiction, and the spirits of sexual perversion and thievery*, along with **Alastor** and **Danglathas**, the *principalities of murder,* are going to be the **FIVE MAJOR SINS of the last days**.

The last two strongmen of emotions do **NOT** at first seem to be strongmen of emotions; however, taking a closer look, we can see how they work hand in hand with all of the other spirits.

Ansitif, the *strongman of possession*, and **Rabisu**, the *spirit that lies in wait*, are two very patient spirits. They are more than willing to wait patiently for a crack to appear in your armor so they can slip in and set up camp in you and keep the door open wide for all the others to enter.

These are what used to be called the doorkeepers.

When a pastor would do deliverance they would seek out the spirits that kept the doors open so the lead spirit could enter with others. Once these spirits were revealed, they would be cast out and the door sealed so they could no longer enter in. In **Genesis 4**, the Lord warned Cain that sin waits at the door patiently for a chance to enter in.

We must always be on our guard.
Remember, Satan goes about as a roaring lion seeking whosoever he can devour.

◆Chart of the Emotional Strongmen◆

1. **Aclahayr** – spirit behind mental anguish and disorders	30. **Chil Gazi** – seducer of women
2. **Aeshma** – controlling spirit behind violence, wrath, anger, rage and fury	31. **Daevas** – spirit behind drunkenness, envy, and impure sexuality
3. **Afrit** – relentless spirit of revenge	32. **Danglathas** – spirit behind violent crimes and murder
4. **Agares** – spirit behind false courage	33. **Dantalion** – three-face spirit of sexual perversion, bisexualism, gender confusion, mind reading and the worship of the occult
5. **Agathodemon** – driving force behind deception	34. **Druj** – spirit that works through perversion and corruption
6. **Agramon** – powerful spirit behind fears	35. **Erzulie** – spirit of fornication and adultery
7. **Aka Manah** – spirit behind the perverted mind and evil deeds	36. **Furfur** – spirit that works through perversion and corruption
8. **Akatash** – spirit behnd evil thoughts	37. **Gresil/Gressil** – spirit behind laziness
9. **Aku Aku** – spirit behind unstable, troubled, aggravated mind	38. **Incubus** – male demon of sexual lusting
10. **Alastor** – spirit behind murder	39. **Indra** – Iranian name for spirit of violence
11. **Alperer** – spirit that preys and troubles lonely women	40. **Inguma** – Biskian name for the spirit of fear
12. **Alu-Demon** – night spirit behind nightmares and bad dreams	41. **Jaldabaoth** – spirit of lust
13. **Ammit** – spirit behind spiritual torment	42. **Jezebeth** – spirit of falsehood and lies
14. **Andras** – spirit who works through quarrels and strife	43. **Joetun** – giant spirit of emotional chaos and destruction
15. **Angra Mainyu** – spirit behind pain, suffering, and torment	44. **Malphas** – spirit that works through deception and lies
16. **Ansitif** – spirit that possesses people	45. **Mammon** – New Testament spirit of greed
17. **Aosoth** – spirit that works through passion and death	46. **Mastema** – spirit behind hostility
18. **Apasmara** – spirit of mindlessness and glare (staring, daze) and belief in reincarnation	47. **Murmur** – spirit of lies, slander, accusations, falsehood, and deceit
19. **Ardat-Lile** – spirit behind destruction of families	48. **Ornias** – spirit of homosexuality
20. **Arioch** – spirit that works behind revenge	49. **Philatanus** – Jewish strongman of sodomy

21. **Ashtaroth** – spirit of lust and seduction	50. **Proserpine** – spirit who helps in establishing the act of sodomy
22. **Aspis** – Hebrew snake-like spirit of evil and stubbornness	51. **Pruflas/Busas** – spirits of war, discord, quarrels, and poverty
23. **Awar** – spirit behind laziness	52. **Pyro** – spirit that works behind falsehood
24. **Az** – spirit of extreme evil	53. **Rabisu – strongman who lies in wait, the doorkeeper (Genesis 4:6)**
25. **Azathoth** – powerful spirit of chaos	54. **Samael** – Hebrew spirit, which is a former Watcher who works through slander, accusation, and seduction
26. **Bael** – spirit of shrewdness and deception	55. **Sonneillon** – spirit of hate
27. **Belial** – Hebrew spirit of emotional darkness, uselessness, and desperation	56. **Succorbenoth** – Hebrew spirit behind jealousy
28. **Bilwis** – German name of the spirit of envy and absolute meanness	57. **Succubus** – female demon of sexual lusting
29. **Caym** – spirit of vain logic and puns	58. **Uphir** – spirit of pharmaceutical drug abuse and chemical and substance addictions

Recommended Reading: The Secret Names of the Strongmen by H.A.Lewis

Prayer Against the Strongmen of Emotions

*Dear Lord, we thank You for the precious blood that covers us [**1 John 1:7**] and closes all doors or entryways to the enemy and his allies. We thank You, Father, for Your love and mercy and for Your forgiveness and compassion. We thank You, Lord, because You are our Good Shepherd. You are the One who protects us from the roaring lion. We thank You, Father that Jesus came to give us peace – that wonderful peace which passes all understanding. He was more than willing to heal our troubled minds as well as our bodies and spirits.*

We no longer have to depend on our troubled minds, but by faith we can have the mind of Christ.
*[**1 Corinthians 2:16**] It is having the mind of Christ that no strongman can prevail against and brings peace to everyone who believes, even in the midst of the most chaotic emotional storms we will ever go through. In Jesus name, Amen.*

*In Jesus' name I renounce all suicidal thoughts and any attempts I've made to take my own life or in any way injure myself. I confess (**name each sin of self-destruction that comes to mind**) and put it under the blood of Jesus. I renounce the lie that life is hopeless and that I can find peace and freedom by taking my own life. Satan is a thief and comes to steal, kill and destroy. I put any access any demons claim to my life or to my family under the blood of Jesus. In Jesus' name I cover all that with the blood of Jesus.*

*I choose life in Christ who came to give me life and give it more abundantly [**John 10:10**]*

Thank You for Your forgiveness that allows me to forgive myself. I choose to believe that there is always hope in Christ. In Jesus' name I pray. Amen.

Psalm 27

The Lord is my light and my salvation – whom shall I fear? The Lord is the stronghold of my life – of whom shall I be afraid?

When the wicked advance against me to devour me, it is my enemies and my foes who will stumble and fall.

Though an army besiege me, even then I will be confident.

One thing I ask from the Lord, this only do I seek: that I may dwell in the house of the Lord all the days of my life, to gaze on the beauty of the Lord and to seek Him in His temple.

For in the day of trouble He will keep me safe in His dwelling; He will hide me in the shelter of His sacred tent and set me high upon a rock.

Then my head will be exalted above the enemies who surround me; at his sacred tent I will sacrifice with shouts of joy; I will sing and make music to the Lord.

Hear my voice when I call, Lord be merciful to me and answer me.

My heart says of you, "Seek his face!" Your face, Lord, I will seek.

Do not hide your face from me, do not turn your servant away in anger; you have been my helper. Do not reject me or forsake me, God my Savior.

Though my father and mother forsake me, the Lord will receive me.

Teach me your way, Lord; lead me in a straight path because of my oppressors.

Do not turn me over to the desire of my foes, for false witnesses rise up against me, spouting malicious accusations.

I remain confident of this: I will see the goodness of the Lord in the land of the living.

Wait for the Lord; be strong and take heart and wait for the Lord.

Heavenly Father, I desire to be obedient by being strong in the Lord and the power of Your might. I see that this is Your will and purpose for me. I recognize that is essential to put on the armor that You have provided, anad I do so now with gratitude and praise that You have provided all I need to stand in victory against Satan and his kingdom. Grant me wisdom to discern the tactics and sneakiness of Satan's strategy against me. I delight to take the armor You have provided and by faith to put it on as effective spiritual protection against the spiritual forces of darkness present in the world today.

I confidently take the belt of truth that You offer me. I take Him who is the truth as my strength and protection. I reject Satan's lies and deceiving ways to gain advantage against me. Grant me discernment and wisdom to recognize the subtle and sneaky ways in which Satan seeks to cause me to accept his lies as truth. I desire to believe only the truth, to live the truth, to speak the truth, and to know the truth. I worship and praise You that You lead me only in the ways of truth. Thank You that Satan cannot stand against the truth.

Thank You for the breastplate of righteousness which you offer me.

I eagerly accept it and put it on as my protection. Thank You for reminding me again that all of my righteousness comes from You. I embrace that righteousness which is mine by faith in the Lord Jesus Christ. It is His righteousness that is mine through justification. I reject and repudiate all trust in my own righteousness, which is as filthy rags. I ask You to cleanse me of all the times I have counted my own goodness as being acceptable before You. I bring the righteousness of my Lord directly against all of Satan's workings against me. I express my desire to walk in righteousness before God today. By faith I appropriate the righteousness of Christ and invite Him to walk His holiness in my life today that I might experience His righteousness in total context of ordinary living. I count upon the righteousness of my Lord to be my protection. I know that Satan must retreat from before God's righteousness.

*Thank You Lord, for the sandals of peace You have provided. I desire that my feet should stand on the solid rock of the peace that You have provided. I claim the peace with God which is mine through justification. I desire the peace of God which touches my emotions and feelings through prayer and sanctification [**Philippians 4:6**]. Thank You that as I walk in obedience to You the God of peace promises to walk with me [**Philippians 4:9**], I thank You that as the God of peace You are putting Satan under my feet [**Romans 16:20**]. I will share this good news of peace with all others that Your Spirit will bring into my life today. Thank You that You have not given me a spirit of fear but of love and power and a sound mind [**2 Timothy 1:7**]. Thank You that Satan cannot stand against Your peace.*

NOTES

Chapter 6
Scriptures to Combat Emotional Areas

◆Scriptures Against Fear◆

The following is a list of scriptures on fear. Use them when fear is attempting to come. Fear does not necessarily mean danger. It simply means fear. We associate fear with danger because that is how our body interacts with our God-given motivation for self-preservation. When we go into a dark room, we might sense fear, especially if we are apprehensive about the dark, but that does not mean that there actually is a danger. It only means that there is an unknown, and that unknown can breed fear – fear of the unknown. To fight the fear of the unknown, counteract it with faith based on the known – the known will of God. All Scriptures are from the King James Version.

❖ **Psalm 23:1-6** The Lord is my shepherd; I shall not want. He makes me to lie down in green pastures: he leads me beside the still waters. He restores my soul: he leads me in the paths of righteousness for his name's sake. Yea, though I walk through the valley of the shadow of death, I will fear no evil: for thou art with me; thy rod and thy staff they comfort me. Thou preparest a table before me in the presence of mine enemies: thou anoints my head with oil; my cup runs over. Surely goodness and mercy shall follow me all the days of my life: and I will dwell in the house of the Lord forever.

❖ **Psalm 27:1-6** The Lord is my light and my salvation; whom shall I fear? The Lord is the strength of my life; of whom shall I be afraid? When the wicked, even mine enemies and my foes, came upon me to eat up my flesh, they stumbled and fell. Though a host should encamp against me, my heart shall not fear: though war should rise against me, in this will I be confident. One thing have I desired of the Lord, that will I seek after; that I may dwell in the house of the Lord all the days of my life, to behold the beauty of the Lord, and to inquire in his temple. For in the time of trouble he shall hide me in his pavilion: in the secret of his tabernacle shall he hide me; he shall set me up upon a rock. And now shall mine head be lifted up above mine enemies round about me: therefore will I offer in his tabernacle sacrifices of joy; I will sing, yea, I will sing praises unto the Lord.

❖ **Psalm 46:1-3** God is our refuge and strength, a very present help in trouble. Therefore will not we fear, though the earth be removed, and though the mountains be carried into the midst of the sea; Though the waters thereof roar and be troubled, though the mountains shake with the swelling thereof. Selah.

❖ **Psalm 55:22** Cast thy burden upon the Lord, and he shall sustain thee: he shall never suffer the righteous to be moved.

❖ **Psalm 56:3, 4** What time I am afraid, I will trust in thee. In God I will praise his word, in God I have put my trust; I will not fear what flesh can do unto me.

- **Psalm 56:9-11** When I cry unto thee, then shall mine enemies turn back: this I know; for God is for me. In God will I praise his word: in the Lord will I praise his word. In God have I put my trust: I will not be afraid what man can do unto me.

- **Psalm 118:5, 6** I called upon the Lord in distress: the Lord answered me, and set me in a large place. The Lord is on my side; I will not fear: what can man do unto me?

- **Proverbs 3:25, 26** Be not afraid of sudden fear, neither of the desolation of the wicked, when it comes. For the Lord shall be thy confidence, and shall keep thy foot from being taken.

- **Proverbs 29:25** The fear of man brings a snare: but whoso puts his trust in the Lord shall be safe.

- **Jeremiah 17:7, 8** Blessed is the man that trusts in the Lord, and whose hope the Lord is. For he shall be as a tree planted by the waters, and that spreads out her roots by the river, and shall not see when heat comes, but her leaf shall be green; and shall not be careful in the year of drought, neither shall cease from yielding fruit.

- **Isaiah 12:2** Behold, God is my salvation; I will trust, and not be afraid: for the Lord Jehovah is my strength and my song; he also is become my salvation.

- **John 14:27** Peace I leave with you, my peace I give unto you: not as the world gives, give I unto you. Let not your heart be troubled, neither let it be afraid.

- **Romans 8:15** For ye have not received the spirit of bondage again to fear; but ye have received the Spirit of adoption, whereby we cry, Abba, Father.

- **Romans 8:28-33** And we know that all things work together for good to them that love God, to them who are the called according to his purpose. For whom he did foreknow, he also did predestinate to be conformed to the image of his Son, that he might be the firstborn among many brethren. Moreover whom he did predestinate, them he also called: and whom he called, them he also justified: and whom he justified, them he also glorified. What shall we then say to these things? If God be for us, who can be against us? He that spared not his own Son, but delivered him up for us all, how shall he not with him also freely give us all things? Who shall lay anything to the charge of God's elect? It is God that justifies.

- **2 Timothy 1:7** For God hath not given us the spirit of fear; but of power, and of love, and of a sound mind.

- **Hebrews 13:5, 6** Let your conversation be without covetousness; and be content with such things as ye have: for he hath said, I will never leave thee, nor forsake thee. So that we may boldly say, The Lord is my helper, and I will not fear what man shall do unto me.

❖ **1 Peter 5:5-7** Likewise, ye younger, submit yourselves unto the elder. Yea, all of you be subject one to another, and be clothed with humility: for God resists the proud, and gives grace to the humble. Humble yourselves therefore under the mighty hand of God, that he may exalt you in due time: Casting all your care upon him; for he cares for you.

♦Scriptures Against Suicide♦

TAKE HOPE! You have options that you cannot see right now! It is not that you do not have options; it is just that you cannot see them. Evil forces cloud our minds from seeing the hope of a better day. Only the word of God can strip away the darkness so that we can see the brightness. You are in the dark simply because you cannot see the light. Hurt and hopelessness work together to block the light. The light is actually all around you. MAKE YOURSELF read the following scriptures, even if you feel absolutely nothing. The deadness will leave. Hope and light will seep into your heart. Do it!

Anyone who is among the living has hope.
Ecclesiastes 9:4

Suicidal thoughts only survive within an outlook of complete hopelessness. Hope, true Biblical hope, is the best antidote for hopelessness. Take the hope that is resident in the promises of God and put it into your heart. Your outlook will change. God has a wonderful habit of raising individuals out of impossible situations. He enjoys doing it, and it brings Him glory. The Bible is full of stories of people, just like you, that were delivered out of extremely dangerous and potentially embarrassing situations – including His own son, Jesus. You are no different. Reject the guilt and shame, and absorb His love, forgiveness, and hope. You will make it out of this situation! The darkness will not last. That is the real truth, but for it to work, you must see it as truth and believe it. This is where reading, speaking, and meditating on God's promises comes in. They will grow hope and belief in your heart.

⇒Helping others is God's prescription for depression.⇐

Anxiety in a man's heart weighs it down (depression), but a good word cheers it up.
Proverbs 12:25 [Holman Christian Standard Bible]

Allow God's good word to cheer you up. God's word is the only true source of hope because it shows the will of Him who can help. Allow the hope of a good result to seep back into your heart. Suicide is the extreme dead-end of hopelessness. Allowing thoughts of hopelessness to control your thinking narrows and darkens your path till suicide appears to be the only option, BUT IT IS NOT. There are plenty of other solutions; you just can't see them now because hopelessness has blinded you to them. The hope that is resident in the promises of God will open the eyes of your heart, and you will be able to see again. It will get brighter.

Suicide only appears like an option when the devil has hidden all your other options. Allow the Bible to open your eyes.

You will have to work at it. You will not feel like it. Do it anyway, your life depends on it, and contrary to what you are feeling, YOUR LIFE IS WORTH IT. Suicide is a permanent solution to an intense but short-term problem. Don't do it!

>>Do not be a fool–why die before your time?<<
Ecclesiastes 7:17b

This may sound harsh but the hard truth is this – the thought to end one's life is foolish – and once you step back and see it for what it really is, you will understand. Do not despair; it will get better. The power to deliver is resident in His word. Put it to work for you. Relax! Make yourself read these scriptures and let God's word do the rest.

❖ **2 Samuel 22:29** You are my lamp O Lord; the Lord turns my darkness into light.

❖ **2 Chronicles 20:17** But you will not need to fight! Take your places; stand quietly and see the incredible rescue operation God will perform for you, Oh people of Judah and Jerusalem! Don't be afraid or discouraged! Go out there tomorrow, for the Lord is with you!

❖ **Job 10:12** You have granted me life and favor, and Your care has preserved my spirit.

❖ **Psalm 4:8** I will lie down in peace and sleep, for though I am alone, Oh Lord, you will keep me safe.

❖ **Psalm 5:12** For You, O Lord, will bless the righteous; with favor You will surround him as with a shield.

❖ **Psalm 25:3** No one whose hope is in you will ever be put to shame.

❖ **Psalm 25:5** You are God my Savior, and my hope is in you all day long.

❖ **Psalm 32:7-9** You are my hiding place from every storm of life; You even keep me from getting into trouble! You surround me with songs of victory. I will instruct you (says the Lord) and guide you along the best pathway for your life; I will advise you and watch your progress. Don't be like a senseless horse or mule that has to have a bit in its mouth to keep it in line!

❖ **Psalm 34:18, 19** The LORD is close to the brokenhearted and saves those who are crushed in spirit. A righteous man may have many troubles, but the Lord delivers him from them all.

❖ **Psalm 37:23, 24** If the Lord delights in a man's way, he makes his steps firm; though he stumbles, he will not fall, for the Lord upholds him with his hand.

❖ **Psalm 42:5** Why are you downcast, O my soul? Why so disturbed within me? Put your hope in God, for I will yet praise him, my Savior and my God.

❖ **Psalm 55:22** Cast your cares on the Lord and he will sustain you; he will never let the righteous fall.

❖ **Psalm 62:5** Find rest, O my soul, in God alone; my hope comes from him.

❖ **Psalm 65:5** You answer us with awesome deeds of righteousness, O God our Savior, the hope of all the ends of the earth and of the farthest seas.

❖ **Psalm 71:5** For you have been my hope, O Sovereign LORD, my confidence since my youth.

❖ **Psalm 71:4** But as for me, I will always have hope; I will praise you more and more.

❖ **Psalm 119:74** I have put my hope in your word.

❖ **Psalm 119:116a** Sustain me according to your promise, and I will live....

❖ **Psalm 145:14** The Lord upholds all those who fall and lifts up all who are bowed down.

❖ **Psalm 147:3** He heals the brokenhearted and binds up their wounds.

❖ **Proverbs 23:18** Surely, there is a future, and your hope will not be cut off.

❖ **Isaiah 26:3, 4** Thou wilt keep him in perfect peace, whose mind is stayed on Thee: because he trusts in Thee. Trust ye in the Lord forever: for in the Lord Jehovah is everlasting strength. (Perfect means complete. If I keep my part of the promise by staying steadfastly focused on the Lord Jesus Christ, He will keep His promise to give me His perfect peace.)

❖ **Isaiah 35:10** And the ransomed of the Lord will return. They will enter Zion with singing; everlasting joy will crown their heads. Gladness and joy will overtake them, and sorrow and sighing will flee away.

❖ **Isaiah 40:31** But they that wait upon the LORD shall renew their strength; they shall mount up with wings as eagles; they shall run, and not be weary; and they shall walk, and not faint.

❖ **John 14:18** No, I will not abandon you or leave you as orphans in the storm – I will come to you.

❖ **John 14:27** I am leaving you with a gift – peace of mind and heart! And the peace I give isn't fragile like the peace the world gives. So don't be troubled or afraid.

❖ **Romans 8:24, 25** We are saved by trusting. And trusting means looking forward to getting something we don't yet have – for a man who already has something doesn't need to hope and trust that he will get it. But if we must keep trusting God for something that hasn't happened yet, it teaches us to wait patiently and confidently.

❖ **Romans 15:4** For everything that was written in the past was written to teach us, so that through endurance and the encouragement of the Scriptures we might have hope.

❖ **Romans 15:13** May the God of hope fill you with all joy and peace as you trust in him, so that you may overflow with hope by the power of the Holy Spirit.

❖ **2 Corinthians 3:12** Therefore, since we have such a hope, we are very bold.

❖ **2 Corinthians 7: 6, 7** Nevertheless God, that comforts, those that are depressed, comforted us by the coming of Titus; And not by his coming only, but by the consolation wherewith he was comforted in you, when he told us your earnest desire, your mourning, your fervent mind toward me; so that I rejoiced the more.

❖ **Ephesians 1:18, 19** I pray also that the eyes of your heart may be enlightened in order that you may know the hope to which he has called you, the riches of his glorious inheritance in the saints, and his incomparably great power for us who believe.

❖ **Ephesians 4:4-6** There is one body and one Spirit – just as you were called to one hope when you were called–one Lord, one faith, one baptism; one God and Father of all, who is over all and through all and in all.

❖ **Philippians 4:6, 7** Be anxious for nothing, but in everything by prayer and supplication with thanksgiving let your requests be made known to God. And the peace of God, which surpasses all comprehension, will guard your hearts and your minds in Christ Jesus.

❖ **2 Thessalonians 2:16, 17** May our Lord Jesus Christ himself and God our Father, who loved us and by his grace gave us eternal encouragement and good hope, encourage your hearts and strengthen you in every good deed and word.

❖ **Titus 3:4-7** But when the kindness and the love of God our Savior toward man appeared, not by works of righteousness which we have done, but according to His mercy He saved us, through the washing of regeneration and renewing of the Holy Spirit, whom He poured out on us abundantly through Jesus Christ our Savior, that having been justified by His grace we should become heirs according to the hope of eternal life.

❖ **James 4:10** Humble yourselves before the Lord, and he will lift you up.

❖ **1 Peter 1:3** Praise be to the God and Father of our Lord Jesus Christ! In his great mercy he has given us new birth into a living hope through the resurrection of Jesus Christ form the dead.

❖ **1 Peter 5:7** Cast all your anxiety on him because he cares for you.

❖ **2 Peter 1:2, 3** Grace and peace be multiplied to you in the knowledge of God and of Jesus our Lord, as His divine power has given to us all things that pertain to life and godliness, through the knowledge of Him who called us by glory and virtue,

❖ **2 Peter 2:9** The Lord knows how to rescue godly men from trials.

◆Scriptures Against Terror◆

❖ **2 Chronicles 7:14** If my people who are called by my name humble themselves, and pray and seek my face and turn from their wicked ways, then I will hear from heaven and will forgive their sin and heal their land.

❖ **Psalm 91:5** Thou shall not be afraid for the terror by night; nor for the arrow that flies by day…

❖ **Proverbs 1:33** …but whoever listens to me will live in safety and be at ease, without fear of harm.

❖ **Isaiah 19:17** And the land of Judah shall be a terror unto Egypt, every one that makes mention thereof shall be afraid in himself, because of the counsel of the Lord of hosts, which he hath determined against it.

❖ **Isaiah 54:14** In righteousness shall thou be established: you shall be far from oppression; for thou shall not fear: and from terror; for it shall not come near thee.

❖ **Isaiah 58:11** The Lord will guide you always; he will satisfy your needs in a sun-scorched land and will strengthen your frame. You will be like a well-watered garden, like a spring whose waters never fail.

❖ **Jeremiah 32:21** And hast brought forth thy people Israel out of the land of Egypt with signs, and with wonders, and with a strong hand, and with a stretched out arm, and with great terror…

❖ **Romans 12:19-21** Beloved, never avenge yourselves, but leave it to the wrath of God, for it is written, "Vengeance is mine, I will repay, says the Lord." To the contrary, "if your enemy is hungry, feed him; if he is thirsty, give him something to drink; for by so doing you will heap burning coals on his head." Do not be overcome by evil, but overcome evil with good.

❖ **Romans 13:1-7** Let every person be subject to the governing authorities. For there is no authority except from God, and those that exist have been instituted by God. Therefore whoever resists the authorities resists what God has appointed, and those who resist will incur judgment. For rulers are not a terror to good conduct, but to bad. Would you have no fear of the one who is in authority? Then do what is good, and you will receive his approval, for he is God's servant for your good. But if you do wrong, be afraid, for he does not bear the sword in vain. For he is the servant of God, an avenger who carries out God's wrath on the wrongdoer. Therefore one must be in subjection, not only to avoid God's wrath but also for the sake of conscience…

❖ **1 Peter 3:14** But and if ye suffer for righteousness' sake, happy [are ye]: and be not afraid of their terror, neither be troubled…

◆Scriptures Against Worry◆

The following is a list of scriptures on worry. Use them when worry and anxiety are attempting to come in. Remember, most of the time worry only means worry, and not the real probability of calamity. Fight anxiety and worry with all you have; they can lead to a loss of hope and then depression. The war is in our head. All Scriptures are from the King James Version.

❖ **John 14:27** Peace I leave with you, my peace I give unto you: not as the world giveth, give I unto you. Let not your heart be troubled, neither let it be afraid.

❖ **1 Peter 5:6, 7** Humble yourselves therefore under the mighty hand of God, that he may exalt you in due time: Casting all your care upon him; for he careth for you.

❖ **Psalm 55:22** Cast thy burden upon the LORD, and he shall sustain thee: he shall never suffer the righteous to be moved.

❖ **Isaiah 26:3, 4** Thou wilt keep him in perfect peace, whose mind is stayed on thee: because he trusteth in thee. Trust ye in the LORD for ever: for in the LORD JEHOVAH is everlasting strength:

❖ **Romans 8:28** And we know that all things work together for good to them that love God, to them who are the called according to his purpose.

❖ **Philippians 4:19** But my God shall supply all your need according to his riches in glory by Christ Jesus.

❖ **Philippians 4:6, 7** Be careful for nothing; but in everything by prayer and supplication with thanksgiving let your requests be made known unto God. And the peace of God, which passeth all understanding, shall keep your hearts and minds through Christ Jesus.

❖ **Matthew 6:24-34** No man can serve two masters: for either he will hate the one, and love the other; or else he will hold to the one, and despise the other. Ye cannot serve God and mammon. Therefore I say unto you, Take no thought for your life, what ye shall eat, or what ye shall drink; nor yet for your body, what ye shall put on. Is not the life more than meat, and the body than raiment? Behold the fowls of the air: for they sow not, neither do they reap, nor gather into barns; yet your heavenly Father feedeth them. Are ye not much better than they? Which of you by taking thought can add one cubit unto his stature? And why take ye thought for raiment? Consider the lilies of the field, how they grow; they toil not, neither do they spin: And yet I say unto you, That even Solomon in all his glory was not arrayed like one of these. Wherefore, if God so clothe the grass of the field, which today is, and tomorrow is cast into the oven, shall he not much more clothe you, O ye of little faith? Therefore take no thought, saying, What shall we eat? or, What shall we drink? or, Wherewithal shall we be clothed? (For after all these things do the Gentiles seek:) for your heavenly Father knoweth that ye have need of all these things. But seek ye first the kingdom of God, and his righteousness; and all these things shall be added unto you. Take therefore no thought for the morrow: for the morrow shall take thought for the things of itself. Sufficient unto the day is the evil thereof.

❖ **1 Corinthians 14:33** For God is not the author of confusion, but of peace, as in all churches of the saints.

◆Scriptures On Forgiveness◆

❖ **1 John 1:9** If we confess our sins, He is faithful and righteous to forgive us our sins and to cleanse us from all unrighteousness.

❖ **Matthew 5:9-12** Blessed are the peacemakers, for they shall be called sons of God. Blessed are those who have been persecuted for the sake of righteousness, for theirs is the kingdom of heaven. Blessed are you when people insult you and persecute you, and falsely say all kinds of evil against you because of Me. Rejoice and be glad, for your reward in heaven is great; for in the same way they persecuted the prophets who were before you.

❖ **Matthew 5:44** But I say to you, love your enemies and pray for those who persecute you.

❖ **Matthew 6:12** And forgive us our debts, as we also have forgiven our debtors.

❖ **Matthew 6:14, 15** For if you forgive others for their transgressions, your heavenly Father will also forgive you. But if you do not forgive others, then your Father will not forgive your transgressions.

❖ **Matthew 7:2-5** For in the way you judge, you will be judged; and by your standard of measure, it will be measured to you. Why do you look at the speck that is in your brother's eye, but do not notice the log that is in your own eye? Or how can you say to your brother, 'Let me take the speck out of your eye,' and behold, the log is in your own eye? You hypocrite, first take the log out of your own eye, and then you will see clearly to take the speck out of your brother's eye.

❖ **Matthew 18:21** Then Peter came and said to Him, Lord, how often shall my brother sin against me and I forgive him? Up to seven times? Jesus said to him, I do not say to you, up to seven times, but up to seventy times seven. [Read the whole parable Matthew 18:21-35]

❖ **Matthew 18:35** My heavenly Father will also do the same to you, if each of you does not forgive his brother from your heart.

❖ **Mark 11:25, 26** Whenever you stand praying, forgive, if you have anything against anyone, so that your Father who is in heaven will also forgive you your transgressions. But if you do not forgive, neither will your Father who is in heaven forgive your transgressions.

❖ **Luke 6:35-37** But love your enemies, and do good, and lend, expecting nothing in return; and your reward will be great, and you will be sons of the Most High; for He Himself is kind to ungrateful and evil men. Be merciful, just as your Father is merciful. Do not judge, and you will not be judged; and do not condemn, and you will not be condemned; pardon, and you will be pardoned.

❖ **Luke 11:4** And forgive us our sins, For we ourselves also forgive everyone who is indebted to us. And lead us not into temptation.

❖ **Luke 15:27** And he said to him, 'Your brother has come, and your father has killed the fattened calf because he has received him back safe and sound.' But he became angry and was not willing to go in; and his father came out and began pleading with him. But he answered and said to his father, 'Look! For so many years I have been serving you and I have never neglected a command of yours; and yet you have never given me a young goat, so that I might celebrate with my friends; but when this son of yours came, who has devoured your wealth with prostitutes, you killed the fattened calf for him.'

❖ **Luke 17:3, 4** Be on your guard! If your brother sins, rebuke him; and if he repents, forgive him. And if he sins against you seven times a day, and returns to you seven times, saying, 'I repent,' forgive him.

❖ **Luke 23:34** But Jesus was saying, Father, forgive them; for they do not know what they are doing. And they cast lots, dividing up His garments among themselves.

❖ **Romans 5:8** But God demonstrates His own love toward us, in that while we were yet sinners, Christ died for us.

❖ **Romans 12:9, 10** Let love be without hypocrisy. Abhor what is evil; cling to what is good. Be devoted to one another in brotherly love; give preference to one another in honor…

❖ **Romans 12:16** Be of the same mind toward one another; do not be haughty in mind, but associate with the lowly. Do not be wise in your own estimation.

❖ **Romans 12:20, 21** But if your enemy is hungry, feed him, and if he is thirsty, give him a drink; for in so doing you will heap burning coals on his head. Do not be overcome by evil, but overcome evil with good.

❖ **Romans 14:1** Now accept the one who is weak in faith, but not for the purpose of passing judgment on his opinions.

❖ **Romans 15:1, 2** Now we who are strong ought to bear the weaknesses of those without strength and not just please ourselves. Each of us is to please his neighbor for his good, to his edification.

❖ **1 Corinthians 3:1** And I, brethren, could not speak to you as to spiritual men, but as to men of flesh, as to infants in Christ. I gave you milk to drink, not solid food; for you were not yet able to receive it. Indeed, even now you are not yet able, for you are still fleshly. For since there is jealousy and strife among you, are you not fleshly, and are you not walking like mere men?

❖ **1 Corinthians 6:7** Actually, then, it is already a defeat for you, that you have lawsuits with one another. Why not rather be wronged? Why not rather be defrauded?

❖ **1 Corinthians 13:4-8** Love is patient, love is kind and is not jealous; love does not brag and is not arrogant, does not act unbecomingly; it does not seek its own, is not provoked, does not take into account a wrong suffered, does not rejoice in unrighteousness, but rejoices with the truth; bears all things, believes all things, hopes all things, endures all things. Love never fails…

- ❖ **1 Corinthians 14:20** Brethren, do not be children in your thinking; yet in evil be infants, but in your thinking be mature.

- ❖ **2 Corinthians 2:6, 7** Sufficient for such a one is this punishment which was inflicted by the majority, so that on the contrary you should rather forgive and comfort him, otherwise such a one might be overwhelmed by excessive sorrow.

- ❖ **Galatians 6:1** Brethren, even if anyone is caught in any trespass, you who are spiritual, restore such a one in a spirit of gentleness; each one looking to yourself, so that you too will not be tempted.

- ❖ **Ephesians 4:1-3** Therefore I, the prisoner of the Lord, implore you to walk in a manner worthy of the calling with which you have been called, with all humility and gentleness, with patience, showing tolerance for one another in love, being diligent to preserve the unity of the Spirit in the bond of peace.

- ❖ **Ephesians 4:32** Be kind to one another, tender-hearted, forgiving each other, just as God in Christ also has forgiven you.

- ❖ **Philippians 2:3, 4** Do nothing from selfishness or empty conceit but with humility of mind regard one another as more important than yourself; do not merely look out for your own personal interests, but also for the interests of others.

- ❖ **Philippians 3:15** Let us therefore, as many as are perfect, have this attitude; and if in anything you have a different attitude, God will reveal that also to you…

- ❖ **Colossians 3:12, 13** So, as those who have been chosen of God, holy and beloved, put on a heart of compassion, kindness, humility, gentleness and patience; bearing with one another, and forgiving each other, whoever has a complaint against anyone; just as the Lord forgave you, so also should you.

- ❖ **2 Timothy 2:24-26** The Lord's bond-servant must not be quarrelsome, but be kind to all, able to teach, patient when wronged, with gentleness correcting those who are in opposition, if perhaps God may grant them repentance leading to the knowledge of the truth, and they may come to their senses and escape from the snare of the devil, having been held captive by him to do his will.

- ❖ **James 1:5** But if any of you lacks wisdom, let him ask of God, who gives to all generously and without reproach, and it will be given to him.

- ❖ **James 1:12** Blessed is a man who perseveres under trial; for once he has been approved, he will receive the crown of life which the Lord has promised to those who love Him.

- ❖ **James 2:13** For judgment will be merciless to one who has shown no mercy; mercy triumphs over judgment.

- ❖ **James 3:13-18** Who among you is wise and understanding? Let him show by his good behavior his deeds in the gentleness of wisdom. But if you have bitter jealousy and selfish ambition in your heart, do not be arrogant and so lie against the truth. This wisdom is not that which comes down from above, but is earthly, natural, demonic. For where jealousy and selfish ambition exist, there is disorder and every evil thing. But the wisdom from above is first pure, then peaceable, gentle, reasonable, full of mercy and good fruits, unwavering, without hypocrisy. And the seed whose fruit is righteousness is sown in peace by those who make peace.

- ❖ **James 5:19, 20** My brethren, if any among you strays from the truth and one turns him back, let him know that he who turns a sinner from the error of his way will save his soul from death and will cover a multitude of sins.

- ❖ **1 Peter 2:17** Honor all people, love the brotherhood, fear God, honor the king.

- ❖ **1 Peter 2:23** …and while being reviled, He did not revile in return; while suffering, He uttered no threats, but kept entrusting Himself to Him who judges righteously…

- ❖ **1 Peter 3:8, 9** To sum up, all of you be harmonious, sympathetic, brotherly, kindhearted, and humble in spirit; not returning evil for evil or insult for insult, but giving a blessing instead; for you were called for the very purpose that you might inherit a blessing.

- ❖ **1 Peter 4:8** Above all, keep fervent in your love for one another, because love covers a multitude of sins.

- ❖ **1 John 3:15** Everyone who hates his brother is a murderer; and you know that no murderer has eternal life abiding in him.

- ❖ **1 John 3:18** Little children, let us not love with word or with tongue, but in deed and truth.

- ❖ **Psalm 51:1-19 [ESV]** Have mercy on me, O God, according to your steadfast love; according to your abundant mercy blot out my transgressions. Wash me thoroughly from my iniquity, and cleanse me from my sin! For I know my transgressions, and my sin is ever before me. Against you, you only, have I sinned and done what is evil in your sight, so that you may be justified in your words and blameless in your judgment. Behold, I was brought forth in iniquity, and in sin did my mother conceive me. Behold, you delight in truth in the inward being, and you teach me wisdom in the secret heart. Purge me with hyssop, and I shall be clean; wash me, and I shall be whiter than snow. Let me hear joy and gladness; let the bones that you have broken rejoice. Hide your face from my sins, and blot out all my iniquities. Create in me a clean heart, O God, and renew a right spirit within me. Cast me not away from your presence, and take not your Holy Spirit from me. Restore to me the joy of your salvation, and uphold me with a willing spirit. Then I will teach transgressors your ways, and sinners will return to you. Deliver me from blood guiltiness, O God, O God of my salvation, and my tongue will sing aloud of your righteousness. O Lord, open my lips, and my mouth will declare your praise. For you will not delight in sacrifice, or I would give it; you will not be pleased with a burnt offering. The sacrifices of God are a broken spirit; a broken and contrite heart, O God, you will not despise. Do good to Zion in your good pleasure; build up the walls of Jerusalem; then will you delight in right sacrifices, in burnt offerings and whole burnt offerings; then bulls will be offered on your altar.

◆ Scriptures Against Depression ◆

Depression is real. If you are fighting it, you are not alone. Depression seems to have been the bane of many of life's great leaders. In the Bible Moses, Elijah, David, and Job had to deal with it. In the world Sir Winston Churchill called depression his 'black dog', and Ernest Hemingway referred to it as 'the artist's reward'.

President Abraham Lincoln battled depression and suicide all his adult life. There were times when for his own safety he would not allow himself to carry a knife. Instead Lincoln turned to the Bible to relieve His depression. Let the Scriptures help you just like they have helped so many of us.

Sometimes depression can be a purely spiritual thing. Rex Rouls wrote that Depression Is a Spirit – It Must Be Fought with the Word of God. Depression is the physical and emotional result of hopelessness – the 'feeling' of hopelessness. We live in a world devoid of hope, and depression is the emotional product of that reality. The only thing that will actually change one's life sufficiently as to destroy the cause, mechanics, and effects of depression is God's hope and His word of hope. The answer is to get God's hope back inside of you.

Hope will let you again see the 'future positive possibility' of your life. Without seeing it you will have no motivation or strength. The good Word of God and the good word of others to you can change the outlook and condition of your heart. Fight for God's outlook with all you have. Fight it with the Word of God. Anyone who is among the living has hope.

God's hope encourages, motivates, and keeps you on the road to faith, peace, and victory. And if you suffer from deep ongoing depression, seek and get help. Sometimes assisting another person keeps you from looking inward according to Rex Rouls who also wrote Helping Others Is God's Prescription for Depression. You are important and you have value. You are not alone. With God's help, you will climb out of this hole.

Anxiety in a man's heart weighs it down (depression), but a good word cheers it up.
***Proverbs 12:25** [Holman Christian Standard Bible]*

These scriptures on depression will give you hope and will build your faith. Confess and meditate on them to win the fight against depression. **The key is NOT losing hope.** Allow the hope of God to seep back into you. Remember, there is a real person (God) behind each and every one of these promises. He promised them to you for a reason – to help you.

- ❖ **Deuteronomy 31:8** The Lord himself goes before you and will be with you; he will never leave you nor forsake you. Do not be afraid; do not be discouraged.

- ❖ **Deuteronomy 33:27** The eternal God is your refuge, and underneath are the everlasting arms.

- ❖ **2 Samuel 22:17-22** He sent from above, he took me; he drew me out of many waters; He delivered me from my strong enemy, and from them that hated me: for they were too strong for me. They prevented me in the day of my calamity: but the Lord was my stay. He brought me forth also into a large place: he delivered me, because he delighted in me. The Lord rewarded me according to my righteousness: according to the cleanness of my hands hath he recompensed me. For I have kept the ways of the Lord, and have not wickedly departed from my God.

- ❖ **2 Samuel 22:29** You are my lamp O Lord; the Lord turns my darkness into light.

- ❖ **Ecclesiastes 9:4** Anyone who is among the living has hope…

- ❖ **Psalm 9:9** The Lord is a refuge for the oppressed, a stronghold in times of trouble.

- ❖ **Psalm 27:14** Wait on the Lord: be of good courage, and He shall strengthen thine heart: wait, I say, on the Lord.

- ❖ **Psalm 31:22, 24** You heard my cry for mercy when I called to you for help… Be strong and take heart, all you who hope in the Lord.

- ❖ **Psalm 34:18, 19** The Lord is close to the brokenhearted and saves those who are crushed in spirit. A righteous man may have many troubles, but the Lord delivers him from them all.

- ❖ **Psalm 37:23, 24** If the Lord delights in a man's way, he makes his steps firm; though he stumbles, he will not fall, for the Lord upholds him with his hand.

- ❖ **Psalm 43:5** Why are you downcast, O my soul? Why so disturbed within me? Put your hope in God.

- ❖ **Psalm 55:22** Cast your cares on the Lord and he will sustain you; he will never let the righteous fall.

- ❖ **Psalm 62:5** Find rest, O my soul, in God alone; my hope comes from him.

- ❖ **Psalm 126:5** Those who sow in tears will reap with songs of joy.

- ❖ **Psalm 143:7, 8** Answer me quickly, O Lord; my spirit fails. Do not hide your face from me or I will be like those who go down to the pit. Let the morning bring me word of your unfailing love, for I have put my trust in you. Show me the way I should go, for to you I'll lift up my soul.

- ❖ **Psalm 147:3** He heals the brokenhearted and binds up their wounds.

- ❖ **Psalm 145:14** The Lord upholds all those who fall and lifts up all who are bowed down.

- ❖ **Isaiah 26:3, 4** Thou wilt keep him in perfect peace, whose mind is stayed on Thee: because he trusts in Thee. Trust ye in the Lord forever: for in the Lord Jehovah is everlasting strength. (Perfect means complete. If I keep my part of the promise by staying steadfastly focused on the Lord Jesus Christ, He will keep His promise to give me His perfect peace.)

- ❖ **Isaiah 35:10** And the ransomed of the Lord will return. They will enter Zion with singing; everlasting joy will crown their heads. Gladness and joy will overtake them, and sorrow and sighing will flee away

- ❖ **Isaiah 40:31** But they that wait upon the LORD shall renew their strength; they shall mount up with wings as eagles; they shall run, and not be weary; and they shall walk, and not faint.

- ❖ **Isaiah 53:4** Surely he took up our sicknesses and carried our sorrows.

- ❖ **Mark 9:23** Everything is possible for him who believes.

- ❖ **Romans 4:18-22** Who against hope believed in hope, that he might become the father of many nations, according to that which was spoken, so shall they seed be. And being not weak in faith, he considered not his own body now dead, when he was about an hundred years old, neither yet the deadness of Sarah's womb: He staggered not at the promise of God through unbelief; but was strong in faith, giving glory to God. And being fully persuaded that, what he had promised, he was able to perform. And therefore it was imputed to him for righteousness.

- ❖ **Romans 15:13** May the God of hope fill you with all joy and peace as you trust in him, so that you may overflow with hope by the power of the Holy Spirit.

- ❖ **2 Corinthians 7:6, 7** Nevertheless God, that comforts, those that are depressed, comforted us by the coming of Titus; And not by his coming only, but by the consolation wherewith he was comforted in you, when he told us your earnest desire, your mourning, your fervent mind toward me; so that I rejoiced the more.

- ❖ **Philippians 4:6, 7** Be anxious for nothing, but in everything by prayer and supplication with thanksgiving let your requests be made known to God. And the peace of God, which surpasses all comprehension, will guard your hearts and your minds in Christ Jesus.

- ❖ **James 4:8** Come near to God and he will come near to you. Wash your hands, you sinners, and purify your hearts, you double-minded.

- ❖ **James 4:10** Humble yourselves before the Lord, and he will lift you up.

- ❖ **2 Peter 2:9** The Lord knows how to rescue godly men from trials.

- ❖ **1 Peter 4:12** Dear Friends, do not be surprised at the painful trial you are suffering, as though something strange were happening to you.

- ❖ **1 Peter 4:13** But rejoice that you participate in the sufferings of Christ, so that you may be overjoyed when his glory is revealed

- ❖ **1 Peter 5:7** Cast all your anxiety on him because he cares for you.

NOTES

Chapter 7
Overcoming Generational Curses

How can we break the power of curses over our family and us? [Matthew 12:29]

Proclamation: For me and house [**my generation**], we will serve the Lord....
[**Joshua 24:15**]

When we get born again and filled with the Holy Spirit, we have a new nature and a new life. The things concerning us change daily as we read the word and learn God's promises to us. Sometimes there are things we try to get free from and no matter how hard we try or what we do such as confessing the word, using Jesus' name, pleading the blood, praying, and using our authority, nothing works. It may be because of something known as a generational curse.

~ Lesson 1 ~
Examples of Generational Curses from the Bible
In **Genesis 9:20-27 Noah got drunk**. *Alcohol is one of the devil's favorite tools* used in *opening the door to a curse*. When people get drunk, they do things they would not normally do because their will is broken down. What happened to Noah is that he was ***uncovered in his tent***. ***Uncovered*** in this sense means there was a *homosexual act committed*.

The passage indicates that Canaan, the son of Ham, is the one who committed this sexual sin. Therefore, Noah spoke a curse on Canaan because of what he had done. Noah, on the other hand, broke the curse from his life caused by drunkenness by repenting, which was making a sacrifice and presenting the blood to cover him (the way it was done in the Old Testament). Noah was forgiven, but Canaan did not repent.

When a father commits a sin, his son picks it up. There is a weakness already to sin when the old nature, which is passed on from the father to the son. The devil comes and tempts the son and he falls into it also. [**Exodus 20:5**] says the iniquity of the fathers is visited upon the children to the third and fourth generation. Let's follow the curse of sexual sin through the generations of the Canaanites, the descendants of Canaan.

⇒*Inhabitants of Sodom and Gomorrah*⇐
Those living in Sodom and Gomorrah were Canaanites. **Genesis 19** tells us that two angels were sent by God to check out Sodom and Gomorrah because an outcry had come to Him against them because their sin was very bad.

When they entered the city Lot insisted they stay with him. However, the men of the city came to Lot's house because they wanted to have sex with the two angels (though they didn't know they were angels). The next day after Lot and his family left the city, God destroyed Sodom and Gomorrah.

These cities were involved in the same sexual sin as Canaan had been (homosexuality). However as generations of sin goes on the sin gets worse in the people. And the people of Sodom and Gomorrah were exceedingly wicked.

⇒*Rahab from Jericho*⇐

Rahab [generations after Sodom and Gomorrah] was a Canaanite and a prostitute living in the city of Jericho during the time of Joshua. By now the Canaanites were involved in other sexual sins besides homosexuality. They included incest, prostitution, and sex with animals.

When Joshua sent two men to Jericho to 'spy out the land' they were found out and the men sought to kill them. Rahab hid them and then helped them escape. She asked that she and her family be spared when they destroyed the city. They agreed to spare her and her family if she tied a scarlet cloth (representing blood) in her window. She did as she was told and all within her home were saved from destruction.

Somehow Rahab got hold of the Word of God and believed it and broke the curse. The curse was not only broken over her life but her descendants lives also. Rahab's great great grandson was King David. And Jesus came from the line of David.

Deuteronomy 7:9 Know therefore that the Lord thy God, He [is] God, the faithful God, which keepeth covenant and mercy with them that love Him and keep His commandments to a thousand generations;

We may have grandparents or parents or our children or ourselves that are involved in all kinds of problems, but we do not have to be defeated by it. In fact, we can break the family curse and its power over our families and us.

When there is a curse on a generation it did not just happen to occur; there has to be a cause behind it. Of course the cause behind a curse is ALWAYS sin. When there is a curse, there is a **root sin**. Some root sins are worshiping other gods (such as money, power, and career), lust for power, rebellion, cruelty, sexual sin, and violence. Root sins can cause physical problems.

What we find is that our mother/father, grandmother/grandfather, or aunt/uncle were the same way or did the same thing. We must also remember that not all sicknesses are spiritual; however, the spiritual **can** affect the physical.

♦The following are several examples of generational curses.♦

♦ General ill health [spirit of infirmity]: you claim healing in one part of your body and are healed but the next day you experience pain and sickness in another part of your body.

♦ Adultery: you lust after the opposite sex even though you are married

♦ Alcoholism	♦ Dishonesty	♦ Arthritis
♦ Unbelief	♦ Fear	♦ Lust
♦ Unforgiveness		♦ Drugs
♦ Homosexuality/Lesbianism		♦ Witchcraft
♦ False Religions - Cults, Occult		♦ Stealing
♦ Poverty and low mentality (lack of money management)		♦ Gambling
♦ Lying	♦ Mental disorder	♦ Diabetes
♦ High blood pressure	♦ Broken bones (bones easily broken)	
♦ Cancer	♦ Ear problems	♦ Heart disease

♦ Infertility (when seen in more than one generation)

♦ Blindness (glaucoma, near and/or farsightedness) and much more

Let's say you get born again and filled with the Holy Spirit, you have a new life in you and a new nature. However, your children can inherit the weakness.

Your generation may be cleansed but the curse must be broken over future generations or they will inherit the weakness of your family.

Accept Jesus is your life and heart today.

[**John 11:25**] Jesus said to her, "I am the resurrection and the life. The one who believes in me will live, even though they die;

God will roll the stone away in your life and bring you freedom. His resurrection power will live inside of you,

~ Lesson 2 ~
How to Break the Power of Curses Over our Family and Us

Matthew 12:29 …how can one enter into a strong man's house, and spoil his goods, except he first **bind the strong man**?

Mark 3:27 NIV *In fact, no one can enter a strong man's house without first tying him up. Then he can plunder the strong man's house*

Matthew 12:29 NIV *Or again, how can anyone enter a strong man's house and carry off his possessions unless he first ties up the strong man? Then he can plunder his house.*

And then he will spoil his house. "**House**" can mean – **generation**.

In order to break the curse of the generations after us, such as addictions, habits, sins, and physical weaknesses etc. we have to go in and bind the strongman who has brought that curse from generation to generation before us. The strongman is Satan and we can bind him in the name of Jesus and then take that house, that generation away from him. It is broken by Jesus' blood.

We say by faith, "We are not going to have heart problems/diabetes/etc. We do not have to have this problem even though our parents did. We are not going to be alcoholics or have a weakness for immorality because our parents were involved in that. The curse is not going to come on us. It will not come on our children because we break the curse and bind the strongman in Jesus' name. The curse of generations is broken."

Even though we break it, the devil will try to convince us that it is not broken. We have got to get serious and do spiritual warfare. He will try to attack us again and again. He may even try to attack our children. We must stand our ground and do not let him do it. Know therefore that the Lord thy God, he [is] God, the faithful God, which keepeth covenant and mercy with them that love him and keep his commandments to a thousand generations [**Deuteronomy 7:9**].

Therefore we can tell the devil, "You do not get our children. You do not get our grandchildren. And you do not get our great grandchildren. If Jesus tarries in returning, you do not get anyone who belongs to my house for a thousand generations. This curse will not go on. It will stop in Jesus' name."

What about when we have married somebody before we were Christians, then we become Christians and they do not, do we have a family curse that cannot be broken? Great news! One believing mate sanctifies the household and the children are freed from any generational curse.

Psalm 68:6 God setteth the lonely in families: He bringeth out those which are bound with chains: but the rebellious dwell in a dry [land]

1 Corinthians 7:13, 14 And the woman which hath an husband that believeth not, and if he be pleased to dwell with her, let her not leave him. For the unbelieving husband is sanctified by the wife, and the unbelieving wife is sanctified by the husband: else were your children unclean; but now are they holy.

God tells us in [**Genesis 12:3**] that He wants to turn our curses into blessings. When we come to Jesus, we come by faith. We also believe His word by faith and when we use our faith, the thing that cursed you is now going to turn around and bless you. We've got God's blessing in our new spiritual family even though your old natural family may have had lots of curses.

We negate the curse by the blood of the Lamb. We turn it to a blessing by the word of our testimony, which is testifying how God set us free so that others can become free. [**Revelation 12:11**] says, "(You) overcame him by the blood of the Lamb, and by **the word** of your testimony…"

For me and House, [**my generation**] we will serve the Lord.... [**Joshua 24:15**]

~ Lesson 3 ~
>>>A Warfare Declaration: Generational Curses<<<
The spirit of "**Rabisu**" looks for a crack in your armor.

Note: The following is an example of how to command Satan and his evil spirits.

⇒Satan, I came against you in the name of my Lord Jesus Christ. I am His child and redeemed by His blood. I have repented of all my sins and have received God's forgiveness. In obedience to God's command, I have forgiven each person who has ever trespassed against me and all for whom I have held resentment.

⇒I have confessed the sins of my ancestors, and have renounced every inherited curse. I take back from you all the ground that you ever gained in my life. You have no rights of dominion over me. Jesus has given me authority to bind you and to cast you out, and you cannot harm me. All of your plans against me are frustrated and cancelled. Every strong man assigned against me is bound.

⇒I command every evil spirit that has gained entrance to me to leave me now in the mighty name of Jesus. *(Press into the battle until you are free.)*

<u>Note:</u> Personalize specific things that you recognize (or even suspect) to be attacks of demons against you, your family, your church, your community, your nation and other nations.

Make your personal list of evil spirits to be bound. Then pray a deliverance prayer, and make your declaration against Satan.

⇒Satan, I remove all ground or advantage that you and your forces have taken in my life, and now cover it completely with the blood of Jesus Christ. I declare broken all power structures of evil, all hierarchies of demonic energy, all schemes ever devised against me for any cause, through any source, at any time. I bind, rebuke and command the departure of all familiar spirits that have come against me from my ancestral bloodline. I command the departure of all enemy spirits that have come against me to hinder my effectiveness as a servant of the Lord Jesus Christ, In His name, which is supreme, I command you to leave me now.

~ Lesson 4 ~
Scriptures Concerning Curses

⇒Reasons for Curses from God⇐

Daniel 9:11: Transgression and disobedience of God's Law leads to curses and sworn judgments.
Deuteronomy 11:26-28: God sets before us a choice. We decide whether we obey or disobey His commandments.
Deuteronomy 28: Many curses listed for disobedience.

⇒First Curses in the Bible⇐

Genesis 3:14: To the serpent: cursed above all animals, crawl on belly, eat dust, head crushed.
Genesis 3:16: To the woman: greatly increased pain in childbearing,…desire husband, be ruled over.
Genesis 3:17-18: To the ground: cursed because of Adam, hard to produce good food, easy to produce thorns.
Genesis 3:17-19: To the man, painful toil, sweating work, eat plants of the ground.

⇒First Curse Spoken by a Man⇐

Genesis 9:25: And (Noah) said, Cursed be Canaan; a servant of servants shall he be unto his brethren. (KJV)

⇒Jews Cursing Themselves and Their Children⇐

Matthew 27:25: Let his (Jesus') blood be on us and on our children. (NIV)

⇒General Statements About Curses⇐

Proverbs 3:33: The Lord's curse is on the house of the wicked, (NIV)
James 3:9-10: With the tongue we curse men. Out of the same mouth proceeds blessing and cursing. (KJV)
Proverbs 26:2: Like a fluttering sparrow or a darting swallow, an undeserved curse does not come to rest. (NIV)

⇒Jesus has the Last Word about Curses⇐

Matthew 5:43-44; Luke 6:27-28: …But I say unto you, Love your enemies, bless them that curse you, do good to them that hate you, and pray for them which despitefully use you, and persecute you… (KJV)

⇒Jesus Provides Freedom from the Curse⇐

Galatians 3:13: Christ redeemed us from the curse of the law by becoming a curse for us,…(NIV)

⇒Last Statement about Curses in the Bible⇐

Revelation 22:3: No longer will there be any curse. (NIV)

NOTES

Chapter 8
God, Angels & Their Assignment

Though the spiritual world is not always seen with the natural eye, it is very real and very present. Essentially the spiritual world is made up of the triune God and His angelic host and Satan and his demonic angels.

God is a triune being. Our way of understanding this is by saying that He is three persons in One. There is:

♦ **God the Father:** He is the Creator of heaven and of earth. He is also the Creator of man and is the Father of His children. He is omnipresent [everywhere and all seeing], omniscient [all knowing], and omnipotent [all powerful].

♦ **God the Son:** We know Him as Yeshua (Jesus the Messiah), the Son of God. He is our brother, our living example, and the supreme chief of all principalities and powers.

♦ **God the Holy Spirit:** He resides with us after Jesus returned to heaven. He is our Comforter, our Guide, our Counselor, and our Help.

Daniel 11:32 (KJV) …the people that do know their God shall be strong, and do exploits.
(NASV) …the people who know their God will display strength and take action.
(RSV) …the people who know their God shall stand firm and take action.

~Lesson 1~
Know What God's Angels Do

Angels are other beings that make up the spiritual world. Before the beginning of earth, they were created by God [**Colossians 1:14-17**]. They are immortal and innumerable. In fact one report says that there are enough Godly angels for every human being to have ten thousand at his disposal.

God is **not** the author of confusion [**1 Corinthians 14:33**]. He created the angels in ranks, each with a specific assignment. For instance in the Greek a prince is the head person of any rank, especially of soldiers, then there are captains, generals, or commanders. Even though Satan and one-third of the angels fell, it did not change their rank. The Bible speaks of the various classifications of the angels [**Romans 8:38; Ephesians 1:21; 3:10; 6:12; Colossians 1:16; 2:10, 15; 1 Peter 3:22**]

Angelic Angels	Demonic Angels
Prince of Peace Jesus	Prince of Darkness [demonic forces] Satan
Archangel (chief) Michael	Principalities & powers (chief)
Thrones & Dominions	Thrones & dominions Rulers of territories
Angels (messenger) Hosts (militant)	Wicked angels – **Psalm 103:20, 21** Demon ministers (ministering)
Seraphim & Cherubim (They protect God's throne)	

There are specific attributes of the *Godly angels* and their assignments.
- They are wise – **2 Samuel 14:20**
- They have emotions – **Job 38:7; Luke 15:10**
- They are sexless – **Matthew 22:20**
- They are invisible to the natural eye except when they become visible for God's purposes – **Hebrews 3:2**
- They mostly appear as men but one account in the Bible, an angel appeared as a woman – **Zechariah 5:9**
- They have knowledge, but they are not all knowing – **Matthew 13:32**
- They are powerful and have great strength – **Psalm 103:20**
- They do not need rest – **Revelation 4:8**
- They can speak and have their own language – **1 Corinthians 13:1**
- They minister for us – **Hebrews 1:14**
- They strengthen us in trials – **Luke 22:43**
- They protect believers – **Psalm 34:7**
- They impart God's will –**Acts 5:19, 20**
- They bring answers to prayer – **Acts 10**
- They control nature and the elements – **Revelation 7:1; 8:9; 16:3** [Note: If we do not activate our angels to take control of the elements, the fallen angels are the ones who will have control over the elements.]
- There are guardian angels: some believe they are assigned to each child at birth and minister to that person throughout life except when that person hardens their heart against God and determines to do evil.
- There are messenger angels that bring messages from God.

The angels seem so awe-inspiring; however, they are *not* to be worshiped [**Colossians 2:18**]. The fact is that we really are above the angels [**Ephesians 1:20, 21**]. It is also in Ephesians that we find where we are raised up and seated with Christ in the heavenly places. This means we also have power over the demonic angels [**Luke 10:19, 20**].

And when we speak the Word of God we activate the Godly angels to minister for us.

Where are the angels? We can say heaven and hell; however, there are three heavens to consider. There is the third heaven where God's throne is [**2 Corinthians 12:2**]. Then there is the second heaven where demonic angels are 'in heavenly places' [**Ephesians 6:12**]. Finally, there is the first heaven, which is the earth's atmosphere [**Matthew 16:1-3**].

~ Lesson 2 ~
The Doctrine of Angels

There is an order of celestial beings that occupy a position quite distinct from that of either God or man. Although they far below the Godhead, they dwell in an estate above that of fallen man. The only source of information that we have of their existence and activities is the Holy Scriptures; mysticism and philosophy have no word of authority whatsoever. The Sadducees, a prominent group in the Jewish Sanhedrin at the time of Christ, did not believe in angels. For the Sadducees say there is no resurrection, neither angel, nor spirit...[Acts 23:8]. Inasmuch as all our information about them comes from the Bible, we do well to learn from all that it says about them, but we must not go beyond that which is revealed. The Old Testament refers to angels 108 times, while the New Testament mentions them 165 times.

>>The Hebrew word for angel is *mal'ak* and the Greek word is *angelos*.<<
>>They both mean **messenger**.<<

Psalm 148:2, 5 Praise ye him, all his angels: praise ye him, all his hosts...Let them praise the name of the Lord: for he commanded, and they were created.

Colossians 1:16 For by him were all things created, that are in heaven, and that are in earth, visible and invisible, whether they be thrones, or dominions, or principalities, or powers: all things were created by him, and for him...

Genesis 1:1 In the beginning God created the heaven and the earth.

Job 38:4-7 Where wast thou when I laid the foundations of the earth? Declare, if thou hast understanding. Who hath laid the measures thereof, if thou knowest? Or who hath stretched the line upon it? Whereupon are the foundation thereof fastened? Or who laid the corner stone thereof; when the morning stars sang together, and all the sons of God shouted for joy?

Angels are created beings with their main abode in heaven [**Matthew 22:30; Luke 2:13-15; John 1:51**]. It is believed they were probably created on the first day of Creation immediately after the creation of heaven. They are not corporal because they do have a physical body. However, they do not have bodies in the sense that man does because they are spirits, ministering spirits [**Psalm 104:4; Hebrews 1:14**].

Any angel (spirit), whether good or evil, can be present at one time but in a very limited space like Legion in the demoniac of Gadara [**Luke 8:30**]. Now they have on occasion assumed the form of human bodies. [**Hebrews 13:2; Genesis 19:1; Luke 1:26, 27; John 20:12; Acts 8:26; 12:7, 8**] It is extremely important to note that angels are NOT to be worshiped [**Colossians 2:18; Revelation 19:10**].

There is no propagation among angels because they all were created at one time. They do not die; therefore, they neither increase nor decrease in number [**Luke 20:34-36**]. And they are referred to in the masculine gender. Even though the angels cannot reproduce there is a vast number of them. They have been referred to as an innumerable company [**Hebrews 12:22**] and as legions [**Matthew 26:53**] and as ten thousand upon ten thousand [**Revelation 5:11**].

Angels are individual rational beings [**2 Samuel 14:20**] that render intelligent worship [**Psalm 148:2**] and possess emotions [**Luke 15:10**].

They are also moral beings and know to do that which is right or wrong.

According to **Matthew 24:36**, it is implied that their knowledge is above man's knowledge. Though they are represented as having superhuman wisdom and intelligence, they are not omniscient [**1 Peter 1:12**] or omnipotent because their power is derived from God [**Psalm 103:20; 2 Thessalonians 1:7; 2 Peter 2:11; Acts 12:7; Matthew 28:2; Revelation 20:1, 2**].

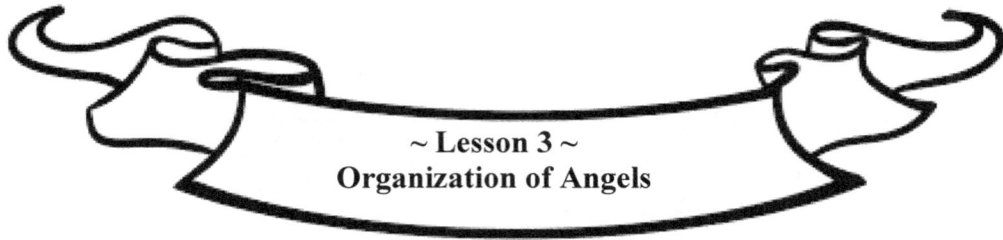

~ Lesson 3 ~
Organization of Angels

◆CHERUBIM◆

[Genesis 3:24; Exodus 37:6-9]

◆SERAPHIM – 'burning ones'◆

[Isaiah 6:1-7]

◆MICHAEL◆
{'who is like God'; one of the chief princes; an archangel; a warring angel}
[Daniel 10:13; 12:1; Jude 9; Revelation 12:7-9]

◆GABRIEL◆
{'the mighty one'; bearer of great tidings concerning God's purposes}
[Daniel 8:15-27; 9:20-27; Luke 1:13, 19, 26-38]

>>>The ministry of angels in relation to believers:<<<

➢ Protection from accidental harm – **Psalm 91:11, 12**
➢ Deliverance from enemies – **Psalm 34:7; 2 Kings 6:15-17**
➢ Encouragement in times of extreme trial – **1 Kings 19:5; Acts 27:22-24**
➢ Grant wisdom and guidance – **Matthew 1:20; 2:13, 19, 20; Acts 8:26**
➢ Escort a soul at death – **Luke 16:22**
➢ Rejoice over salvation – **Luke 15:10**

~ Lesson 4 ~
His Angels Battle for You

Psalm 34:7 The angel of the Lord encamps all around those who fear Him, and delivers them.

Psalm 91:11 For He shall give His angels charge over you, to keep you in all your ways.

Psalm 35:5-8 And let the angel of the Lord chase him … And let the angel of the Lord pursue him … Let the destruction come upon him unexpectedly.

Exodus 23:20 Behold, I send an angel before you to keep you in the way and to bring you into the place which I have prepared.

Hebrews 1:14 Are they not all ministering spirits sent forth to minister for those who will inherit salvation?

1 Chronicles 21:27, 29 Then the Lord commanded the angel, and he returned his sword to its sheath … but David could not go before it to inquire of God, for he was afraid of the sword of the angel of the Lord.

2 Kings 19:35 And it came to pass on a certain night that the angel of the Lord went out, and killed in the camp of the Assyrians one hundred and eighty-five thousand; and when the people arose early in the morning, there were the corpses – all dead.

Acts 12:23 Then immediately an angel of the Lord struck him, because he did not give glory to God. And he was eaten by worms and died.

Hebrews 13:2 Do not forget to entertain strangers, for by doing so some have unwittingly entertained angels.

NOTES

Archangel

743 = Ariyadatha - Persons;
Anchaggelon = Chief Angel

Gabriel
Luke 1:19, 26 Daniel 9:21

Michael
Daniel 12:1; 10:13
Jude 9 Rev 12:7

Hyiel (Lucifer)
Isaiah 14:12-13
Job 1:6; 2:1

Copyright protected by Joshua International

Chapter 9
Satan and his Demonic Forces

~ Lesson 1~
Know Who Your Enemy Is ~ The Origin of Satan

Satan is also part of the spiritual world. He was originally an archangel named Lucifer, who exalted himself above God because of pride. This created being wanted to be higher than the Creator. He led a rebellion in heaven with one-third of the angelic host. As a result they ALL were cast out of heaven. **[Ezekiel 28:12-19; Isaiah 14:12-15; Revelation 12:3, 4, 9]**

He now rules in the world system as the god of this world [2 Corinthians 4:4]. He has spiritual authority and a hierarchy **[Ephesians 6:12]**. Today Satan and his demons are actively going around destroying **[1 Peter 5:8]** and accusing the brethren **[Revelation 12:10]**.

Do not forget that Jesus conquered Satan **[Colossians 2:15]**. And He gave us all authority over Satan AND his evil spirits **[Matthew 28:18-20; Mark 16:15-20; Luke 10:19]**. We must be led by the Holy Spirit to effectively counter these evil spirits. We cannot be ignorant of his devices unless he gets an advantage over us **[2 Corinthians 2:11]**

WHO is Satan?
- ~ He is a spiritual enemy → **Ephesians 6:12**
- ~ He is able to disguise himself. → **2 Corinthians 11:14**
- ~ He is a rebellious angel. → **Isaiah 14:12-15; Ezekiel 28:11-19; Revelation 12:7-9**
- ~ He is a murderer and a liar.→ **John 8:44**
- ~ He is a limited being. → **Job 1:7; 2:2**
- ~ He can be cast out, bound, and spoiled. → **Matthew 12:28, 29**
- ~ He can be held back/restrained. → **2 Thessalonians 2:7**
- ~ He is a deceiver. → **Revelation 20:12**
- ~ He is NOT omnipresent. → **Job 1:7**
- ~ He is defeated. → **Colossians 2:15**
- ~ He CANNOT read your mind.

WHAT Satan has?
- ~ He has tools he operates with called deception, perversion, and fear
  - Lies = perverted truth
  - Sickness = perverted health
  - Fear = perverted faith
  - Death = perverted life
  - Lust = perverted love

SEVEN ASSIGNMENTS AGAINST YOU

- Regression: to go backward; to backslide; reverse
- Repression: not expressive; introverted; silent; sulk; won't talk about problems
- Suppression: to abnormally squeeze down; to conceal; hide feelings and emotions
- Depression: a broken spirit; crushed; confused; angry; no peace; no happiness; suicidal; staring into space; no energy; no enthusiasm
- Oppression: to weigh you down with something so heavy you can't carry it; sickness; disease; sorrow; fear
- Obsession: a complex; phobia; lies becoming truth; truth becoming a lie; cannot think of anything else; need outside help to get free
- Possession: (Final Step) the devil controlling completely; hearing voices; insanity; eyes having demonic glare; only outside help can set them free

~ **He has four methods of control**. These are usually manifested through spiritual and/or mental oppression, depression, suppression, and possession.

- Intimidation: to strike fear into, especially by threats
    [1 Kings 19:1-4; 2 Chronicles 20:1-2]
- Manipulation: to work or handle skillfully; to manage shrewdly or artfully, often in an unfair way, to alter for one's own purpose
    [Genesis 3:1-7]
- Domination: to control or rule by strength; to hold a commanding position over – **[Hebrews 2:14-17]**
- Condemnation: to pronounce guilty; to censure or blame – **[Revelation 12:10]**

WHAT can Satan do?
~ He can steal, kill, and destroy. → **John 10:10**
~ He can deceive. → **Revelation 12:9; 20:1-10; John 8:44**
~ He can accuse and divide. → **James 3:16; Revelation 12:10**
~ He can intimidate. → **1 Peter 5:8**
~ He can counterfeit. → **2 Corinthians 11:13-15**
~ He can tempt. → **Mark 1:13; 1 Corinthians 7:5**
~ He can cause offense. → **Matthew 16:23**
~ He can hinder the gospel. → **Acts 13:10**
~ He can steal the word. → **Matthew 13:19; Luke 8:12**
~ He can cause delay and compromise. → **Acts 24:25; 26:28**
~ He can make war on the saints. → **Ephesians 6:12; Revelation 13:7**

One of the greatest hindrances to the Body of Christ is not knowing or recognizing the enemy. He is great at condemning us. In other words he gives us feelings of inadequacy, shame, fearfulness, guilt, inferiority and by not measuring up to expectations (whether actual or imagined). Our sense of being is judged all the time.

When we don't' recognize it is the enemy at work, we won't walk in faith. When we're not operating in faith then we will not be apt to flow in or with the anointing. When we're not operating in faith, then we'll not be speaking the Word. Jesus used the Word of God against the wiles of the devil. By keeping us preoccupied with ourselves then we'll not do anything about burdens or yokes. We won't have the faith for it. {**Romans 8:1**]

The Bible uses a variety of other names that describe who Lucifer, now Satan really is:

- Abaddon (Apollyon) – **Revelation 9:11 12:10**
- Adversary – **1 Peter 5:8**
- Anointed Cherub – **Ezekiel 28:14**
- Belial – **2 Corinthians 6:15 11:3**
- Devil (Deceiver) – **Revelation 12:9**
- Dragon – **Revelation 12:3; 20:2-7**
- Evil Spirit – **1 Samuel 16:14**
- King – **Revelation 9:11; Ephesians 6:12**
- Lying spirit – **1 Kings 22:22**
- Murderer – **John 8:44**
- Oppressor – **Acts 10:38**
- Prince of Darkness – **Ephesians 6:12 16:11**
- Roaring Lion – **1 Peter 5:8**
- Satan – **Job 1:6; Revelation 12:9**
- Serpent – **2 Corinthians 11:3; Genesis 3:1, 14; Revelation 12:9**
- Tempter – **Matthew 4:3**
- Unclean spirit – **Matthew 12:43**

- Accuser of the brethren – **Revelation**
- Angel of Light – **2 Corinthians 11:14**
- Beelzebub – **Matthew 10:25; 12:24**
- Corrupter of Minds – **2 Corinthians**
- Deceitful – **2 Corinthians 11:4**
- Enemy – **Matthew 13:39**
- God of this world – **2 Corinthians 4:4**
- Liar – **John 8:44**
- Lucifer – **Isaiah 14:12**
- Old Serpent – **Revelation 12:9**
- Prince of the Air – **Ephesians 2:1, 2**
- Prince of This World – **John 12:31;**
- Ruler of demons – **Matthew 12:24**
- Thief – **John 10:10**
- Wicked One – **Matthew 13:19, 38**

I really hate Satan, don't you? Understand, I do not FEAR him, but I do HATE him! I do not fear him because the one who has all power over him lives in me. And the devil responds to the Word, not us. Knowing the Word, I can respond with, "It is written…"

John 4:4 Greater is He that is in you than he that is against you.

KNOW WHO YOUR GOD IS [**Chapter 2**] AND KNOW WHO LIVES IN YOU

Recommended Reading: The Secret Names of the Strongmen by H.A.Lewis

~ Lesson 2 ~
Names of Demon Spirits

There are also specific attributes to *Satan's demonic forces* as well as what they are attracted to.

➢ They have personalities – **Luke 8:6-23**
➢ They are intelligent – **1 Timothy 4:11**
➢ They have feelings and desires – **Matthew 8:28-31**
➢ They are afraid of God – **James 2:19**
➢ They are attracted to all images worshiped by cults and the occult – **Exodus 2:3**
➢ They are also attracted to movies of violence, movies dealing with the occult, fortune telling, drugs, alcohol, all forms of abuse, ESP, meditation, rock music, singing about rebellion, and illicit sex.

>>>The demon spirits also have names.<<<

➢ *Spirit of Infirmity* – **Luke 13:11; John 5:4, 5; Acts 3:2; 4:9; 10:38** [bent body/spine, impotent/frail/lame, asthma/hay fever/ allergies, arthritis, weakness, lingering disorder, oppression, cancer]
TAKING ACTION: **John 10:10; James 1:7; Matthew 18:18**
        Bind the spirit of infirmity and loose the Spirit of God

➢ *Deaf and Dumb spirit* – **Mark 5:5; 9:17, 18, 20, 20, 22, 25, 26, 29, 39; Matthew 9:32, 33; 12:22; 15:30, 31; 17:15; Luke 9:39; 11:14; Isaiah 35:5, 6;** [dumb/mute, crying, abusive, tearing, blindness, ear problems, mental illnesses, suicidal, foaming at the mouth, seizures/epilepsy, burn, gnashing of teeth, pining away/frustration]
TAKING ACTION: **Matthew 18:18; Romans 8:11; 1 Corinthians 12:9**
        Bind the deaf and dumb spirit and loose resurrection life and gifts of healing

➢ *An angel [Deceiving spirit]* – **2 Corinthians 11:14**

➢ *A lying spirit* – **1 Kings 22:22, 23; 2 Chronicles 18:21, 22; 2 Thessalonians 2:9-13; Psalms 78:36; 31:18; Proverbs 20:19; 10:18; 26:28; 29:5; 6:16-19; 1 Timothy 4:7; 6:20; 2 Timothy 2:16 Galatians 5:1; Jeremiah 23:16, 17; 27:9, 10; Matthew 7:15; Revelation 12:10; 2 Peter** [strong deception, flattery, superstitions, religious bondages, false prophecy, accusations, slander, gossip, lies, false teachers]

➢ *Seducing spirits* – **1 Timothy 4:1; Proverbs 1:10; 12:22, 26; James 1:14; Mark 13:22; Romans 7:11; 2 Timothy 3:13; 2 Thessalonians 2:10; 1 John 2:18-26; Deuteronomy 13:6-8** [hypocritical lies, seared conscience, attractions and fascination by false prophets, deception, wander from the truth, fascination with evil ways, objects, and persons, seduces/enticers, lust, adultery, fornication, homosexuality]

TAKING ACTION: **Matthew 18:18; John 16:13**
        Bind the seducing spirit and loose Holy Spirit

➢ *Foul spirit* – **Mark 9:25; Revelation 18:2**

➢ *Spirit of jealousy* – **Numbers 5:14, 30; Genesis 4:8; 37:3, 4, 8; Proverbs 6:34; 10:12; 13:10; 14:29, 30; 22:24, 25; 27:4; 29:22, 23; 1 Thessalonians 4:18; Song of Solomon 8:6;**

Galatians 5:19 [anger and rage, hatred, depression, murder, revenge and spite, jealousy, cruelty, strife, contention, extreme competition, envy, cause division]

➤ *Spirit of fear* – **2 Timothy 1:7; Isaiah 13:7, 8; 54:14; Psalms 55:4, 5; 91:5, 6; Luke 21:26; John 14:1, 27; Proverbs 29:25; Jeremiah 1:17-19; Ezekiel 2:6, 7; 2:3-9; Hebrews 2:14, 15; 1 Peter 5:7; Matthew 8:26; Revelation 21:8** [fears/phobias, torment, heart attacks, nightmares/terrors, fear of man, fear of death, anxiety/stress, untrusting/doubt]

TAKING ACTION: **Matthew 18:18; 2 Timothy 1:7**
Bind the spirit of fear and loose love, power, and a sound mind

➤ *Spirit of Divination* – **Acts 16:16; Micah 5:12; Isaiah 2:6; 19:3; 47:13; Exodus 7:11; 8:7; 9:11; 22:18; Leviticus 19:26; Jeremiah 10:2; 1 Samuel 15:23; Deuteronomy 18:11; Galatians 5:20; Revelation 9:21; 18:23; 21:8; 22:15; Hosea 4:12** [fortune teller, warlock/witch/sorcerer, stargazer/zodiac/horoscopes, rebellion, hypnotist/enchanter, drug (Greek – Pharmakos), water witching/divination/magic]

➤ *Familiar spirit* – **Leviticus 19:31; Deuteronomy 18:11; 1 Chronicles 10:13; 1 Samuel 28:7, 8; Isaiah 8:19; 29:4; 59:3; Jeremiah 23:16; 25:32; 27:9, 10; 29:8; Galatians 5:20; Revelation 9:21; 18:23; 21:8; 22:15** [necromancer, medium, peeping and muttering, yoga, clairvoyant, drug, spiritist, passive mind dreamers, false prophecy]

➤ *Perverse Spirit* – **Isaiah 19:14; Proverbs 1:22; 15:4; 14:2; 17:20, 23; 19:1; Romans 1:17-32; Exodus 21:22-25; 20:13; Proverbs 2:12; 19:3; 23:33; 1 Timothy 3:7, 8; 6:4, 5; 2 Timothy 3:2; Acts 13:10; 2 Peter 2:14; Philippians 2:14-16; Titus 3:10, 11** [broken spirit, evil actions, atheist, abortion, child abuse, filthy mind, doctrinal error, sexual perversion, foolishness, twisting the word, chronic worrier, contentious]

➤ *Spirit of Haughtiness/Pride* – **1 Samuel 15:23; 22:8; Jeremiah 43:2; 48:29; 49:16; Isaiah 2:11, 17; 5:15; 16:6; Proverbs 1:22; 3:34; 6:16, 17; 13:10; 16:18, 19; 21:24; 24:9; 28:5, 25; 29:1, 8; Ezekiel 16:49, 50; Daniel 5:20; Obadiah 1:3; Luke 18:11, 12; Psalm 10:4** [arrogant/smug, pride, idleness, strife, obstinate, self-deception, scornful, contentious, self-righteousness, rebellion, rejection of God]

➤ *Spirit of Heaviness* – **Isaiah 61:3; Luke 4:18; Nehemiah 2:2; Proverbs 12:18; 15:3, 13; 18:14; Psalm 69:20; Luke 4:18; 2 Corinthians 1:18, 19; Mark 9** [excessive mourning, sorrow/grief, insomnia, self-pity, broken heart, despair/dejection/hopelessness, depression, suicidal thoughts, heaviness]

➤ *Spirit of Whoredom* – **Hosea 5:4; 4:13-19; Ezekiel 16:15, 28; Proverbs 5:1-14; 15:27; Galatians 5:19; Deuteronomy 23:17, 18; 1 Timothy 6:7-14; Judges 2:17; Leviticus 17:7; 1 Corinthians 6:13-16; Philippians 3:19; James 4:4** [unfaithfulness/adultery, prostitution, chronic dissatisfaction, love of money, fornication, idolatry, excessive appetite, worldliness]

TAKING ACTION: roots of the flesh **Galatians 5:19-21; Matthew 7:20; 18:18; Ephesians 3:16; Psalm 51** Bind the spirit of whoredom and loose the spirit of God, pure spirit

> ➤ *Spirit of Bondage* – **Romans 6:16; 7:23; 8:15; 2 Peter 2:19; Hebrews 2:14, 15; Luke 8:26-29; John 8:34; Acts 8:23; Proverbs 5:22; 2 Timothy 2:26** [fears, addictions, fear of death, captivity to Satan, servant of corruption, compulsive sin, bondage to sin]

TAKING ACTION: **Matthew 18:18**
> Bind the spirit of bondage and loose liberty and the spirit of adoption

> ➤ *Spirit of Antichrist* – **1 John 2:18, 19; 4:3, 5, 13; 2 John 7; 2 Thessalonians 2:3-12; Revelation 13:7** [denies deity of Christ, denies atonement, against Christ and His teaching, humanism, worldly speech and actions, teachers of heresies, anti-Christian, deceiver and lawlessness]

TAKING ACTION: **Matthew 18:18; 1 John 4:6**
> Bind the spirit of antichrist and loose the Spirit of Truth

> ➤ *Spirit of Error* – **1 John 4:1-6; Proverbs 10:17; 12:1; 13:18; 14:22; 15:10, 12, 32; 29:1; 2 Peter 2:10; 3:16, 17, 19; 1 Timothy 6:20, 21; 2 Timothy 4:1-4; Titus 3:10; James 3:16** [error, unsubmissive, false doctrines, unteachable, servant of corruption, contentions (defensive/argumentative, defend God's revelations to them personally), New Age movement]

TAKING ACTION: **Matthew 18:18; 1 John 4:6; Psalm 51:10**
> Bind the spirit of error and loose the Spirit of Truth

> ➤ *Spirit of Death* – **1 Corinthians 15:26; Mark 5:9, 42; Luke 22:3** [physical death, emotional death, and spiritual death]

TAKING ACTION: **Matthew 18:18; John 10:28**
> Bind the spirit of death and loose the Spirit of Life

Being able to identify our adversary ought to be a simple task, at least if he looked like what many people believe he looks like: *red suit – horns – long pointed tail – carries a pitchfork.* Definitely couldn't miss that look at all! However, he doesn't look like that. He is not some mystical, imaginary creature that is bent on mischief. He is the adversary of our souls. And he hates and despises everything that is good and holy. He is perverted in all his manners and is altogether evil.

He often works with very slow and calculated movements. He is so good at plotting and scheming that his abilities, slyness, and craftiness will often go undetected until something major occurs. If he can lull his victims into a spiritual sleep, then he can draw them in under his control. And he can do this without them even being able to realize what is happening. [**1 Timothy 4:1-4**]

Satan wants to keep the Word hidden from the world [**2 Corinthians 4:3, 4**]. His lies and perversion keep men's eyes and focus off of the truth. He will appeal to men's fleshly, carnal appetites [**1 John 2:15-17**]. Adam and Eve wanted power, prestige, influence, and intellect [**Genesis 3:1-7**]. Judas Iscariot wanted money [**John 12:1-6; Matthew 26:14-16; John 13:1, 2, 25-30; 1 Timothy 6:9, 10**]

His ploy for man is not so much that they worship him as much as it is that they worship themselves. He doesn't want man to worship God. If men crowned themselves as their own god, then the same end is accomplished, which is the rejection of Jesus Christ as Lord and the enthroning of one's own rights to themselves. This equals the lordship and exaltation of self as master of their life, and this was the beginning of the end for Satan. Those who follow the same pattern will reap the same results.

The subject of demonology occupies a fairly substantial place in the revelations of Holy Scripture. The King James Version has somewhat obscured the subject by a poor translation of the words *daimonion* and *daimon*, rendering them as **devil** or **devils**. Later versions have properly translated these as demons. There is only one devil [*diabolos*] while there are multitudes of demons.

- ❖ Jesus recognized their reality. [**Matthew 12:27, 28; 10:8; Mark 16:17**]
- ❖ The seventy believed in their reality. [**Luke 10:17**]
- ❖ The Apostle Paul recognized their reality. [**1 Corinthians 10:20; 1 Timothy 4:1**]

~ Lesson 3 ~
Origin of Demons

God is the Creator of all things and after He had finished His work of Creation, He pronounced that everything in Creation was good [**Genesis 1:1**]. It seems quite certain that the demons were not created sinful. If we are assuming that demons are angels, "which kept not their first estate, but left their own habitation…" [**Jude 6**], and are those referred to when we read: "For if God spared not the angels that sinned, but cast them into hell…" [**2 Peter 2:4**], then we can conclude that they were once perfect, sinless beings. The cause of their fall and how they became demons has been the subject of much conjecture. Conservative Christian scholars, endeavoring to demonstrate scriptural authority, have advanced three principle theories.

1. *Demons are disembodied spirits of inhabitants of a Pre-Adamic earth.* Some believe that something catastrophic occurred between **Genesis 1:1** and **Genesis 1:2**. Satan's attempted overthrow of God led to his being cast out of heaven, which caused a convulsive action in the earth by sending it into a chaotic state of turmoil, and thus destroying the Pre-Adamite race who were somehow involved in the rebellion, and they lost their material bodies and became disembodied spirits.

2. *Demons are the offspring of angels and antediluvian women.* This theory is based on **Genesis 6:1-4** and **Jude 6, 7**. This theory concludes that because the angels had sexual intercourse with these women that they were sentenced to the punishment mentioned in Jude. This perversity caused God to flood the whole earth, destroying their monstrous offspring, and then their disembodied spirits became demons.

3. *Demons are fallen angels.* This view is supported from the fact that a number of scriptures refer to a great host of spirits who are variously designated as under the authority of Satan.
   Matthew 12:24 ⇒ Beelzebub, the prince of demons.
   Matthew 25:41 ⇒ the devil and his angels
   Revelation 12:7, 9 ⇒ the dragon…and his angels
   Revelation 12:3, 4 ⇒ one third of heaven's angels were caught in the rebellion in heaven and were cast down along with Satan

~ Lesson 4 ~
Demon Activity

Demons have strength [**Mark 5:2-4**], and wisdom [**James 2:19**]. They are not omniscient even though their wisdom appears to be above man's wisdom [**Matthew 8:29; Mark 1:21-24; Acts 19:15**]. They are wicked, unclean, and vicious [**Matthew 8:28; 10:1**]. And there seems to be degrees of wickedness among them [**Matthew 12:43-45**]. They seek to hinder the purposes of God and to extend the power of Satan.

Demons are quite active. They oppose the saints [**Ephesians 6:12; 1 Thessalonians 2:18**], induce departure from the faith [**1 Timothy 4:1**], encourage formalism as the result of false teaching [**1 Timothy 4:1-3**], and back all idol worship [**1 Corinthians 10:19-21; Revelation 9:20**]. They also cause various physical ailments such as dumbness [**Matthew 9:32, 22**], blindness [**Matthew 12:22**], insanity [**Luke 8:26-35**], suicidal mania [**Mark 9:22**], personal injuries [**Mark 9:18**], and defects and deformities [**Luke 13:11-17**].

All demon activity does not result in demon possession. In demon possession the person's spirit, soul, and body are entered and dominated by a demon or demons. In demon influence it could be described as warfare from without that is carried on by suggestion, temptation, and influence [**Ephesians 6:16**].

Essentially how do demons gain access over or into a person's life? They are always invited in. And they can be invited in through a variety of ways such as:

• Music • Drugs • Pornography • Occult/demonic movies • Alcohol
• False doctrine/teaching   • Familiar spirits/generational curses
• Emotional trauma • Words • Yielding to carnal lusts • Sin
• Dwelling on negative thoughts (having a defeated attitude)
• Fascination with occult powers (video/board games, tarot cards, ouiji board, books, séances, astrology, spiritism, horoscopes, good luck charms, fortune telling)

≈Occult means 'hidden things' = magic.≈

During Jesus' ministry, He dealt with the reality of demon possession [**Matthew 8:16; 9:32, 33; 12:26-28; Mark 5:2-13**] The Early Church dealt with the reality of demon possession as well [**Mark 16:15-17; Acts 5:16; 8:6, 7; 16:16-18; 19:13-16**]. Therefore we do not need to be ignorant of Satan's devices. Never give him a place. It is the blood of the Lamb and the word of your testimony that makes you an over comer.

NOTES

Understanding the Spiritual Kingdom

Angel
Jude 9; Hebrews 1:13,14
Acts 27:23; Luke 1:30

7 Archangels
1 Thessalonians 4:16; Jude 9

1. *Uriel* - over the world & tartarus
2. *Raphael* - over the spirits of men
3. *Raguel* - take vengeance on the world of luminaries
4. *Micheal* - over past, part of man and chaos - *Israel defender*
5. *Saragel* - over the spirits who sinned in the spirit
6. *Gabriel* - over paradise, the serpent and the cherubims *(God's faithful messenger)*
7. *Remeel* - over those who rise

* Mystery angel - *Zotiel*
Historical reference: Book of Enoch 1&2

The Book of Enoch was once canonized but was thrown out by the Roman Catholic church. Although not considered spiritually accurate, it is historically and culturally a reliable source of information.

Demons
Luke 8:2, 26, 27; 9:49
Daimon = Demons, Inferior deity, evil spirits

Fallen Angels
Watchers - Genesis 6:2
Satan - Job 1:6; 2:1

Leader	Semjaza	Asakiba	Rameel
Kokabiel	Tamiel	Daniel	Ezeqeel
Baraqijal	Asael	Armaros	Batarel
Ananel	Zaqiel	Samaopeel	
Satarel	Turel	Jomjael	Sariel

Copyright protected by Joshua International

Unclean Spirits
Mark 1:26-27, 32-34
Luke 4:33, 35; 6:18
Matthew 10:1

169 Greek Akathartos = mean, foul, impure

Chapter 10
Principalities and Powers in High Places – The Second Heaven
Opposition to God's Kingdom

What are they? What is their assignment against God's kingdom? Do they influence people for generations to generations?

~ Lesson 1 ~
The Assignment of Principalities and Powers

Principalities and powers in high places control certain governments of the world with secret societies like Illuminati, Processed Church, Masonry, Rosicrucian, etc. Michael and his angels protect certain governments as in the case of Jerusalem. Those who participate in these governments and societies are under the influence because they have surrendered to these principalities and powers to be able to perform the bidding of Satan's will, which opposes the kingdom of God and brings destruction to the land and its people.

Many countries and many cities throughout the world are experiencing serious strongholds that are producing spiritually evil fruit. There is spiritual wickedness, murderous spirits, and death from religions that oppose the God of the Bible. There are false religions that keep people from having a relationship with Christ and instead follow traditions and in turn develop addictions. There are wars, all sorts of destruction, unnatural storms, humanism, unbelief, abortion, and much more.

These fruits are manifested by invitation from corrupt governments, false religions, secret societies etc. This causes the atmosphere to inhabit the power from the second heaven which influence the people of the land they live in.

These creatures in high places mention in [**Ephesians 6: 10-20**] are like the prince of countries mentioned in the book of Daniel. They were in heaven along with Satan before the fall. These angels were known as the sons of God. They followed Satan in his rebellion against God and were thrown out of heaven by Michael and his angels.

When Lucifer entered the Garden of Eden and successfully tempted Eve, then Eve tempted Adam; the lordship of this planet was given over to Satan. By legal spiritual law the ownership of the world was rightfully his and in turn Satan placed certain spirits over the entire world as rulers and principalities, powers and wicked spirits.

These creatures ruled every area with the permission of Satan AND by invitation of humans that worshiped them through idolatry. The Babylonians invited their spiritual prince over them through idol worship, as did the Medes and Persians, the Greeks and the Romans. The false gods became the rulers and principalities over nations, cities, towns, churches, and families. As false religions are established, powers take over and these dark powers rule over the people who worship them.

The Heavens

3rd Heaven: The Throne of God

**The Four
Living Creatures**
Ezekiel 1:5

Wheel

**Cherubims
Seraphims
Arch Angels**

**Redeemed
Mankind**

2nd Heaven: The Throne of Satan

Principalities

**Powers of
this world**

**Rulers of
Darkness**

**Wicked Spirits
in high places**

1st Heaven: The Air Around Us

Wind

**Rain
Snow**

Clouds

Storms

**The air
we breathe**

The Earth

Mankind

**Animals
Birds**

**Creatures of
he waterways**

Demons

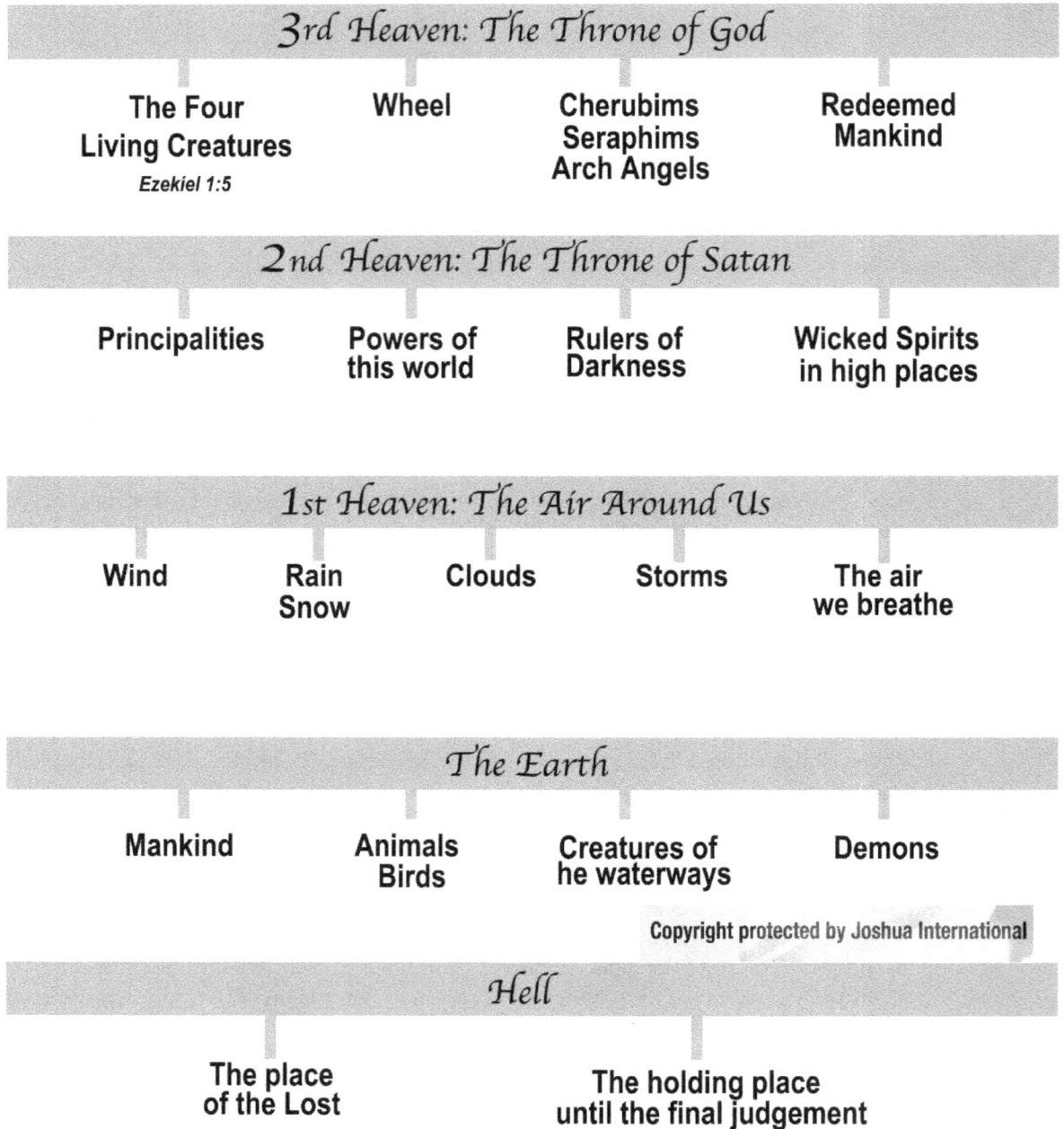

Hell

**The place
of the Lost**

**The holding place
until the final judgement**

~ Lesson 2 ~
>>Wicked spirits counterfeit the act of the Holy Spirit by false religions<<

As signs and miracles are sought after, the **wicked spirits** begin to try to **counterfeit** the acts of the Holy Spirit in religions such as spiritualism and the worshiping of the dead. Those participating in the worshiping of the dead believe that the dead can come back to speak the living. The followers of Hinduism believe in reincarnation.

All false religions have been established to worship false gods giving the wicked spirits (principalities) permission to rule over cities and individuals. Now with the increase of alcohol and drug addictions, prostitution, witchcraft, sexual perversion (pornography, homosexuality, bestiality), thievery, and murder wicked spirits are given authority to operate in those who are enslaved to these lifestyles. The only way to break the power and ruler ship is to turn away from them and turn to God.

Note: The wicked spirits and principalities are invited into our lives and to be delivered and set free from these creatures, we must invite God into our lives. Spiritual laws are set up to protect us from these spirits. Unless we break these laws and invite them into our lives, they will have no power over us.

Therefore, we must be careful who we listen to and come into agreement with

Satan's Influence on Mankind

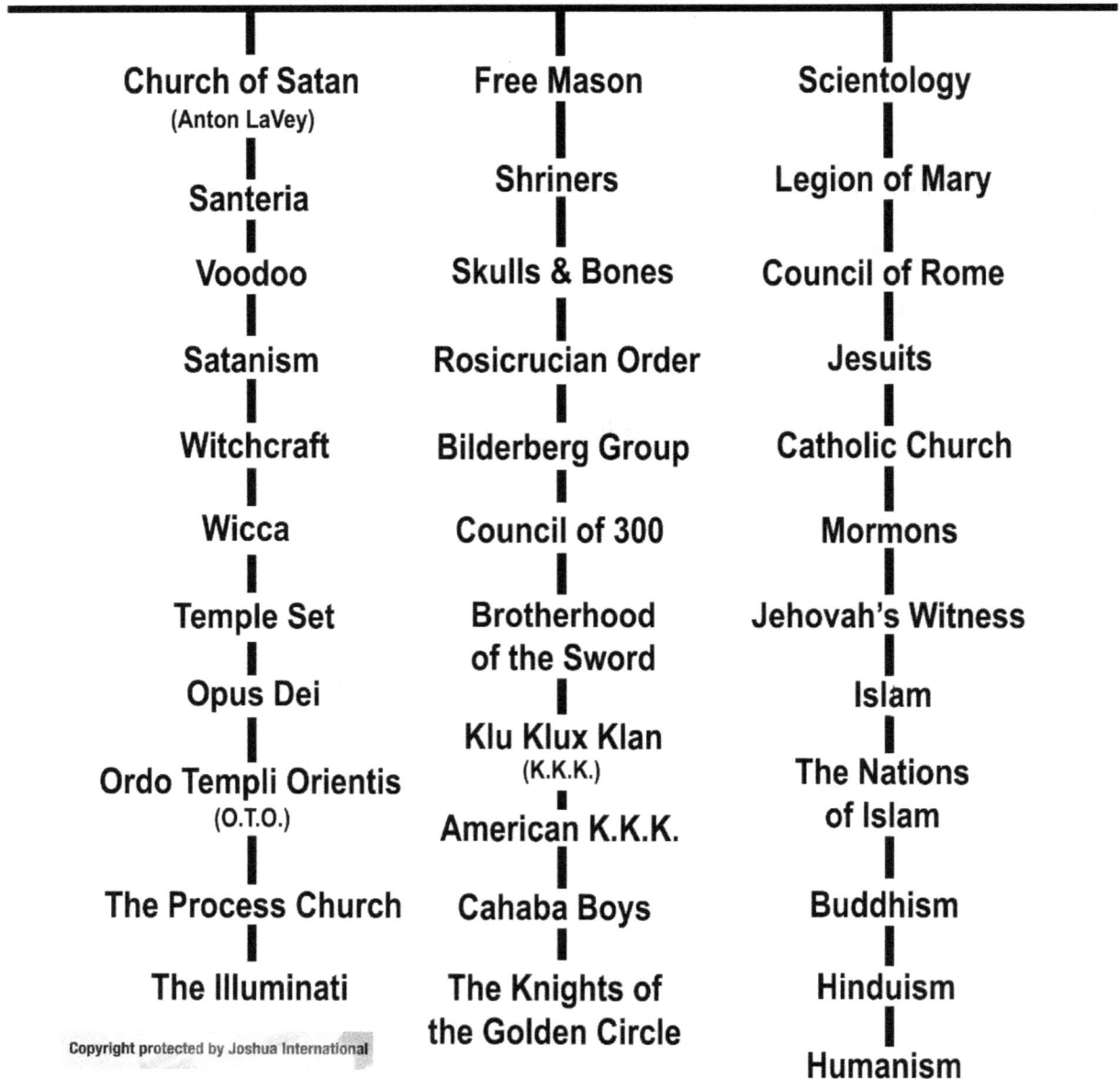

Church of Satan (Anton LaVey)	**Free Mason**	**Scientology**
Santeria	**Shriners**	**Legion of Mary**
Voodoo	**Skulls & Bones**	**Council of Rome**
Satanism	**Rosicrucian Order**	**Jesuits**
Witchcraft	**Bilderberg Group**	**Catholic Church**
Wicca	**Council of 300**	**Mormons**
Temple Set	**Brotherhood of the Sword**	**Jehovah's Witness**
Opus Dei	**Klu Klux Klan** (K.K.K.)	**Islam**
Ordo Templi Orientis (O.T.O.)	**American K.K.K.**	**The Nations of Islam**
The Process Church	**Cahaba Boys**	**Buddhism**
The Illuminati	**The Knights of the Golden Circle**	**Hinduism**
		Humanism

The Purpose of these Groups is:
1. to bring about the one world government
2. to bring unity amongst all false religions that are **not** Hebrew and biblically based
2. prepare the way of the anti-christ
3.prepare satan to rule the earth

~ Lesson 3 ~
>> False Religions and their Foundations Bring Deception >>

PLEASE do your research. STUDY [**2 Timothy 2:15**] Work hard so you can present yourself to God and receive his approval. Be a good worker, one who does not need to be ashamed and who **correctly explains the word of truth.**

There are religions that appear to hold the name of 'Christ' in their services and teachings **BUT** their foundations is NOT biblical which shows that Christ is NOT recognized as the FULL redeemer BUT leading them in their religion and NOT a relationship with God and his word.

Instead: we pray to other deities to make intercession and follow religious acts that are dead and NOT BIBLICAL and Non Relationship with God.[**II Tim 3:5**] which brings **soul ties [Lesson 5]** and **causes the biblical believer to agree emotionally saying that ITS OKAY to agree with this.**

Please note: A form of Godliness[religion] denying the power thereof is truly a scripture that needs understanding. [**II Tim 3:5**]   [**I Tim 2:5**] For there is one mediator between God and man **but denying its power. Have nothing to do with such people.**

The spirit behind it has a mission to bring FALSE UNITY [**Spirit of Seduction**] amongst all men and women and religions.[**The Spirit of the Anti Christ**]

Please Note: [The roots of these religions are located in ancient Babylonian and Egyptian roots]
Ref: The Two Babylon's by Alexander Hyssop]

Important Note: [**The Christian church is rooted in the Hebrew scriptures**]

++**Reference:** *Nimrod, where religions began by H.A.Lewis*++

"**Nevertheless**, the firm foundation of God stands, having this seal, 'The Lord knows those who are HIS,' and, 'Let everyone who names the name of the Lord abstain from wickedness.'" [**2 Timothy 2:19-21**]

[**I Timothy 2:5**] For there is one God and one mediator between God and mankind, the man Christ Jesus

[**Hebrews 9:15**] For this reason Christ is the mediator of a new covenant, that those who are called may receive the promised eternal inheritance--now that he has died as a ransom to set

~ Lesson 4 ~
>>>Test the Spirits that Speak.<<<
A spirit can appear in a dream, a vision, a voice, or through a human medium. It can be disguised as an angel of light, Jesus, God, a Bible personality, or a deceased family member. However, there are a few things we need to remember:

- ***Demons CANNOT confess Jesus Christ came in the flesh***. When asked if they can confess: "Jesus Christ came in the flesh", their disguise will vanish and their demonic identity will be revealed.

1 John 4:1-3 (NKJV) Beloved, do not believe every spirit, but test the spirits, whether they are of God; because many false prophets have gone out into the world. By this you know the Spirit of God: Every spirit confesses that Jesus Christ has come in the flesh is of God, and every spirit that does not confess that Jesus Christ has come in the flesh is not of God. And this is the spirit of the Antichrist, which you have heard was coming, and is now already in the world.

- ***The Holy Spirit of God CANNOT say Jesus is accursed.*** God the Holy Spirit cannot speak of the Lord Jesus in anything but loving, admiring, and honoring terms. Anything negative about the person or character of Christ, His work or sacrifice, is NOT the *Spirit of God* who is speaking.

1 Corinthians 12:3 (NKJV) Therefore, I make known to you that no one speaking by the Spirit of God calls Jesus accursed, and no one can say that Jesus is Lord except by the Holy Spirit.

- ***Demon spirits CANNOT say Jesus is their Lord.*** Regardless of whether the evil spirit is speaking through a medium (prophet, necromancer, etc) or directly in a vision or dream, when asked to confess Jesus is their Lord, its disguise will vanish and its evil identity will be revealed.

These three objective tests work when faithfully done.
John 17:17 (KJV) Sanctify them through thy truth: thy word is truth.

~ Lesson 5 ~
Wicked Spirits and Powers: Charismatic Witchcraft and Soul Ties

Charismatic witchcraft and soul ties are areas of life that fall under the leadership of wicked spirits and powers. Charismatic witchcraft is just as evil as regular witchcraft; however, many people do not believe in it or know how it works. Basically this form of witchcraft is when someone tries to insert their personal desires and wants over others.

It happens through self-centered prayers to govern and control the lives of others. The person praying these kinds of prayers are trying to make others do what he/she wants them to do and be, which is usually contrary to God's will in their life. I have heard people praying curses into the lives of others so that the person prayed for surrenders their will to the person who is trying to control them by their unbiblical prayers. This is why it is extremely important to ask God to protect us from the prayers of the immature, carnal Christian and the curses of the wicked.

Soul ties happen when we become *'soulishly'* connected to another, usually through sexual ties and/or idol worship. It occurs when we surrender our intellect, will, and emotions to someone else. We become slaves to these people. Soul ties can also be connected to substance abuse like drugs, alcohol, sex, and cigarettes. Essentially whatever we surrender to becomes our master and we become the slaves.

Charismatic witchcraft coincides with soul ties. When someone wishes to dominate the life of another, it can end up in a strong soul tie. Anything we may have done that tries to control our minds, our wills, and our emotions, we must ask God to break the power over us TO SET US FREE from these wicked spirits and power over our life.

If the soul tie is a result of a sexual tie to another, we must confess it as sin, which it is. We must ask God to forgive us and to set us free from its powers. All doors must be closed to all ungodly ties of yesterday, and we must bring our 'self/souls' under the Lordship and authority of God.

When we have a sexual experience outside of marriage, we become one with that person. Until the ties are broken through confession, we will continue our soul tie with that person, which can involve familiar spirits. It can become a vicious ongoing cycle in our lives and if it is not broken, then familiar spirits will try to pass it on to our children and future generations to come – generational curses.

It isn't just sexual experiences that this can happen with, it also applies to those who are continually controlled by substance abuse such as alcohol, drugs, tobacco, and even over eating. These ties must be broken! Behind all these addictions there are wicked spirits that work to keep us enslaved and eventually bring us to death.

See Lesson 3 on Soul Ties

Strongmen

Lucifer
(Ezekiel 28:1-19)
god of this world
(2 Cor 4;4)

Abaddon - Apollyon
Hebrew   Greek
(Revelation 9:11)

Beelzebub
prince of devils
(Matthew 10:25; 12:24)

Prince of Darkness
(Ephesians 6:12)

Prince of this World
(John 12:31; 16:11)

Behemoth
(Job 40:15-24)

Leviathon
(Job 41:1-10)

Rahab
(Psalms 87:4; 89:10 & Ezekial 29:2-5)

Prince of Babylon (Daniel 7:4)
Prince of Mede & Persia (Daniel 7:5)
Prince of Greece (Daniel 7:6)
Prince of Rome (Daniel 7:7)

Lion - Bear   Leopard - Fierce Beast

Recommended Reading: The Secret Names of the Strongmen by H.A.Lewis

~ Lesson 6 ~
Names of Principalities

Meni: god of destiny and fortune worshiped by ancient Hebrews [**Isaiah 65:11**]

Merodach: head god of the Babylonian people, was worshiped by Nebuchadnezzar, the Assyrians, and Cyrus the Great. He is also known as Merodach-baladan and Evil-Merodach. [**Jeremiah 51:44; Isaiah 46:1**]

Milcom: the national god of the Ammonites and is called the abomination of the Ammonites. [**1 Kings 11:5; 2 Kings 23:13**]

Molech: a detestable god of the Semitic deity worship through child sacrifice. [**Leviticus 18:21; 20:15**]

Nebo: Babylonian god of wisdom and literature

Nehushtan: the brazen serpent [**2 Kings 18:4**]

Nergal: Babylonian sun god and god of the underworld, also the god of pestilence and war, same as Beelzebub [**2 Kings 17:30**]

Satyr: demonic beings which will dance among the ruins of Babylon. They are half goats and half men.

Tammuz: Babylonian deity worshiped by Hebrew women [**Ezekiel 8:14**]. He was called Dumuzi, god of pasture and flocks, subterranean water and vegetation. He was the husband and brother of Isthar, a fertility goddess. [**Jeremiah 22:18; Amos 8:10; Zechariah 12:10**]

REMEMBER These counterfeit beings who work false miracles and acts of power are only trying to imitate the works of the Holy Spirit and the true source of God's power.

These wicked spirits in high places [**Ephesians 6:12**] are fallen angels who rule along with the principalities and powers in high places, the second heaven – the seat of Satan's throne. These spirits are behind all acts of destruction, murders, suicides, and perversion deeds and acts.

Recommended Reading: The Secret Names of the Strongmen by H.A.Lewis

~ Lesson 7~
Engaging With Demons in the 2nd Heaven

Warning – Do Not Engage With Demons [Principalities} in the 2nd Heaven Unless Directly Authorized by the Lord

In the area of spiritual warfare, one very controversial issue you will come across is whether or not we, as born-again believers, have the power and authority to try and attempt to engage with demons who are in the 2nd heaven, who are in what the Bible calls the **"heavenly places."**

After researching both sides of this very controversial issue, it is our personal opinion that unless God Himself directly authorizes and commissions you to engage in this kind of very special, high level type of spiritual warfare, that you stay completely away from this kind of activity. If you try to step into this kind of arena without God's direct approval and protection, you could open both yourself and possibly the members of your immediate family to major attacks from these higher-ranking demons.

Reference Reading: The Spiritual Opposition to the Five Fold Ministry, H.A.Lewis

Chapter 11
Spiritual Warfare Preparation

~ Lesson 1 ~
Religious Pride

PRIDE – AMORITE
(publicity-prominence)

LEGALISM: Adonizedec – Lord of Justice Legal
SECTARIANISM: Hebron – Compacted by a Spell or Enchantment
LAWLESSNESS: Piram – Running Wild; Wild Ass
RATIONALISM: Japhia – Shine Bright, Shew Self
RITUALISM: Debir – Shrine-Innermost Sanctuary, Rehearse
(Interpretation of Strong's Hebrew root meanings)

Joshua 10:3-5 Wherefore Adonizedec, king of Jerusalem sent unto Hoham, king of Hebron, and unto Piram, king of Jarmuth, and unto Japhia, king of Lachish, and unto Debir, king oi Eglon, saying, "Come up unto me, and help me, that we may smite Gibeon; for it hath made peace with Joshua and with the children of Israel." Therefore the five kings of the Amorites, the king of Jerusalem, the king of Hebron the king of Jarmuth, the king of Lachish, and the king of Eglon, gathered themselves together, and went up, they and all their hosts, and encamped before Gibeon, and made war against it.

Ephesians 6:12 For we wrestle not against flesh and blood, but against principalities, against powers, against the rulers of darkness of this world, against spiritual wickedness in high places.

Joel 2:7-11 They shall run like mighty men; they shall climb the wall like men of war; and they shall march every one on his ways, and they shall not break their ranks; Neither shall one thrust another; they shall walk every one in his path: and when they fall upon the sword, they shall not be wounded. They shall run to and from in the city; they shall run upon the wall, they shall climb up upon the houses; they shall enter in at the windows like a thief. The earth shall quake before them; the heavens shall tremble: the sun and the moon shall be dark, and the stars shall withdraw their shining: And the Lord shall utter his voice before his army: for his camp is very great: for he is strong that executeth his word: for the day of the Lord is great and very terrible; and who can abide it?

◆What are these ruler spirits and where will we find them?◆

❖ Every nation, state, city, congregation and household has a demon prince, ruler spirit or strongman assigned to it, whose job it is to kill, steal or destroy.

❖ The same is true of kingdoms, such as the kingdoms of finance, industry, oil, politics, science, etc.

Daniel 10:12-13 Then said he unto me, Fear not, Daniel: for from the first day that thou didst set thine heart to understand, and to chasten thyself before thy God, thy words were heard, and I am come for thy words. But the prince of the kingdom of Persia withstood me one and twenty days: but, lo, Michael, one of the chief princes, came to help me; and I remained there with the king of Persia.

❖ The kings hid in the cave of Makkedah.

Joshua 10:17-19 And it was told to Joshua, saying, The five kings are found hid in a cave at Makkedah. And Joshua said, Roll great stones upon the mouth of the cave, and set men by it for to keep them: And stay ye not, but pursue after your enemies, and smite the hindmost of them; suffer them not to enter into their cities: for the LORD your God hath delivered them into your hand.

Maqqedah (mak-kay-daw') – from the same meaning as a sense of herding; fold; Makkedah – a place in Palestine

❖ The sheepfold is a type of institutional religion, which is also a type of grave. After fueling the battle, the spirits go into hiding. Only by exercising the 'discerning of spirits' can they be located. Joshua, a type of Jesus, told the men to bind the strongmen by putting great stones upon the mouth of the cave. This type of binding and loosing is accomplished through high praise and the two-edged sword. The parallel to this in the New Testament is worshiping in spirit and in truth.

Psalms 149:6-9 Let the high praises of God be in their mouth, and a two-edged sword in their hand; To execute vengeance upon the heathen, and punishments upon the people; To bind their kings with chains, and their nobles with fetters of iron; To execute upon them the judgment written: this honour have all his saints. Praise ye the Lord.

John 4:23-24 But the hour cometh, and now is, when the true worshippers shall worship the Father in spirit and in truth: for the Father seeketh such to worship him. God is a Spirit: and they that worship him must worship him in spirit and in truth.

❖ The goal is that every member of the body of Christ truly becomes a "lively stone", each one reflecting or declaring a definite ray of spiritual light.

1 Peter 2:5-9 Ye also, as lively stones, are built up a spiritual house, an holy priesthood, to offer up spiritual sacrifices, acceptable to God by Jesus Christ. Wherefore also it is contained in the scripture, Behold, I lay in Sion a chief corner stone, elect, precious: and he that believeth on him shall not be confounded. Unto you therefore which believe he is precious: but unto them which be disobedient, the stone which the builders disallowed, the same is made the head of the corner, And a stone of stumbling, and a rock of offence, even to them which stumble at the word, being disobedient: whereunto also they were appointed. But ye are a chosen generation, a royal priesthood, an holy nation, a peculiar people; that ye should shew forth the praises of them who hath called you out of darkness into his marvelous light.

❖ Stones or rocks are always types of revelation beyond flesh and blood sense knowledge.

Matthew 16:15-19 He saith unto them, "But whom say ye that I am?" And Simon Peter answered and said, "Thou art the Christ, the Son of the living God." And Jesus answered and said unto him, "Blessed art thou, Simon Barjona: for flesh and blood hath not revealed it unto thee, but my Father which is in heaven. And I say also unto thee, that thou art Peter, and upon this rock I will build my church; and the gates of hell shall not prevail against it. And I will give unto thee the keys of the kingdom of heaven: and whatsoever thou shalt bind on earth shall be bound in heaven: and whatsoever thou shalt loose on earth shall be loosed in heaven."

❖ Peter, the one who received this great spiritual revelation from the Father, was said to be Satan's mouthpiece later.

Matthew 16:23 But he turned, and said unto Peter, "Get thee behind me, Satan: thou art an offence unto me: for thou savourest not the things that be of God, but those that be of man."

❖ Speaking things that sound good to the natural mind, such as religious sayings, does not bind the devils but causes them to manifest even more.

Acts 19:13-16 Then certain of the vagabond Jews, exorcists, took upon them to call over them which had evil spirits the name of the Lord Jesus, saying, "We adjure you by Jesus whom Paul preacheth." And there were seven sons of one Sceva, a Jew, and chief of the priests, which did so. And the evil spirit answered and said, "Jesus I know; but who are ye?" And the man in whom the evil spirit was leaped on them, and overcame them, and prevailed against them, so that they fled out of that house naked and wounded.

❖ Jacob and Laban could only bind the spirits of contention (which had been between them for 20 years) by placing a heap of stones in the midst of them.

Genesis 31:44-49 Now therefore come thou, let us make a covenant, I and thou; and let it be for a witness between me and thee. And Jacob took a stone, and set it up for a pillar. And Jacob said unto his brethren, gather stones; and they took stones, and made an heap: and they did eat there upon the heap. And Laban called it Jegar-sahadutha: but Jacob called it Galeed. And Laban said, "This heap is a witness between me and thee this day." Therefore was the name of it called Galeed; And Mizpah; for he said, "The Lord watch between me and thee, when we are absent one from another."

❖ Unity is possible only when Jesus, the Living Word, is the foundation and the lively stones allow His glory to shone upward to the glory of the Father.

❖ Satan, the master counterfeiter, illegally dwells in the midst of the lively stones.

Ezekiel 28:13-16 Thou hast been in Eden the garden of God; every precious stone was thy covering, the sardius, topaz, and the diamond, the beryl, the onyx, and the jasper, the sapphire, the emerald, and the carbuncle, and gold: the workmanship of thy tabrets and of thy pipes was prepared in thee in the day that thou wast created. Thou art the anointed cherub that covereth; and I have set thee so: thou wast upon the holy mountain of God; thou hast walked up and down in the midst of the stones of fire. Thou was perfect in thy ways from the day that thou wast created, tin iniquity was found in thee. By the multitude of thy merchandise they have filled the midst of thee with violence, and thou hast sinned: therefore I will cast thee as profane out of the mountain of God: and I will destroy thee, O covering cherub, from the midst of the stones of fire.

~ Lesson 2 ~
Spirit of Legalism

Joshua 10:3-5 Wherefore Adonizedek, king of Jerusalem sent unto Hoham, king of Hebron, and unto Piram, king of Jarmuth, and unto Japhia, king of Lachish, and unto Debir, king of Eglon, saying, "Come up unto me, and help me, that we may smite Gibeon: for it hath made peace with Joshua and with the children of Israel." Therefore the five kings of the Amorites, the king of Jerusalem, the king of Hebron, the king of Jarmuth, the king of Lachish, the king of Eglon, gathered themselves together, and went up, they and an their hosts, and encamped before Gibeon, and made war against it.

❖ Adonizedek gathered four other kings together against the peace of the children of Israel.

Definition: *Adoniy-Tsedeq* (ad-o'-nee-tseh'-dek) – meaning lord of justice; *Adoni-Tsedek* a Canaanite king
– *adown* (aw-done'); or (shortened) *adon* (awdone'); from the unused root (meaning to rule); sovereign; for example, controller (human or divine) -- lord, master, owner.
– *tsedeq* (tseh-dek); the right (natural, moral or legal); justice, justify, clear self.

❖ In my opinion the spirit of legalism is the leading religious spirit attacking the Church today. This spirit grips Christian minds so that only the letter of the law, without mercy or grace, can be understood. Scriptures are searched out and selected in such a sequence that they will justify their own thinking or actions, with little regard for what the Spirit of Truth is saying. This goes all the way back to the choice in the Garden of Eden between the tree knowledge of good and evil and the tree of life. This choice means the difference between life and death, both naturally and spiritually.

Deuteronomy 30:14-15, 19 But the word is very nigh unto thee, in thy mouth, and in thy heart, that thou mayest do it. See, I have set before thee this day life and good, and death and evil; I call heaven and earth to record this day against you, that I have set before you life and death, blessing and cursing: therefore choose life, that both thou and thy seed may live.
2 Corinthians 3:6 Who also hath made us able ministers of the new testament; not of the letter, but of the spirit: for the letter killeth, but the spirit giveth life.

❖ Satan knows, believes and quotes scripture.

Luke 4: 9-11 And he brought him to Jerusalem, and set him on a pinnacle of the temple, and said unto him, "If thou be the Son of God, cast thyself down from hence: For it is written, He shall give his angels charge over thee, to keep thee: And in their hands they shall bear thee up, lest at any time thou dash thy foot against a stone."
James 2:19 Thou believest that there is one God; thou doest well: the devils also believe, and tremble.

2 Corinthians 11:14-15 And no marvel; for Satan himself is transformed into an angel of light. Therefore it is no great thing if his ministers also be transformed as the ministers of righteousness; whose end shall be according to their works.

❖ This is a problem of demonic spells, not one of flesh and blood.

Galatians 3:1-2 0 foolish Galatians, who hath bewitched you, that ye should not obey the truth, before whose eyes Jesus Christ hath been evidently set forth, crucified among you? This only would I learn of you, Received ye the Spirit by the works of the law, or by the hearing of faith?

1 Timothy 4:1 Now the Spirit speaketh expressly, that in the latter times some shall depart from the faith, giving heed to seducing spirits, and doctrines of devils.

❖ This spirit of law, or legalism, was an ongoing hindrance to Jesus through the Pharisees, Sadducees and lawyers.

Luke 11:52-54 Woe unto you, lawyers' for ye have taken away the key of knowledge: ye entered not in yourselves, and them that were entering in ye hindered. And as he said these things unto them, the scribes and the Pharisees began to urge him vehemently, and to provoke him to speak of many things: Laying wait for him, and seeking to catch something out of his mouth, that they might accuse him.

Matthew 23:23-26 Woe unto you, scribes and Pharisees, hypocrites! For ye pay tithe of mint and anise and cumin, and have omitted the weightier matters of the law, judgment, mercy and faith: these ought ye to have done, and not to leave the other undone. Ye blind guides, which strain at a gnat, and swallow a camel. Woe unto you, scribes and Pharisees, hypocrites! For ye make clean the outside of the cup and of the platter, but within they are full of extortion and excess.

❖ Jesus never responded according to their religious expectations but always put the *Holy Spirit Rock* on them to bind them.

Matthew 12:9-15 And when he was departed thence, he went into their synagogue: And, behold, there was a man which had his hand withered. And they asked him, saying, "Is it lawful to heal on the sabbath day?", that they might accuse him. And he said unto them, "What man shall there be among you, that shall have one sheep, and if it fall into a pit on the sabbath day, will he not lay hold on it, and lift it out? How much then is a man better than a sheep? Wherefore it is lawful to do well on the sabbath days." Then saith he to the man, "Stretch forth thine hand." And he stretched it forth; and it was restored whole, like as the other. Then the Pharisees went out, and held a council against him, how they might destroy him. But when Jesus knew it, he withdrew himself from thence: and great multitudes followed him, and he healed them all.

Matthew 12:22-24 Then was brought unto him one possessed with a devil, blind, and dumb: and he healed him, insomuch that the blind and dumb both spake and saw. And all the people were amazed, and said, "Is not this the son *of* David?" But when the Pharisees heard it, they said, "This fellow doth not cast out devils, but by Beelzebub the prince of the devils."

Matthew 12:31-32 Wherefore I say unto you, "All manner of sin and blasphemy shall be forgiven unto men: but the blasphemy against the Holy Ghost shall not be forgiven unto men. And whosoever speaketh a word against the Son of man, it shall be forgiven him: but whosoever speaketh against the Holy Ghost, it shall not be forgiven him, neither in this world, neither in the world to come."

⇒*It is a dangerous thing to attribute the work of the Holy Spirit to devils.*⇐

❖ The man who was blind only said what he knew for sure, "I was blind but now I see." This word divided the enemy's ranks.

John 9:14-16 And it was the sabbath day when Jesus made the clay, and opened his eyes. Then again the Pharisees also asked him how he had received his sight. He said unto them, "He put clay upon mine eyes, and I washed and do see." Therefore said some of the Pharisees, "This man is not of God, because he keepeth not the sabbath day." Others said, "How can a man that is a sinner do such miracles?" And there was *a* division among them.

❖ The crippled man bound the spirit by speaking truth that he knew at the time. After further questioning the man revealed that it was Jesus who made him whole.

John 5:10-11 The Jews therefore said unto him that was cured, "It is the sabbath day: it is not lawful for thee to carry thy bed." He answered them, "He that made me whole, the same said unto me, Take up thy bed, and walk."

❖ The same Spirit of God at work in the early church is at work in today's Church.

Acts 15:1-2 And certain men, which came down from Judea, taught the brethren, and said, "Except ye be circumcised after the manner of Moses, ye cannot be saved." When therefore Paul and Barnabas had no small dissention and disputation with them, they determined that Paul and Barnabas, and certain other of them should go up to Jerusalem unto the apostles and elders about this question.

❖ After the leaders had tried to settle the question through debate, they were able to hear what the Holy Spirit had to say. The Holy Spirit allowed liberty to the Gentiles.

Acts 15:28-29 For it seemed good to the Holy Ghost, and to us, to lay upon you no greater burden than these necessary things; That ye abstain from meats offered to idols, and from blood, and from things strangled, and from fornication: from which if ye keep yourselves, ye shall do well. Fare ye well.

❖ Where the law of the Spirit is applied, there is freedom and liberty.

Romans 8:2 For the law of the Spirit of life in Christ Jesus hath made me free from the law of sin and death.

2 Corinthians 3:17 Now the Lord is that Spirit; and where the Spirit of the Lord is, there is liberty.

Romans 14:4-5 Who art thou that judgest another man's servant? to his own master he standeth or falleth. Yea, he shall be holden up: for God is able to make him stand. One man esteemeth one day above another: another esteemeth every day alike. Let every man be fully persuaded in his own mind.

James 1:25 But whoso looketh into the perfect law of liberty, and continueth therein, he being not a forgetful hearer, but a doer of the work, this man shall be blessed in his deed.

James 2:12 So speak ye, and so do, as they that shall be judged by the law of liberty.
Matthew 7:2 For with what judgment ye judge, ye shall be judged: and with what measure ye mete, it shall be measured to you again.

❖ Some of the most common points of legalism in the midst of people who worship God are:
- Church government
- Dress, hair and make-up
- Water baptism
- Music
- Kingdom of God
- Deliverance
- Use of money (tithing, spending, borrowing)
- Gifts of the Holy Spirit (tongues, miracles)
- Marriage and divorce
- Worship day
- Discipleship
- Healin

~ Lesson 3 ~
Spirit of Sectarianism

◆HEBRON◆

Definition: *chebrown* (kheb-rone') meaning seat of association; Chebron – a place in Palestine, also the name of two Israelites

–*cheber* (kheh'-ber) – a society; also a spell; charmer (-ing), company, enchantment

–*chabar* (khaw-bar') – a primitive root; to join (literally or figuratively); specifically (by means of spells) to fascinate: -- charm (-er), be compact, couple (together), have fellowship with, heap up, join (self, together), league.

By the words spell, enchantment, charmer and fascinate, we could conclude that these are groups joined and held together by devils rather than the Spirit of unity. This could also apply to a denomination, congregation, race, family, fraternity, nation, state, city, legal doctrine or philosophy, etc.

❖ Jesus said John was of a wrong spirit.

Luke 9:49-55 And John answered and said, "Master, we saw one casting out devils in thy name; and we forbad him, because he followeth not with us." And Jesus said unto him, "Forbid him not: for he that is not against us is for us." And it came to pass, when the time was come that he should be received up, he steadfastly set his face to go to Jerusalem, And sent messengers before his face: and they went, and entered into a village of the Samaritans, to make ready for him. And they did not receive him, because his face was as though he would go to Jerusalem. And when his disciples James and John saw this, they said, "Lord, wilt thou that we command fire to come down from heaven, and consume them, even as Elias did?" But he turned, and rebuked them, and said, "Ye know not what manner of spirit ye are of."

❖ A sect can form around one person.

1 Corinthians 3:4 For while one saith, I am of Paul; and another, I am of Apollos; are ye not carnal?

Definition: *Sect* – (Greek) – *hairesis* (hah'ee-res-is) – properly, a choice, specifically a party or (abstractly) disunion; heresy [which is the Greek word itself, sect]

❖ Manifestation of indignation of the sect of Sadducees followed the witness of healing and deliverance by the Spirit of God.

Acts 5:16-17 There came also a multitude out of the cities round about unto Jerusalem, bringing sick folks, and them which were vexed with unclean spirits: and they were healed every one. The high priest rose up, and all they that were with him, (which is the sect of the Sadducees), and were filled with indignation.

❖ Sect formed around the letter of the law.

Acts 15:5 But there rose up certain of the sect of the Pharisees, which believed, saying, That it was needful to circumcise them, and to command them to keep the law of Moses.

❖ Paul split the ranks with a word of wisdom.

Acts 23:6-7 But when Paul perceived that the one part of the Sadducees, and the other Pharisees, he cried out in the council, Men and brethren, I am a Pharisee, the son of a Pharisee: of the hope and resurrection of the dead I am called in question. And when he had so said, there arose a dissension between the Pharisees and the Sadducees: and the multitude was divided.

❖ Paul was accused of being a ringleader of the sect of the Nazarenes because Jesus came from Nazareth.

Acts 24:5 For we have found this man a pestilent fellow, and a mover of sedition among all the Jews throughout the world, and a ringleader of the sect of the Nazarenes.

❖ Paul's testimony of how he was of the sect gamed the attention of King Agrippa.

Acts 26:5 Which knew me from the beginning, if they would testify, that after the most straitest sect of our religion I lived a Pharisee.

❖ In Rome Paul testified that the "sect", as they called it, is the kingdom of God.

Acts 28:22-23 But we desire to hear of thee what thou thinkest: for as concerning this sect, we know that everywhere it is spoken against. And when they had appointed him a day, there came many to him into his lodging; to whom he expounded and testified the kingdom of God, persuading them concerning Jesus, both out of the law of Moses, and out of the prophets, from morning till evening.

❖ Instead of seeing the beginning of the glorious church, Peter wanted to build a building in honor of man. The Father rebuked him.

Matthew 17:4 Then answered Peter, and said unto Jesus, Lord, it is good for us to be here: it thou wilt, let us make here three tabernacles; one for thee, and one for Moses, and one for Elias.

❖ A sect can form even around a holy place.

Acts 7:48-49 Howbeit the most High dwelleth not in temples made with hands; as saith the prophet, Heaven is my throne, and earth is my footstool: what house will ye build me? saith the Lord: or what is the place of my rest?
1 Corinthians 6:19-20 What? know ye not that your body is the temple of the Holy Ghost which is in you, which ye have of God, and ye are not your own? For ye are bought with a price: therefore glorify God in your body, and in your spirit, which are God's.

❖ Christianity cannot be a mere performance behind walls that are often called a "sanctuary". The boundaries of the new covenant are flexible.

Matthew 9:17 Neither do men put new wine into old bottles: else the bottles break, and the wine runneth out, and the bottles perish: but they put new wine into new bottles, and both are preserved.
Isaiah 54:2 Enlarge the place of thy tent, and let them stretch forth the curtains of thine habitations: spare not, lengthen thy cords, and strengthen thy stakes.

2 Corinthians 3:17 Now the Lord is that Spirit: and where the Spirit of the Lord is, there is liberty.

❖ Peter battled with sectarian thinking.

Acts 10:15 And the voice spake unto him again the second time, "What God hath cleansed, that call not thou common."

Acts 10:34-35 Then Peter opened his mouth, and said, "Of a truth I perceive that God is no respecter of persons:

But in every nation he that feareth him, and worketh righteousness, is accepted with him."
Galatians 2:11-12 But when Peter was come to Antioch, I withstood him to the face, because he was to be blamed. For before that certain came from James, he did eat with the Gentiles: but when they were come, he withdrew and separated himself, fearing them which were of the circumcision.

❖ The Church is the "garden enclosed".

Song of Solomon 4:12-16 A garden enclosed is my sister, my spouse; a spring shut up, a fountain sealed. Thy plants are an orchard of pomegranates, with pleasant fruits; camphor, with spikenard, Spikenard and saffron; calamus and cinnamon, with all trees of frankincense; myrrh and aloes, with all the chief spices; A fountain of gardens, a well of living waters, and streams from Lebanon. Awake, O north wind; and come, thou south; blow upon my garden, that the spices thereof may flow out. Let my beloved come into his garden, and eat his pleasant fruits.

❖ We must earnestly cry out for the "strong winds" of the Holy Spirit to blow us so that the ministry may arise above all walls of sectarianism.

John 3:8 The wind bloweth where it listeth, and thou hearest the sound thereof, but canst not tell whence it cometh, and whither it goeth: so is every one that is born of the Spirit.

❖ Will we allow it to happen suddenly?

Acts 2:2 And suddenly there came a sound from heaven as of a rushing mighty wind, and it filled all the house where they were sitting.

❖ Paul was taken to Rome by the wind.

Acts 27:7 And when we had sailed slowly many days, and scarce were come over against Cnidus, the wind not suffering us, we sailed over Crete, over against Salmone.

❖ Sometimes God allows a soft wind in the beginning because of our weakness in courage.

Acts 27:13-14 And when the south wind blew softly, supposing that they had obtained their purpose, loosing thence, they sailed close by Crete. But not long after there arose against it a tempestuous wind, called Euroclydon.

❖ Going against the flow of the Holy Spirit wind is "tough sailing".

Acts 27:15 And when the ship was caught, and could not bear up into the wind, we let her drive.

❖ There comes the time when we pull up anchor and say, "If I die, I'll die trusting God."

Acts 27:40 And when they had taken up the anchors, they committed themselves unto the sea, and loosed the rudder bands, and hoised up the mainsail to the wind, and made toward shore.

Because of the wind, Paul was able to see a shipload of people saved, praying together in one accord, fasting and carrying out a ministry together on the island of Melita. They had to leave the ship, which had brought them this far, because it was sinking. They had to float into the "fruitful haven"…so it is with sectarian religion.

❖ The only true unity is having hearts knit together in love.

Colossians 2:2 That their hearts might be comforted, being **knit** together in love, and unto all riches of the full assurance of understanding, to the acknowledgement of the mystery of God, and of the Father, and of Christ.

1 Samuel 18:1-3 And it came to pass, when he had made an end of speaking unto Saul, that the soul of Jonathan was knit with the soul of David, and Jonathan loved him as his own soul. And Saul took him that day, and would let him go no more home to his father's house. Then Jonathan and David made a covenant, because he loved him as his own soul.

Definition: *Knit* (Greek) – *sumbibazo* (soom-bib-ad'-zo); *bibazo* (to force; causative [by reduplication; to drive together; unite (in association or affection), (mentally) to infer, show, teach: compact, assuredly gather, entrust, knit together, prove.
– *sun* (soon); a primary preposition denoting union; with or together; by association, companionship, process, resemblance, possession, instrumentality, addition, etc.: beside, with. In composition it has similar applications, including completeness.

Definition: *Knit* (Hebrew) –*qashar* (kaw-shar'); a primitive root: to tie, physically (gird, confine, compact) or mentally (in love, league): bind (up), (make a) conspire (-acy, -ator), join together, knit, stronger, work [treason].

Endeavoring to keep the unity of the Spirit in the bond of peace.
Ephesians 4:3

~ Lesson 4 ~
Spirit of Lawlessness
Joshua 10

Definition: *pere* (peh'-reh); or pereh [**Jeremiah 2:24**] (peh'reh); the sense of running wild; the onager; wild (ass).

❖ Submitting to the ordinances of man as a witness to the world.

1 Peter 2:13-16 Submit yourselves to every ordinance of man for the Lord's sake: whether it be to the king, as supreme; Or unto governors, as unto them that are sent by him for the punishment of evildoers, and for the praise of them that do well. For so is the will of God, that with well doing ye may put to silence the ignorance of foolish men: As free, and not using your liberty for a choke of maliciousness, but as the servants of God.

❖ The Church sometimes wants to 'police' the world when our own lifestyle is one of lawlessness.

1 Peter 4:17 For the time is come that judgment must begin at the house of God: and if it first begin at us, what shall the end be of them that obey not the gospel of God?

❖ The royal law of love and liberty

James 2:8-12 If ye fulfill the royal law according to the scripture, Thou shalt love thy neighbor as thyself, ye do well: But if ye have respect to persons, ye commit sin, and are convinced of the law as transgressors. For whosoever shall keep the whole law, and yet offend in one point, he is guilty of all. For he that said, Do not commit adultery, said also, Do not kill. Now if thou commit no adultery, yet if thou kill, thou art become a transgressor of the law. So speak ye, and so do, as they that shall be judged by the law of liberty.

Matthew 22:36-39 "Master, which is the great commandment in the law?" Jesus said unto him, "Thou shalt love the Lord thy God with all thy heart, and with all thy soul, and with all thy mind. This is the first and great commandment. And the second is like unto it, Thou shalt love thy neighbor as thyself."

❖ Love is not just a feeling but Love is a work.

Galatians 5:13 For, brethren, ye have been called unto liberty; only use not liberty for an occasion to the flesh, but by love serve one another.

❖ To have a feeling of love or compassion and to not put it to work is lawlessness or vain.

James 1:25-27 But whoso looketh into the perfect law of liberty, and continueth therein, he being not a forgetful hearer, but a doer of the work, this man shall be blessed in his deed. If any man among you seems to be religious, and bridleth not his tongue, but deceiveth his own heart, this man's religion is vain. Pure religion and undefiled before God and the Father is this, To visit the fatherless and widows in their affliction, and to keep himself unspoiled from the world.

- ❖ Love Feasts

Jude 1:4-8 For there are certain men crept in unawares, who were before of old ordained to this condemnation, ungodly men, turning the grace of our God into lasciviousness, and denying the only Lord God, and our Lord Jesus Christ. I will therefore put you in remembrance, though ye once knew this, how that the Lord, having saved the people out of the land of Egypt, afterward destroyed them that believed not. And the angels which kept not their first estate, but left their own habitation, he hath reserved in everlasting chains under darkness unto the judgment of the great day. Even as Sodom and Gomorrah, and the cities about them in like manner, giving themselves over to fornication, and going after strange flesh, are set forth for an example, suffering the vengeance of eternal fire. Likewise also these filthy dreamers defile the flesh, despise dominion and speak evil of dignities.

Definition: *unspotted* (Greek) – *aspilos* (as'-pee-los); from I (as a negative particle); unblemished (physically or morally): without spot, unspotted.
Definition: *dominion* (Greek) – *kuriotes* (koo-ree-ot'-ace); (concretely and collectively) rulers; dominion, government.

- ❖ Former Christians who have fallen back into spiritual death after being redeemed, and who continue to masquerade as children of the covenant, have no fear of God because they are blinded by a spirit of lawlessness.

Jude 1:12-13 These are spots in your feasts of charity, when they feast with you, feeding themselves without fear: clouds they are without water, carried about of winds; trees whose fruit withereth, without fruit, twice dead, plucked up by the roots; Raging waves of the sea, foaming out their own shame; wandering stars, to whom is reserved the blackness of darkness for ever.

- ❖ Submission to the law of love is the greatest "spot remover".

Ephesians 5:24-27 Therefore as the church is subject unto Christ, so let the wives be to their own husbands in every thing. Husbands, love your wives, even as Christ also loved the church, and gave himself for it; That he might sanctify and cleanse it with the washing of water by the word,
That he might present it to himself a glorious church, not having spot, or wrinkle, or any such thing; but that it should be holy and without blemish.

- ❖ The spirit of lawlessness attempts to convince Christians that there are no boundaries under grace.

Romans 8:2 For the law of the Spirit of life in Christ Jesus hath made me free from the law of sin and death.

Matthew 7:13-14 Enter ye in at the strait gate: for wide is the gate, and broad is the way, that leadeth to destruction, and many there be which go in thereat: Because strait is the gate, and narrow is the way, which leadeth unto life, and few there be that find it.

- ❖ Iniquity is better translated "lawlessness".

Matthew 7:21-25 Not every one that saith unto me, Lord, Lord, shall enter into the kingdom of heaven; but he that doeth the will of my Father which is in heaven. Many will say to me in that day, Lord, Lord, have we not prophesied in thy name? and in thy name have cast out devils? and in thy name done many wonderful works? And then will I profess unto them, I never knew you: depart from me, ye that work iniquity. Therefore whosoever heareth these sayings of mine, and doeth them, I will liken him unto a wise man, which built his house upon a rock: And the rain descended, and the floods came, and the winds blew, and beat upon that house; and it fell not: for it was founded upon a rock.

❖ Gifts of the Holy Spirit must come under love.

1 Corinthians 13:1-2 Though I speak with the tongues of men and of angels, and have not charity, I am become as sounding brass, or a tinkling cymbal. And though I have the gift of prophecy, and understand all mysteries, and all knowledge; and though I have all faith, so that I could remove mountains, and have not charity, I am nothing.

❖ Ananias and Sapphira tempted God with their lawlessness.

Acts 5:3-5 But Peter said, Ananias, why hath Satan pulled thine heart to lie to the Holy Ghost, and to keep back part of the price of the land? Whiles it remained, was it not thine own? and after it was sold, was it not in thine own power? why hast thou conceived this thing in thine heart? thou hast not lied unto men, but unto God. And Ananias hearing these words fell down, and gave up the ghost: and great fear came on all them that heard these things.

❖ Peter asked, "Why did you lie, since you were at liberty?"
❖ We see what happens when two lawless spirits are in agreement.

Acts 5:9-14 Then Peter said unto her, "How is it that ye have agreed together to tempt the Spirit of the Lord? Behold, the feet of them which have buried thy husband are at the door, and shall carry thee out." Then fell she down straightway at his feet, and yielded up the ghost: and the young men came in, and found her dead, and, carrying her forth, buried her by her husband. And great fear came upon all the church, and upon as many as heard these things. And by the hands of the apostles were many signs and wonders wrought among the people; (and they were all with one accord in Solomon's porch). And of the rest durst no man join himself to them: but the people magnified them. And believers were the more added to the Lord, multitudes both of men and women.

❖ Fear of the Lord, signs, wonders and multiplying of the numbers came after the purging of lawlessness.

Isaiah 66:16 For by fire and by his sword will the LORD plead with all flesh; and the slain of the LORD shall be many.
Isaiah 66:18 For I know their works and their thoughts: it shall come, that I will gather all nations and tongues; and they shall come, and see my glory.

❖ Lawlessness is when a Christian commits willful habitual sin against the law of love expecting grace to cover it.

Romans 6:1-2 What shall we say then? Shall we continue in sin, that grace may abound? God forbid. How shall we that are dead to sin, live any longer therein?

❖ Those who continue to break the law of love and liberty may be keeping the religious letter of the law but despise the Spirit of grace.

Hebrew 10:26-28 For if we sin willfully after that we have received the knowledge of the truth there remaineth no more sacrifice for sins. But a certain fearful looking for of judgment and fiery indignation, which shall devour the adversaries. He that despised Moses' law died without mercy under two or three witnesses: 29 Of how much sorer punishment, suppose ye, shall he be thought worthy, who hath trodden under foot the Son of God, and hath counted the blood of the covenant, wherewith he was sanctified, an unholy thing, and hath done despite unto the Spirit of grace?

  ❖ There is a place of no repentance for mature Christians.

Hebrews 6:4-6 For it is impossible for those who were once enlightened, and have tasted of the heavenly gift, and were made partakers of the Holy Ghost, And have tested the good word of God, and the powers of the world to come, If they shall fall away, to renew them against unto repentance; seeing they crucify to themselves the Son of God afresh, and put him to an open shame.
Hebrews 12:16-17 Lest there be any fornicator, or profane person, as Esau, who for one morsel of meat sold his birthright. For ye know how that afterward, when he would have inherited the blessing, he was rejected; for he found no place of repentance, though he sought it carefully with tears.

  ❖ This does not apply to sins of weakness or ignorance, but only to willful and habitual sins.

Hebrew 4:15 For we have not an high priest which cannot be touched with the feeling of our infirmities; but was in all points tempted like as we are, yet without sin.
Hebrews 5:2 Who can have compassion on the ignorant, and on them that are out of the way; for that he himself also is compassed with infirmity.

  ❖ Fear the God who controls hell.

Matthew 10:28 And fear not them which kid the body, but are not able to kill the soul: but rather fear him which is able to destroy both soul and body in hell.

  ❖ The root cause of lawlessness is lack of the fear of God.

Psalms 36:1 The transgression of the wicked saith within my heart, that there is no fear of God before his eyes.

  ❖ Fear of God is where everything begins.

Psalms 111:10 The fear of the LORD is the beginning of wisdom: a good understanding have all they that do his commandments: his praise endureth forever.

  ❖ Fear of God is the conclusion of all things.

Ecclesiastes 12:13 Let us hear the conclusion of the whole manner: Fear God, and keep his commandments: for this is the whole duty of man.

  ❖ The foundation stone which our lives must be built upon is the fear of the Lord. All else is shifting sand.

~ Lesson 5 ~
Japhia, King of Lachish

Definition: *Japhia* – *yapha'* (yaw-fah'); a primitive root; to shine: be light, shewself, (cause to) shine (forth); a Canaanite, an Israelite, and a place in Palestine

❖ New Testament examples of "rationalism":

2 Timothy 3:4-7 Traitors, *heady*, *high minded*, lovers of pleasures more than lovers of God; Having a form of godliness, but denying the power thereof: from such turn away. For of this sort are they which creep into houses, and lead captive silly women laden with sins, led away with divers lusts, Ever learning, and never able to come to the knowledge of the truth.

Definition: *Heady, Rashly* (Greek) – *propetes* (prop-et-ace'); falling forward, headlong (figuratively, precipitate): heady, rash [-ly].
Definition: *High minded* (Greek) – *tuphoo* (toof-o'-o); from a derivative of *tupho*; to envelop with smoke, ie. (figuratively) to inflate with self-conceit: high minded, be lifted up with pride, be proud. – *tupho* (too'-fo); apparently a primary verb; to make a smoke, ie. slowly consume without flame.

Ephesians 4:17 This I say therefore, and testify in the Lord, that ye henceforth walk not as other Gentiles walk, in the *vanity* of their minds.
Hebrews 5:14 But strong meat belongeth to them that are of full age, even those who by reason of use have their senses exercised to discern both good and evil.

Definition: *Vanity* – *mataiotes* (mat-ah-yot'-ace); from *mataios*; inutility; figuratively, transientness; morally, depravity; vanity.
– *mataios* (mat'-ah-yos); from the base of *maten*; empty, ie. (literally) profitless, or (specifically) an idol: vain, vanity.
– *maten* (mat'-ane); (through the idea of tentative manipulation, ie. unsuccessful search, or else of punishment); folly, ie. (adverbially) to no purpose: vain.

NOTE The words **idol**, **transientness**, and **depravity** indicate demonic activity in the mind.

❖ Smoke screens or cover-ups are much the same as were the fig leaves Adam and Eve used to try to cover the fact that they had been feeding from the wrong tree. Characteristics of this spirit include:
  • *Self conceit* -- to be lifted up with pride because of one's own sense of knowledge.
  • *Religiosity* -- to be religious but refusing the let the power of God to flow.
  • *Compulsion* -- to be driven to learn new things but never able to know the Spirit revealed truth.
  • *Vanity of the mind* -- to believe in and trust our own knowledge of good and evil rather than to lean on the Spirit of discernment to convict us daily from the heart.

♦ This <u>spirit</u> says "**seeing is believing**" but the <u>Truth</u> says "**believing is seeing**". ♦

John 11:40 Jesus saith unto her, Said I not unto thee, that, if thou wouldest believe, thou shouldest see the glory of God?

Hebrews 11:1-3 Now faith is the substance of things hoped for, the evidence of things not seen. For by it the elders obtained a good report. Through faith we understand that the worlds were framed by the word of God, so that things which are seen were not made of things which do appear.

Ephesians 3:20 Now unto him that is able to do exceeding abundantly above all that we ask or think, according to the power that worketh in us.

❖ Faith operates by higher revelation than the rational mind can comprehend. The only limiting factor is how much power our natural mind allows to work in us. Faith goes beyond what we can verbalize or even "confess".

Rational Fact or Truth

⟹**What is truth?**
John 17:17 Sanctify them through thy truth: thy word is truth.

⟹**Truth is what the Holy Spirit of Truth is saying and not what the majority is saying. The Truth of God supersedes any rational fact.**

Numbers 13:30-31 And Caleb stilled the people before Moses, and said, Let us go up at once, and possess it; for we are well able to overcome it. But the men that went up with him said, We be not able to go up against the people; for they are stronger than we.
Numbers 14:24 But my servant Caleb, because he had another spirit with him, and hath followed me fully, him will I bring into the land whereunto he went; and his seed shall possess it.

NOTE The vote was 10 to 2 in favor of moving by rational fact over God's revealed truth.
NOTE Caleb was not of a spirit of rationalism.

⟹**Admitting what is the rational fact of the matter does not hinder faith unless we let it govern our walk.**

⟹**When Jesus -- the Living Word -- speaks, it is.**
John 11:4 When Jesus heard that, he said, This sickness is not unto death, but for the glory of God, that the Son of God might be glorified thereby.
John 11:11-15 These things said he: and after that he saith unto them, Our friend Lazarus sleepeth; but I go, that I may awake him out of sleep. The said his disciples, Lord, if he sleep, he shall do well. Howbeit Jesus spake of his death: but they thought that he had spoken of taking of rest in sleep. Then said Jesus unto them plainly, Lazarus is dead. And I am glad for your sakes that I was not there, to the intent ye may believe; nevertheless let us go unto him.

⟹**Jesus speaks both fact and truth; but walks in the light of Truth.**
Joshua 10:12-13 Then spake Joshua to the: LORD in the day when the LORD delivered up the Amorites before the children of Israel, and he said in the sight of Israel, Sun, stand thou still upon Gibeon; and thou, Moon, in the valley of Ajolon. And the sun stood still, and moon stayed, until the people had avenged themselves upon their enemies. Is not this written in the book of Jasher? So the sun stood still in the midst of heaven, and hastened not to go down about the whole day.

NOTE God had compassion on Joshua's lack of knowledge and stopped the rotation of the earth instead of making the sun and moon stand still as he verbally commanded.

Hebrews 4:15 For we have not an high priest which cannot be touched with the feeling of our infirmities; but was in all points tempted like as we are, yet without sin.

Hebrews 5:2 Who can have compassion on the ignorant, and on them that are out of the way; for that he himself also is compassed with infirmity.

1 Corinthians 1:27-29 But God hath chosen the foolish things of the world to confound the wise; and God hath chosen the weak things of the world to confound the things which are mighty; And base things of the world, and things which are despised, hath God chosen, yea, and things which are not, to bring to nought things that are:That no flesh should glory in his presence.

⇒Casting down reasonings and every high thing

2 Corinthians 10:3-5 For though we walk in the flesh, we do not war after the flesh: (For the weapons of our warfare are not *carnal*, but mighty through God to the pulling down of strong holds;) Casting down *imaginations*, and every high thing that exalteth itself against the knowledge of God, and bringing into captivity every thought to the obedience of Christ.

Definition: *Carnal* (Greek) – *sarkikos* (sar-kee-kos'); pertaining to flesh, carnal fleshly (by extension) bodily, temporal or (by implication) animal, unregenerate.
Definition: *Imaginations* (Greek) – *logismos* (log-is-mos'); computation, conceit; (figuratively) reasoning; (conscience) imagination, thought.

Romans 4:17-21 (As it is written, I have made thee a father of many nations,) before him whom he believed, even God, who quickeneth the dead, and calleth those things which be not as though they were. Who against hope believed in hope, that he might become the father of many nations; according to that which was spoken, So shall thy seed be. And being not weak in faith, he considered not his own body now dead, when he was about an hundred years old, neither yet the deadness of Sarah's womb: He staggered not at the promise of God through unbelief; but was strong in faith, giving glory to God; And being fully persuaded that, what he had promised, he was able also to perform.

~ Lesson 6 ~
Spirit of Ritualism

Definition: *Debir* (**Hebrew**) - *Debiyr* (deb-eer'); or (shortened) Debir (**Joshua 13:26**) (deb-er'); Debir, the name of an Amoritish king and of two places in Palestine: Debir.
– *debyr* (deb-eer'); or (shortened) debir (deb-eer'); (apparently in the sense of oracle); the shrine or innermost part of the sanctuary: oracle.
– *dabar* (daw-bar'); a primitive root; perhaps properly, to arrange; but used figuratively (of words), to speak; rarely (in a destructive sense) to subdue: answer, appoint, bid, command, commune, declare, destroy, give, name, promise, pronounce, rehearse, say, speak be spokesman, subdue, talk, teach, tell, think, use [entreaties], utter,

❖ A ritualistic spirit takes short-cuts in our worship and walk with God; a rehearsed, arranged plan centered around a man-made sanctuary or shrine rather than a spiritual entrance which cannot be rushed, projected or programmed on a computer.

❖ In the tabernacle in the wilderness, it was impossible to skip from the entrance of the courtyard to the Holy of Holies.

❖ It was at least 40 years between the time God called Moses and the time he was used as the deliverer.

❖ In the case of Paul it was least 10 years from the road to Damascus experience to being sent out from the church at Antioch.

❖ This does not mean that God only honors long praying, praising, preaching, Bible study or suffering; but the truth is that all spiritual entrances is governed by a sovereign God.

⟹**Stephen was stoned by religious people under the control of this spirit of ritualism, which violently resists change and the removal of shrine or temple worship.**

Acts 6:13-15 And set up false witnesses, which said, This man ceaseth not to speak blasphemous words against this holy place, and the law: For we have heard him say, that this Jesus of Nazareth shall destroy this place, and shall change the customs which Moses delivered us. And all that sat in the council, looking steadfastly on him, saw his face as it had been the face of an angel.

❖ The manifestations of the glory of God always herald change. The time of indecision is over.

Exodus 40:35-36 And Moses was not able to enter into the tent of the congregation, because the cloud abode thereon, and the glory of the LORD filled the tabernacle. and when the cloud was taken up from over the tabernacle, the children of Israel went onward in all their journeys.
2 Corinthians 3:18 But we all, with open face beholding as in a glass the glory of the Lord, are changed into the same image from glory to glory, even as by the Spirit of the Lord.

❖ Adam, Eve, Job and Jonah were all afraid of the presence of (or face to face fellowship with) God.

Genesis 3:8 And they heard the voice of the Lord God walking in the garden in the cool of the day: and Adam and his wife hid themselves from the presence of the Lord God amongst the trees of the garden.
Job 23:15-16 Therefore am I troubled at his presence: when I consider, I am afraid of him. For God maketh my heart soft, and the Almighty troubleth me.
Jonah 1:3 But Jonah rose up to flee unto Tarshish from the presence of the LORD, and went down to Joppa; and he found a ship going to Tarshish: so he paid the fare thereof, and went down into it, to go with them unto Tarshish from the presence of the Lord.

❖ Angry demonic manifestations at the powerful preaching of Stephen:

Acts 7:47-51 But Solomon built him an house. Howbeit the most High dwelleth not in temples made with hands; as saith the prophet, Heaven is my throne, and earth is my footstool: what house will ye build me? saith the Lord: or what is the place of my rest? Hath not my hand made all these things? Ye stiffnecked and uncircumcised in heart and ears, ye do always resist the Holy Ghost: as your fathers did, so do ye.
Acts 7:54, 57 When they heard these things, they were cut to the heart, and they gnashed on him with their teeth.
Then they cried out with a loud voice, and stopped their ears, and ran upon him with one accord.

❖ Ritualism in deliverance ministry:

Acts 19:13 Then certain of the vagabond Jews, exorcists, took upon them to call over them which had evil spirits the name of the Lord Jesus, saying, We adjure you by Jesus whom Paul preacheth.

⟹**United worship in spirit and in truth changes those people who would ordinarily lead rituals.**

2 Chronicles 5:13-14 It came even to pass, as the trumpeters and singers were as one, to make one sound to be heard in praising and thanking the Lord; and when they lifted up their voice with the trumpets and cymbals and instruments of music, and praised the Lord, saying, For he is good; for his mercy endureth for ever: that then the house was filled with a cloud, even the house of the Lord; So that the priests could not stand to minister by reason of the cloud: for the glory of the Lord had filled the house of God.

Haggai 2:6-9 For thus saith the Lord of hosts; Yet once, it is a little while, and I will shake the heavens, and the earth, and the sea, and the dry land; And I will shake all nations, and the desire of all nations shall come: and I will pull this house with glory, saith the Lord of hosts. The silver is mine, and the gold is mine, saith the Lord of hosts. The glory of this latter house shall be greater than of the former, saith the Lord of hosts: and in this place will I give peace, saith the Lord of hosts.

❖ This had not fully happened at the writing of the book of Hebrews and, in my opinion, has not fully happened even at this present time.

Hebrews 12:26-29 Whose voice then shook the earth: but now he hath promised, saying, Yet once more I shake not the earth only, but also heaven. And this word, Yet once more, signifieth the removing of those things that are shaken, as of things which cannot be shaken may remain. Wherefore we receiving a kingdom which cannot be moved, let us have grace, whereby we may serve God acceptably with reverence and godly fear: For our God is a consuming fire.

❖ What once served a good purpose may later become a ritual and must be cast down.

2 Kings 18:4 He removed the high places, and brake the images, and cast down the groves, and brake in pieces the brazen serpent that Moses had made: for unto those days the children of Israel did burn incense to it: and he called it Nehushtan.

This is not a flesh and blood battle with carnal weapons but is the using of spiritual weapons of HIGH PRAISE AND THE TWO EDGED SWORD until the enemy is <u>utterly</u> destroyed.[Hebrew 4:12]

NOTES

Chapter 12
The Nephilim, the Anakim, and the Rephaim

The Nephilim, the Anakim, and the Rephaim are believed to be the children of the sons of God and the daughters of men [**Genesis 6:4; Numbers 13:33**]. In fact, it is in the book of Numbers that many believe prove the existence of giants who were the children of the daughters of men and the sons of God. Essentially the sons of God came down and had relations with the women and as a result their offspring were giants. These scriptures show that the giants mentioned first in **Genesis 6** could reproduce more giants.

In **2 Samuel 21:16-22** and **1 Chronicles 20:4-8** we see the term *children of the giants*. It is said that they were born of the giants in Gath. Of course Gath is where Goliath, the most famous giant in the Bible, came from. He is also the giant slain by David.

~ Lesson 1 ~
Names of the Giants

In **Deuteronomy 2:10-11** the children of Emims lived in the land and they were as large as the children of Anak who were the Anakims. Josephus wrote in book five chapter two of the giants where bodies were so large and their countenances so different from men that they were surprising to the sight and terrible to the hearing.

I agree with others that the giants became the foundation for the Greek gods and goddesses. Nimrod, mentioned in **Genesis 10**, became the root of the Greek and Roman hero known as Hercules.

The very term to describe these being *nephil* means *giant, bully or tyrant* [**Genesis 6:4; Numbers 13:33**]. That these beings were of abnormal size is clearly described in **Numbers 13:33**. As Israel was spying out the land and saw these giants, they saw themselves as grasshoppers. Naturally they were like grasshoppers in the sight of these giants as well.

The Bible speaks of these creatures as a people great and tall in body [**Deuteronomy 1:28; 2:10-11, 21; 9:21; Joshua 11:21-22; 14:12-14**] The father of these beings, Anak, was also a giant. The Emims were according to **Deuteronomy 2:10-11** as large as the Anakims. The Zamzummims were called giants by the Ammonites in **Deuteronomy 2:19-21**. Og, king of Bashan was a giant so large that he had a special bed made that was 18 ½ feet long and 8 ft. 4 in. wide. [**Deuteronomy 3:11; Joshua 12:4; 13:12**]

There was also another land of giants mentioned in **Joshua 15:8; 18:16**. This was the valley of the Rephaim. These giants were mentioned in [**Genesis 14:5; 15:20: 2 Samuel 5:18, 22; 23:13; 1 Chronicles 11:15; 14:9; Isaiah 17:15**]. The Rephaims were well known giants but unfortunately instead of retaining their proper name the translators translated it *dead* [**Job 26:5; Psalm 88:10; Proverbs 2:18; 9:18; 21:6; Isaiah 14:8; 26:17**] and as deceased in **Isaiah 26:14**.

Rephaim is properly translated as *giants* in [**2 Samuel 21:16,18, 20,22; 1 Chronicles 20:4, 6-8**] and as *giants* in [**Deuteronomy 2:11, 20; 3:11, 13; 1 Chronicles 11:15; 14:9; Isaiah 17:5**]. The phrase *'remnant of giants'* should be translated *'remnants of the Rephaim'* for these were many nations of giants besides the Rephaim who filled the whole country trying to contest God's claim on the Promised Land.

They are listed as the following: Kenites, Kenizzites, Kadmonites, Hittites, Perizzites, Rephaims, Amorites, Canaanites, Girgashites, Jebusites, Hivites, Anakims, Emims, Horims (Horites), Avims (Avites), Zamzummims, Caphtorims (Caphtorites), and the Nephilims [**Genesis 6:4; 14:5,6 ; 15:19, 21; Exodus 3:8, 17; 23:23; Deuteronomy 2:10-12, 20-23; 3:11-13; 7:1; 20:17; Joshua 12:4-8; 13:3; 15:8; 17:15; 18:16**]

Og, the giant king of Bashan was of the Rephaim and not any other giant race. All of these giant races are from the union of the sons of God and the daughters of men **after** the flood. Twice this union between fallen angels and the woman of the earth had happened and it will happen again just before the return of our Lord Jesus.
The creatures were of large stature. Some even had six fingers on each hand and six toes on each foot. Their spears weighed anywhere from 10-25 lbs.

Goliath's armor weighed 196 lbs. and he was around 13 ft. tall. His five brothers were even bigger than he was. We will probably not understand how the great pyramids of Egypt and the giant cities of Bashan and other huge monuments of construction happened. It will probably remain a secret or an unsolved mystery unless these colossal constructions are accepted as the result of labor of the fallen angels.

The revelation of the giants in scripture give us a true picture of what Greek, Roman, and Norse mythology tries to give us. Mythology is just the outgrowth of traditions, memories, and legend telling of the acts of the supernatural fathers (fallen angels) and their offspring the giants of Genesis. In mythology, these acts of perversion and total corruption are a transmission of actual facts concerning these mighty beings.
The fact that the Rephaim have no resurrection [**Isaiah 26:14**] proves the reality of giants. They were not mortal men. All mortal men will be resurrected [**John 5:28, 29**]; therefore, giants must be different creatures than the seed of Adam.

Isaiah makes it clear that the Rephaim are in hell [**Isaiah 14:9**]. Solomon confirms this in [**Proverbs 2:18; 9:18; 21:6**] where the Hebrew word for *dead* is ***Rephaim***. The fact that giants came from the union of fallen angels and the daughters of men proves that their fathers were not ordinary men of Adamite stock. No such monstrosities as these creatures were ever a product of a normal man and woman. No matter how righteous the father and how evil the mother, there cannot be a product of that relationship.

~ Lesson 2 ~
Where the Giants Originated

We must understand that if these creatures were a product of relations between an ordinary man and woman before the flood and after the flood, why is it that they are not produced today? Why did it happen so much before the flood and after and doesn't occur today?

It is unscriptural and unhistorical to say that these creatures came from the sons of Seth and the daughters of man. God's law of reproduction has always been – *each after its own kind*. It isn't possible for ordinary men and women to give birth to these monsters.

I know we have large men today. I come from a family that had thirteen men of great size and weight. They were around 7ft. 5 in. tall and weighed nearly 500 lbs. My great grandfather was 6 ft. 8in. tall and weighed 380 lbs. My father was 6 ft. 5in. tall and would stop traffic as he walked the street in the 1950's. Men were not that tall back then. My son is 6 ft. 8 in. and close to 300 lbs. My grandson is also 6ft. 8in. at the age of nineteen; yet, they are not giants, only tall men.

To produce these giants it took an element of supernatural that revealed the plan of Satan and his fallen angels to produce giants of the human race. After these beings came into existence, they produced others like themselves instead of ordinary-sized men. [**Numbers 13:33; 2 Samuel 21:16, 18-20, 22; 1 Chronicles 20:4-8**]

♦The biggest question is: where did the giants get their start? ♦

Genesis 6:4 makes it clear that it was from the union of fallen angels and the daughters of men. Nevertheless there is an opposing side which states that angels cannot produce. Four conclusions the opposing side have voiced are that

1. Ungodly women have the power to produce these monsters if married to godly men.
2. Godly men have the power to produce these monsters if married to ungodly women.
3. A mixture of godliness and ungodliness produce giants.
4. Extreme wickedness on either side will produce giants.

All four conclusions are **wrong** as proven by everyday living. An ungodly spouse with a godly one will not produce giants. Therefore, the theory that the sons of Seth intermarried with the daughters of Cain is disproved. In addition it is proven by scripture that the children of Seth were as ungodly as the daughters of Cain.

In fact from the time of Adam to the time of Noah's flood only three righteous men were recorded in scripture. Could these three men have been responsible to produce the giants?

In fact in Noah's time, he alone was called righteous.

God considered none of Noah's sons righteous and none of his sons were giants. How could Noah have produced the vast number of giants that existed in the days before the flood?

NOTES

Chapter 13
Do the Rephaims Exist Today?

The Rephaims exist today; however, they are using different measures to produce new offspring without the increase in size. They are mutating DNA by intermingling or cross breeding. It is not only animals that this is happening with. This cross breeding is producing creatures that have not been seen since the days of Noah. Amazingly enough, they are cross breeding animal genes with human genes developing creatures that are neither truly animal nor truly human.

~ Lesson 1 ~
Legends are Perversions of the Truth

There was cross breeding of animals and humans before the flood. It produces creatures like the Minotaur, who had the body of a man and the head of a bull, and the centaur, which had the body of a horse and the chest, stomach and head of a man. There is also the companion of Heracles, which was part goat and man.

These stories stretch back hundred of years throughout all nations. They tell us of creatures from werewolves to leopard men. And they can be traced all the way to the days of Noah. If the fallen angels are once again trying to mate with the daughters of man where is the proof?

⇒I WON'T BELIEVE IT UNTIL I SEE IT!⇐

I understand there are many people who are quite unconvinced. It's all right to be skeptical; however, be careful what you ask for. If you were unfortunate enough to encounter these creatures, it would take the power of God to protect you. For those few who have survived an encounter with these creatures, twice as many have died at the hands of these monsters.

I have personally talked to some Native Americans on this topic and they have told me of seeing these kinds of creatures. There is a young man who was working at his job when a Rephaim attacked and shredded his boss to pieces in front of his eyes. He hasn't been the same since. Now he is constantly depressed and walks around talking to himself all day long.

~ Lesson 2 ~
The Tunnels of Brussels
The offspring of the fallen angels are beginning to show themselves openly to man.

Under the city of Brussels, Belgium there are tunnels crossing into Switzerland. The tunnels are where these humanoids are being sent from Belgium to many easily reached European countries like France, Italy, Germany, and Portugal.

Many of the older generation believe these stories of half creatures or humanoids are simply rubbish. After all, how can you cross a man with an animal and get a humanoid? Well I don't blame you for your doubt, we were raised in a generation that taught: "if we don't see it we will not believe it."

Yet our sons, daughters, and grandchildren have been raised in a generation where if a dog talked to them it would acceptable. Therefore a hybrid creature comes and says he is a good creature then this younger generation will accept it and believe it. Why would they do that?

They have watched thousands of stories on television about creatures that are part man and animal that only want to help mankind to develop. They also have hundreds of books in libraries and bookstores telling them witchcraft is good and can answer all your questions. There is no need for God. They are told: you are god and with what you learn, it will help you to develop into your own god self.

The Rephaim will not give up the chance to bring this planet under the ruler ship of their fallen angel fathers and their master, Satan.

There is a powerful war going on in the heavenly realm, which will shortly be brought to earth. Creatures, which your thought only existed in legends and Roman, Greek and Norse mythology are about to be revealed. After all, where did these authors of mythology get their information to write the legend of their gods and goddesses?

There were creatures/giants that truly walked the earth with such strength and power that even the sound of their voices hurt the ear of mortal man. From these creatures came the legends of mythology across all nations. It was not mythology that created these giants. Instead it was the offspring of the fallen angels and the daughters of men that produced the mythology.

Is it not interesting that the father of the gods were often having affairs with earthly women and producing offspring liked Hercules, Thor, and Diana? The offspring of the gods were in themselves demigods – half man and half gods. Brace yourselves for the Rephaim, the Anakim and the other thirteen tribes of giants recorded for all ages to know about and to be strongly warned.

I remember an old television show about a horse named Mr. Ed.
They would open every show with a comical song that had these words: "a horse is a horse of course of course unless it is a talking horse." **IF** it **IS** a talking horse then it is a monster and a creation of the Rephaim.

NOTES

Chapter 14
Secret Societies

→Amaranth order←

To be a member of the order of Amaranth, one must already be a master Free Mason. This order is open to male and female and they consider themselves as a charitable organization.

→American Knights of the Ku Klux Klan←

George Lincoln Rockwell, the founder was born March 9, 1918 and was a legal commander of the US Navy. In the 1950's he formed the American Nazi party, a prejudice organization who sought the destruction of any people who were not white. An ex-party member named John Patler assassinated Rockwell on August 25, 1967.

→Ancient Arabic Order of the Nobles of the Mystic Shrine←

They are also known as the Shriners. This group also considers themselves as a charitable organization.

→Anunnaki←

This is a secret society who believe that ancient astronauts from the planet Nibiru, which was three times larger than earth came here 450,000 years ago. Anu, who was the leader of Nibiru, sent his two sons Enlil and Enki to earth to supervise the colonization of earth. For every major theme in scripture they have a counterfeit from Creation to the creation of Adam and Eve to the Nephilim to the story of Noah and the great flood.

→Aryan Brotherhood←

Within prison it is an organization of the K.K.K. This group has nine churches called the Church of Jesus Christ. They believe that the whites are God's chosen people and that non-whites are on the level of animals and that the Jews are the children of Satan.

H.A.Lewis offers a 2 hr DVD teaching that was recorded on Live TV of the Political and Spiritual Side of the Occult

Government Structure of the Occult

BABYLONIAN BROTHERHOOD
Oldest Secret Society in Existence

Nimrod
believed to
be founder

COUNCIL ON FOREIGN RELATIONS
1921

**Trilateral
Commission
1972**

UNA-UK
1945

ROUNDTABLE
19th century

1954

**THE ROYAL
INSTITUTE OF
INTERNATIONAL AFFAIRS**
1921

THE CLUB OF ROME
1968

Free Masons
England 1717
*Founded by 2
protestant ministers
for universal brotherhood*

Spiritual Side of the Occultic World

First to rebel against God

Known as the father of the occult

Nimrod
anti-God

BABYLONIAN BROTHERHOOD
Oldest Secret Society in Existence

BROTHERHOOD

Grand Leader

Council of the Three

Council of the Five

Council of the Seven

Council of the Nine

Council of the Thirteen

Council of the Thirty-Three

SISTERHOOD

Sister of the Light

The Five Star Generals

Master Counsellors

Keepers of the Books

Keepers of the Seals

Asomodeus

Grand David Council

The Olympians (committee of 300)

The Committee of 500

© 2013 H. A. Lewis Ministries

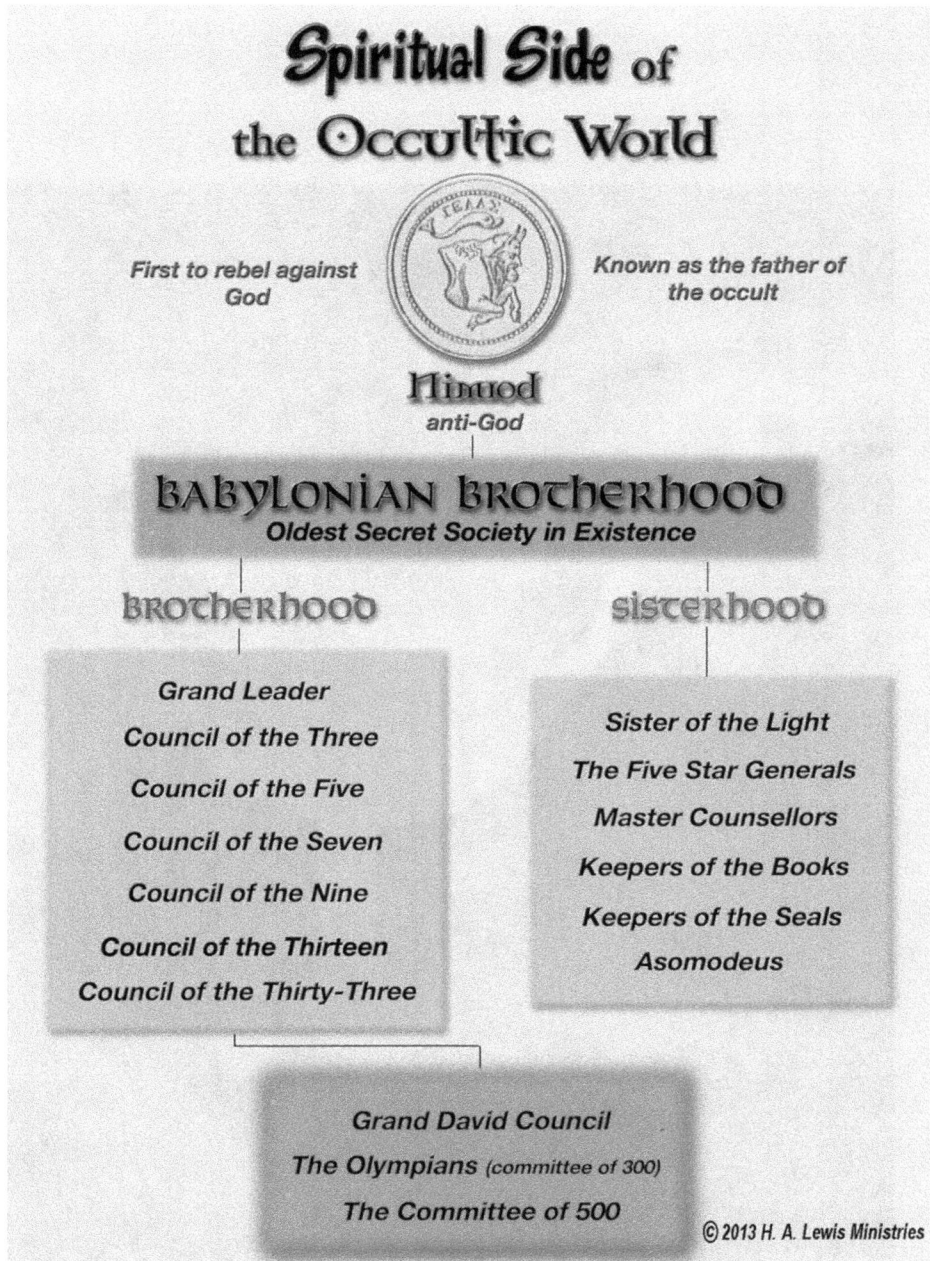

Copyright protected by Joshua International

Recommended Book : Nimrod Where religions began, the ancestral root of Satan, by H.A.Lewis

Chapter 15
The Characteristics and Assignment of the Serpent

I must shed light on how the serpent works today in our families and in the church which brings forth lies, division, defamation of character and more. If a person has been touched due to religious and non-Biblical environments, they will react emotionally, which is not led by the Holy Spirit. Just as a bite of a physical serpent cause its victim to be physically paralyzed and eventually die so the bite of the spiritual serpent causes its victim to be paralyzed spiritually and to die. It causes them not to trust in man and can break the covenant they have with God. This can affect their earthly marriage with their spouse.

As the Holy Spirit gives life, the counterfeit produces destruction and separation from God and His Holy Spirit. It will cause false prophecies to come forth because of the influence it has over a believer. Many believers today do not know about this unseen creature which has been around for decades and if they have been touched or not.

~ Lesson 1 ~
Comparing the Serpent Physically and Spiritually

The serpent or snake is a commonly used metaphor to describe a deceptive or treacherous person. In our culture, serpents have long been identified and associated with evil. Presumably, their association with evil comes from the Bible, where the serpent is one of many names given to Satan himself [**Revelation 12:9**].

So why does the Bible use this metaphor of a serpent to describe evil? What are the salient characteristics of a serpent that would cause God to choose this reptile as opposed to some other creation? It turns out that there is a lot more being said in the serpent metaphor than is common knowledge.

❖ Any general or strategist will tell you that if one wants to have success in dealing with a particular enemy, one must have intelligence or information about that enemy.

❖ One must be able to identify their enemy's habits, motivations, and behaviors. The Bible informs us about our main spiritual enemy through the metaphor of the serpent. Therefore, the serpent metaphor is an insight into the nature of the devil, and how he operates in the world. The serpent metaphor reveals the devil's tactics and modus operandi, through which he takes control of people's lives.

❖ Serpents are essentially ambush predators. They don't chase down or pursue their prey, but instead rely on its own carelessness. [Looking for a crack in your armor.] When the prey happens to get too close, or allows the snake to get too close, the serpent will quickly strike and put its venom into it. The serpent will then back off, and allow its venom to go to work. It waits in the shadows while the venom quickly paralyzes, digests, and destroys the animal from the **inside out**. When its prey finally succumbs, and is completely helpless, then the serpent will swallow it whole. This is the serpent's survival strategy and how it derives sustenance from other creatures. It doesn't use brute force, but relies on its own stealth and the power of its venom.

❖ Naturally the devil doesn't go around literally biting and poisoning people, but he does **overpower and consume them on a spiritual level**. He does go about poisoning the mind of man with deceptions, lies, half-truths, and false doctrines. He increases his power over them in a pattern that is similar to the way that natural serpents hunt and feed. The venom of the Biblical serpent is not a literal poison, but something more insidious and clandestine, that happens to relate to another of a snake's characteristic.

❖ The serpent's poison through which he overpowers mankind is the incredible deceptive power of his lies. The forked tongue of the serpent is a symbol of this propensity for dishonesty and deception. From the beginning, the devil has been a liar and a father of lies [**John 8:44**]. He uses the power of his lies to create dissension between man and God. God is of course more powerful than the devil, but as the spiritual estrangement between man and God becomes greater, man becomes more susceptible to the serpent's authority.

❖ So spiritually speaking, the devil's venom is his lies, and his lies act like a spiritual toxin, working to destroy and incapacitate those listening to him. In this way, the serpent uses his lies and deceptions to hold a place of power over the world, at the top of the spiritual food chain.

◆The Lies of the Serpent create False Thoughts and Perceptions in People◆

How does the serpent actually use his lies to destroy people? In other words, what is the process through which the serpent enslaves people with his venomous lies?

What basically all lies have in common is that they **create false thoughts and distorted perceptions within people**. They cause you to question. Did God truly say? And once this poison is received within you it will lead you to spiritual death and destruction. It will produce within you a counterfeit spirit. It can replace the Holy Spirit with a religious spirit.

As in the Old Testament in the temple when the Holy Spirit left the temple the people were still being religious and did not realize that the presence of God left. The devil creates false perceptions within people so that they think and act in ways that increasingly alienate them from God. God is the truth and the light, and as one drifts away from God, the devil is free to increasingly exercise authority over that person.

That's not to say that the serpent is behind every false perception and mistruth that is in the world, because man can certainly err on his own. However, many of the most destructive lies originate with the serpent, and he is a spiritual trafficker of lies, sowing them throughout the world.

◆The serpent is patient and observes from a distance.◆

There isn't one set type of lie that the serpent uses to deceive, but he tailors them to people's individual dispositions, weaknesses, and insecurities. These false thoughts and perceptions are unique for each person, and operate within them at their **basic spiritual level**. Like the serpent the enemy is patient and willing to stay in the shadow unobserved until his poison takes effect, then he will spring to destroy. The serpent can puff up and flatter people, getting them to think they are special, and have a right to mistreat others. He can get people to feel like victims that are owed something.

◆False Hopes and Lies Can Lead People Away◆

Sometimes he will give false hopes that lead people astray and into traps. Other times he will steal away what has the potential to be real hope. *Those [seeds] by the wayside are they that hear; then cometh the devil, and taketh away the word out of their hearts, lest they should believe and be saved* [**Luke 8:12** (KJV)]

❖ The serpent's lies will tear people down and make them feel worthless and alone, as if they have no place in the world. In some he creates a spirit of self-righteousness and false honor, so that they only see other people's flaws.

❖ The serpent will often influence people's values so that they seek after meaningless things, and deny the people and things that are important.

❖ He will attack any aspect of someone's life that he can, from their self-perceptions to their relationships to the perceptions of the past. Whether positive or negative, all the serpent's lies are distortions of reality that push us toward sin, and sow seeds of destruction in our lives. While some of the serpent's lies are more targeted, there are some that seem to work on a lot of people.

❖ One of his simplest and most common lies is that we'd be happy if only we got our way all the time.

❖ Another common strategy is to make sin look cool and exciting, as if there are no bad consequences for those who revel in it (he gets a lot of help from the entertainment industry on this one). Among groups of people, the serpent will often work to inflame feelings of anger, hatred, and fear so that they react to their false emotions. Many of the serpent's lies have led to great chaos, war, and suffering.

One favorite tactic of the serpent is to appeal to our fleshly desires and weaknesses. And when he had fasted forty days and forty nights, he was afterward an hungered. *And when the tempter came to him, he said, "If thou be the Son of God, command that these stones be made bread."* [**Matthew 4:2, 3** (KJV)]

Here the serpent attempts to corrupt Jesus by getting Him to use His power for personal gain and satisfaction, even for something as simple as bread. Of course his efforts were futile because our Lord cannot be tempted, even when the devil offers Him all the kingdoms of the world [**Matthew 4:8-10**]. Whether building people up on false foundations and promises, or plunging them into hopelessness, the serpent's intention is the same, increasing sin and alienation from God.

Perceptions and beliefs control our thoughts, which in turn control our actions. We grow up in a kingdom of lies and as certain lies take root in our minds, they affect our thoughts. These thoughts then culminate in the temptation and compulsion to sin through our words and actions.

Please Note
The serpent's lies work to constantly blind us to the spiritual reality of our own capabilities.

When our thought process is guided by these lies and false perceptions instead of the truth, we cannot make righteous choices. Then when the lies lead us to sin, the venom has finished its job, and the result is spiritual incapacitation and death. **Romans 6:23** declares …for the wages of sin is death. Thereby the serpent metaphor is complete, and he is able to digest us on a spiritual level.

When we succumb to or embrace the lies of the serpent, we can enter a kind of **death spiral** that we have all experienced to some degree. When our sins increase, we drive an increasingly larger wedge between God and us. **His presence grows dim**. This gives the serpent more power over us, making us more susceptible to his lies. We often respond to the grief and misery that we feel by using sin as an outlet. This can create a downward death spiral, where we try to deal with our grief and misery through sin, but in the end the sin just leads to more grief and misery.

◆ The serpent's lies tell us that it's hopeless to resist. ◆

This is similar to the alcoholic who drinks to drown out his sorrows, but the reason he has so many sorrows is because he drinks. Another example is the overeater who is sad and depressed about his situation and life, and so copes with this grief by overeating even more. The serpent's lies tell us that it's hopeless to resist, and then even if we do resist and overcome one's self-destructive behavior, another pops up to take its place.

However, the self-destructive overeater or alcoholic is at the nobler end of the spectrum. Especially when compared to a person like a pedophile. This type manages his pain by inflicting that same emotional pain on others, thus spreading evil and sin like a spiritual plague throughout the world. Con artists are another example of this type, as they are often motivated by the sense of power that they feel by taking advantage of someone else's vulnerability. There are of course a whole host of methods that people use to cope with their own spiritual chaos at someone else's expense.

So whether it is by the destruction of one's self or others, or often a combination of the two, the very things people instinctively do to feel better, ends up driving them deeper into the serpent's clutches. The resulting destruction is the serpent's food. Crawling on his belly through the dust, the serpent feeds on the remnants of people's lives. *Upon thy belly shalt thou go, and dust shalt thou eat all the days of thy life* [**Genesis 3:14**].

Paul alludes to this devastation when he speaks of the devil's snare in 2 Timothy. *In meekness instructing those that oppose themselves; if God peradventure will give them repentance to the acknowledging of the truth; and that they may recover themselves out of the snare of the devil, who are taken captive by him at his will* [**2 Timothy 2:25, 26**]. Here Paul describes sinners as being spiritually captured in the snare or trap of the devil.

~ Lesson 2 ~
The Serpent's Snares/Traps

There are many different kinds of snares or traps that hunters use; however, a traditional snare trap often involves some kind of noose which the animal runs into or triggers. The snare works like a slipknot that becomes increasingly tighter around the animal as it struggles to get away, sometimes suffocating it. With this and many other kinds of traps, it is the instinctive reactions of the animal that causes it to become more entangled and less likely to get away.

Similarly, the serpent's trap is like a snare that further entangles its victims by their reactions to what has occurred. Their innate responses and actions cause them to become increasingly bound so that they are unwittingly surrendering to him.

The word that is translated her as **recover (Greek: ananayfo)**, means literally to regain one's senses from an intoxicated state. Paul uses this word to describe sinners recovering or escaping from the trap of the serpent. In other words, rather than being physically held captive, they are spiritually trapped in a cloud of lies and delusions that prevent them from thinking and seeing clearly. As opposed to an external trap, a venomous cocktail of lies trap them internally.

This is why the passage says in the Greek that sinners are taken captive _unto his will_, meaning _unto serving the devil's will_. A lot of commentators fumble with this sentence, but it makes sense in the context of this discussion. The devil's trap is a snare of lies that spiritually entangles its victims through their own sins. Once entangled in the serpent's lies, they are held captive according to his will, and the authority that he has gained over them.

♦People can choose to resist the serpent's lies.♦

This might come across as though I am making excuses for the deeds of the wicked. It might seem as if I am saying that because the serpent lies to people and uses them, that their sins are his fault. If sinners are trapped under the serpent's influence, then how can they be held accountable for their own actions? One could argue that they are just doing what seems right, or at least practical, according to their own spurious perceptions.

While it's true that people get used and manipulated by the serpent, it's also true that they will be held responsible for their sins. We know that all people sin, and are susceptible to the serpent's lies in one way or another. However, it's up to the individual how far they are willing to go, and in this respect they are accountable. The serpent doesn't take over and control every aspect of every person's life, but probes for weaknesses and areas of control, through which he can gain a foothold.

Even though the serpent has a foothold in the lives of all the unsaved, many of them have ingrained values and moral codes, and cannot be prodded to do evil things beyond a certain point. Their natural empathies and boundaries of right and wrong create inner conflicts that prevent them from being fully entrapped. _For when the Gentiles, which have not the law, do by nature the things contained in the law, these, having not the law, are a law unto themselves._ [**Romans 2:14**]. Although nonbelievers dwell in spiritual darkness and have no real fellowship with God, some do have an innate revulsion to evil and refuse to be manipulated beyond certain points.

♦Beware you are not drawn into the lies. Renew your mind with the Word of God.♦

All people succumb to sin, but there are some individuals who are drawn to the serpent's lies more than others. For these wicked ones, the devil's lies serve to liberate them through the realization of their innermost desires. The serpent provides them with a spirit of self-righteousness and justification for their wicked deeds.

The wicked embrace the lies of their spiritual father, and willingly render themselves unto his purposes. *Ye are of your father the devil, and the lusts of your father ye will do. He was a murderer from the beginning, and abode not in the truth, because there is no truth in him. When he speaketh a lie, he speaketh of his own: for he is a liar, and the father of it. And because I tell you the truth, ye believe me not* [**John 8:44, 45**].

Loving the wages of unrighteousness, they serve their master and have no yearning for the light and truth of God. They despise the truth because it stands against who they are, and what they feel in their hearts. To the wicked, the serpent's lies are a gospel of power. He is their spiritual overlord, using lies to serve their mutual interests of narcissism and self-glorification.

◆ Christ gives us immunity to the serpent's lies. ◆

The serpent's lies are very sinister because they influence our perceptions, together with our thought processes. The problem with overcoming the serpent's lies, is that we as people have no foundation of truth with which to expose and defeat them. One cannot have the power to reject a lie unless one has some truth or insight that undermines and exposes that lie. There is no innate yardstick within the world or us to spiritually distinguish between the truth and the lies. Just because we want to believe something doesn't make it true and just because we don't want to believe something doesn't make it a lie.

◆ Lies can corrupt our thought process. ◆

Regardless of how intelligent we are, we cannot overcome the false presumptions and errors that entangle us. There are just too many lies, and too many possibilities for us to have a clear vantage point with which to perceive and understand the world. A lot of the lies operate within us at a subconscious level. We aren't even aware of them, much less able to defeat them.

For those of us who have experienced it, salvation is like slowly finding our way out of a dark tomb and into the light of day [**John 5:21**]. In this process, we are drawn out of the confusion and darkness of the world, and in to the light of Christ. In the light, we can perceive what is happening spiritually and distinguish between the truth and lies.

◆ I AM the Light of the World. ◆

Then spake Jesus again unto them saying, "I am the light of the world: he that followeth me shall not walk in darkness, but shall have the light of life." [**John 8:12**] In Christ, we have freedom from the lies, because we are no longer being continually shackled and blinded by our sins. When we understand the Word, He gives us light and life, becoming a true frame of reference within our souls. Therefore, we can identify and uproot the serpent's lies so that they no longer find shelter within us.

Christ is the antidote to the poisoning of lies that has bound and sickened us our entire lives. In Him we are finally cut loose from the serpent's snare, and sobered up from the cloud of deceit that afflicts us. When we believe in the Word, we are spiritually immunized to the serpent's venom.

This is why when a serpent bites Paul he suffers no ill effects. *And when Paul had gathered a bundle of sticks, and laid them on the fire, there came a viper out of the heat, and fastened on his hand. And when the barbarians saw the venomous beast hang on his hand, they said among themselves, no doubt this man is a murderer whom though he hath escaped the sea, yet vengeance suffereth not to live. And he shook off the beast into the fire, and felt no harm.* [**Acts 28:3-5**]

♦The Bite + The Affliction♦

The bite is described as being very sever, with the serpent hanging off his hand. Yet by the power of God Paul is completely unfazed by it. This miracle symbolizes how Christ was immunizing and protecting Paul from the power of the serpent. The Word had formed a foundation of truth within Paul, so that he was spiritually impervious to the enemy's lies. *Behold, I give unto you power to tread on serpents and scorpions, and over all the power of the enemy: and nothing shall by any means hurt you.* [**Luke 10:5**]

When we understand the Biblical usage of the serpent metaphor we can begin to have a more mature perspective on what the Bible really teaches. The Bible is a composite of reality itself, giving us insight into every detail of how the world works on a spiritual level, including the modus operandi of our adversary, the serpent. He's not some cartoon character trying to blow up the world, but he is a predator who can wreak havoc and devastation in the lives of those who succumb to his lies. The Bible guides us to spiritual freedom from these lies, through the light and authority of Jesus Christ.

Prayer: Satan, I come against you in the name of my Lord Jesus Christ. I am His child His blood redeems me. I have repented of all my sins and have received God's forgiveness. In obedience to God's command, I have forgiven each person who has ever trespassed against me and all for whom I have held resentment.

I have confessed the sins of my ancestor, and have renounced every inherited curse. I take back from you all the ground that you ever gained in my life. You have no rights of dominion over me. All of your plans against me are frustrated and cancelled. Every strongman assigned against me is bound.

I command every evil spirit, which has gained entrance to me, to leave me now in the mighty name of Jesus. (Press the battle until you are free.)

Bind the spirit of Rabisu!
→ I ask that you seal all my cracks in my armor.
→ Fill me now with the power of Your Holy Spirit.
→ Remove ALL signs and symptoms of any religious spirit.
→ Heal my emotions and remove all fears.

Note: Personalize specific things that you recognize (or even suspect) to be attacks of demons against you, your family, your church, your community, your nation and other nations. Make you personal list of evil spirits to be bound. Then pray a deliverance prayer, and make your declaration against Satan.

Satan, I remove all ground or advantage that you and your forces have taken in my life, and now cover it completely with the blood of Jesus Christ. I declare…broken all power structures of evil, all hierarchies of demonic energy, all schemes ever devised against me for any cause, through any source, at any time. I bind, rebuke, and command the departure of all familiar spirits that have come against me from my ancestral bloodline. I command the departure of all enemy spirits that have come against me to hinder my effectiveness as a servant of the Lord Jesus Christ. In His Name, which is supreme, I command you to leave me now.

I announce that JESUS IS MY LORD AND MY SAVIOR.

Psalm 18:2 The Lord is my rock, my fortress, and my deliverer; my God is my rock, in whom I take refuge, my shield and the horn of my salvation, my stronghold.
Exodus 20:3 You [I] must not have any other god but Me.
Isaiah 54:17 No weapon formed against me will prosper.

Key Facts to Remember

- GO and make peace to those you may have rumored against.
- ASK for forgiveness to those who you may have offended.
- FORGIVE those who have offended you.

NOTES

Chapter 16
Sins of the Fathers and Curses

There are a number of Biblical examples showing the sins of the fathers and curses in action. However, one example has been ongoing for many generations. It is the family line of Israel. Technically, this nation started with Abraham, and is still on going. But we are going to use King David as the starting point for our illustration.

King David sits as a shining example of king, priest, and prophet. He is the example of the One who was yet to come at that time, the Lord Jesus. As we read about his life in First and Second Samuel, and in First Kings, we see a tremendous number of victories, conquests, favor with the people, and favor with God. It has been said that the peak of David's accomplishments, the peak of his life occurred just before his encounter with Bathsheba. From then on things began to deteriorate.

~ Lesson 1~
David's Descendants

Wait! Wasn't David forgiven? The answer is yes; he was forgiven. However, the sins of the fathers and the resulting curses operating on his family line didn't stop just because he was forgiven. Forgiveness does not normally stop the curses, which are the consequences of sin. The cross stops the curses when we appropriate it into our lives. If we don't appropriate it or if we don't know we need to do so, the consequences/curses continue.

Some consequences continue no matter what because a seed was planted that produced a harvest. The child conceived and born out of wedlock provides a simple example. The child is still with us even after all concerned have repented and received God's forgiveness. At the other extreme, a person murdered does not come back to life after the murderer repents. Forgiveness is a wonderful gift from God, but it is only part of what needs to be done in order to stop curses.

David entered into the sins of *adultery*, *deception*, *conspiracy*, and *murder* [**2 Samuel 11:4, 8, 12-17**]. After David and Bathsheba's sin, Nathan the prophet confronts David. Besides the humiliation of being exposed by Nathan, David receives a multi-part curse from God [**2 Samuel 12:10-14**]. The curses are penalties of like nature as the sins he had committed.

David and his descendants are going to reap what he has sown. As we discussed earlier, this curse includes the death of the child from the affair [**2 Samuel 12:15-19**], but this is only the beginning. God spares David; nevertheless, the penalty for adultery (death by stoning) falls onto the son. Is this fair, or consistent, with the scriptures about each one dying for his sin? David repents. We can read his confessional prayer in **Psalm 51**. This is a great psalm, one with which we can all identify.

Later, one of David's sons, Amnon *rapes* Tamar [**2 Samuel 13:1-18**], which leads to Amnon being *murdered* by Absalom [2 Samuel 13:28, 29]. *Deception*, *lying*, and *conspiracy* are all involved. Then Absalom himself *rebels* against his father, the king, and *conspires* to take over the kingdom [**2 Samuel 15**]. The story ends with Absalom's *death* [**2 Samuel 18:14**], and with much *destruction* in Israel, just as the prophet had spoken. If we continue to follow the history of Israel, and the line of David, we find the same sins of the fathers and outworking of the curses occurring time after time after time.

Solomon, the second son of David and Bathsheba, became king. While he was one of the wisest men to ever live, he was not wise in his later years. He married many foreign women, and fell into the *traps of women*, *gold*, *horses*, and *idolatry* [**1 Kings 11:4, 6**].

While there are both good and bad kings in his descendants (in Judah), the trend is downward, and God finally stops the royal succession coming through Solomon. He does this even though He had promised David: "And thine house and **thy kingdom shall be established** for ever before thee: thy throne shall be established for ever." [**2 Samuel 7:16 KJV**]

God cuts off Solomon's line with Jehoiachin (Coniah or Jeconiah), the son of Jehoiakim, and lets Israel go into captivity [**Jeremiah 22:24-30**].

Jeremiah 22:30 Thus saith the Lord, write ye this man childless, a man [that] shall not prosper in his days: for no man of his seed shall prosper, sitting upon the throne of David, and ruling any more in Judah.

Since we have the benefit of knowing history, we can see that God still fulfilled his promise to David through David's son Nathan, the third son born to David and Bathsheba [**1 Chronicles 3:5; Luke 3:31**]. It is this family line that eventually leads to the birth of Jesus, the 'supposed' son of Joseph [**Luke 3:23**]. Jesus is now sitting upon the throne of David forever.

What a fascinating example of God keeping all of his promises, both the cursing and the blessings, to King David and Israel/Judah! At the same time, the outworking of the curses caused an ever-deepening spiral of wickedness and destruction. David had set up his descendants for a lot of trouble.

What about David's ancestors?

Did he fall into sin for no apparent reason, or were there family pressures setting him up?
Where did all of this sin really begin?

~ Lesson 2 ~
David's Ancestors

We know that David's grandmother was Ruth, a Moabitess [**Ruth 1:22; Matthew 1:5**]. His great grandmother was Rahab [**Matthew 1:5**], a Canaanite, the keeper of the inn in Jericho. We see they come from two heathen nations known for their *idolatry* and *sexual sins*. These nations and what they are known for are now grafted into the Israelite line preceding David, **within four generations**.

Going back further we do not know much about David's ancestors until we get back to Judah, a distance of ten generations. We can read about Judah in **Genesis 38** where he lays with his daughter-in-law, Tamar, thinking she is a harlot. The scriptures don't tell us Tamar's nationality; although, Jewish tradition indicates that she is an Israelite. From this union Perez or Phares as some translations have it is born. *Deception*, *fornication*, and *lying* are involved.

Consider Jacob (Israel) the father of Judah. *Deceit*, *lying*, *cursing*, *cheating*, and etc. are all evident in his life before his encounter with the angel of the Lord at the brook Jabbok [**Genesis 32:22-31**]. His mother, Rebekah entered into *deception* with Jacob, even **calling for the resulting curse to** be upon her [**Genesis 27:12, 13**]. Then his wife, Rachel, *stole* her father's *household gods* and *lied* about them. This resulted in Jacob's *unintentional cursing* of her and her early death [**Genesis 31:30-35; 35:16-20**].

Both Abraham and Isaac were guilty of *lying* [**Genesis 20:2; 26:7**], saying that their wives were their sisters. While the blessings of the fathers far outweighed the cursing, it is clear that David did not have a **PURE** family line. Since we don't know very much about his ten nearest ancestors, except Boaz, who was a righteous man following the Mosaic Law, there is much room for speculation. At least to a degree we can rightly say David was 'setup' by his ancestors.

Even though David had a heart after God, he also chose to enter into the sins of his fathers when he sinned with Bathsheba. David is a reminder to us to always be on guard and to not assume that just because God's favor is on us, just because hundreds or thousands are being saved and/or healed doesn't mean that Satan won't try to bring us down. Right at the pinnacle of our ministry is when we are apt to be the most unguarded. We must always be ready for the counterattack.

~ Lesson 3 ~
Scriptures Concerning Sins Of The Fathers

Sins of the Fathers

Exodus 20:1-17: (Ten Commandments)…visiting the iniquity of the fathers upon the
Deuteronomy 5:9: (Ten Commandments)…children unto the third and fourth generation
Exodus 34:6-7; Numbers 14:18: God's description of Himself, of His goodness, **merciful** and **just.**
Exodus 21:23-2: (Law of Judgment)… eye for an eye …

Sins of the Fathers at Work

Leviticus 26:39: Warning to Israel that they and their children will waste away in a foreign land.
I Kings 15:24-26; 16:25, 26; 22:52, 53: Descendants of Solomon corrupted by iniquity, leading nation into idolatry and corruption. In general, each one was worst than the previous.
Jeremiah 16:10-12: Descendants of Solomon and of Israel just before the Exile.
Lamentations 5:1-15: Children of Israel in Babylon during the Exile.
Matthew 23:30-32 Scribes and Pharisees identifying with their ancestors who killed the prophets (particularly clear in the NIV)

Each Dies for His Own Sin

Deuteronomy 24:16: Original declaration: each dies for own sins.
2 Chronicles 25:3-4: King Amaziah of Judah applies **Deuteronomy 24:16**
Jeremiah 31:29-30: End of a proverb about sour grapes.
Ezekiel 18:1-32: Clear outline of God's judgment and repentance principles.

We Are All Under Iniquity

Romans 3:23: For all have sinned and come short of the glory of God. (KJV)
Romans 3:10-18: Horrible description of the true nature of Man.
Romans 6:23: For the wages of sin is death…(KJV)

Special Exceptions Where Children Die For Their Father's Sin

Numbers 16:27-34: Rebellion of Korah, Dathan and Abiram results in the earth swallowing them and their men, their wives, children, and all of their possessions.

Joshua 7:1, 18-26; 22:18-22: Sin of Achan results in his entire family and all possessions being stones, burned, and buried.

2 Samuel 12:14-18: Death of firstborn son of David and Bathsheba at age 7 days.

Jeremiah 11:21-23; 13:14; 16:3-4: Death of children as well as the fathers: of Anathoth and of Judah.

Lamentations 5:1-16: Our fathers sinned and are no more, and we bear their punishment.

Isaiah 14:20-23: Death of the children of the wicked of Babylon and destruction of the city.

NOTES

Chapter 17
Spiritual Wickedness Against Believers

Finally, my brethren, be strong in the Lord, and in the power of his might. Put on the whole armor of God, that ye may be able to stand against the wiles of the devil. [Ephesians 6:10-11]

Although we are walking in this wicked world, and we are subject to all sorts of trials and temptations, the Lord has made a way of escape and a way to keep us pure and holy. A great many people perhaps feel that once you are saved and sanctified and have the Spirit of the Lord dwelling in your heart, that there is no more warfare or there is no more struggle. But this is not true. Often those who are the closest to the Lord will have the greatest struggles. They seem to have great trials and tribulations, and even temptations, because Satan is out to defeat God's children. And so we have a wonderful scripture here and we should rejoice that the Lord has made a way to escape. And He has provided safety and help against the enemy of our soul.

~ Lesson 1 ~
Paul's Writing About Spiritual Wickedness

Paul is writing Ephesians to the believers and to those who have ever known what it is to have the infilling of the Holy Spirit, which is a great cleansing of the heart and cleansing against the carnal nature and the coming in His fullness – the Spirit of Christ. Some people call the infilling of the Holy Spirit the coming of the gift of tongues. Now we do not see that in the scripture. The infilling of the Holy Spirit has to do with great cleansing and purity.

The gift of tongues is just as we say, a gift. And Paul said it was the least of the gifts, least of all of the gifts, and one that perhaps everybody does not receive. But all of us are to be holy and pure. The scripture says without holiness no man shall see the Lord.

Paul is writing to the Christian, Spirit-filled believer, those who have consecrated and given their hearts to the Lord. They have asked Him to come in, in all of His fullness and cleansing power. So what should this kind of believer expect from the enemy? Would he expect that Satan would turn on his heel and run when he sees a Christian of this kind of faith? Or just what attitude does Satan take?

In[**Ephesians 6:10**] Paul writes – finally! After all the things he has said previously about walking in the Spirit and how we should walk. Then he explains about the church, which are the pure, the sanctified, the redeemed **AND** all the blessings the Lord has for the church. Finally what? What is the last thing, the important thing that he has to add in this epistle? He says, *"Finally, my brethren, be strong in the Lord, and in the power of his might." [Ephesians 6:10]*

Power of his might: these words are interesting words. If you pass over them quickly, you might miss it. But if you want to look into the meaning of ***power*** and ***might***, in a spiritual sense, what does it mean? Paul says, "Be strong in the Lord and in the power of His might."

❖ One translation of this kind of might is the strength, the inward strength that comes to every sanctified believer, the strength, the abiding strength, and the strength of stability that is within every believer because of the presence of the Holy Spirit in his life. It's called in the scripture, **might**, and we might say then that every sanctified believer has a might within him, the might of the Lord, the strength of the Lord which is very mighty, and the power.

❖ Power! The sanctified believers are given power, and this power is a strength that is in operation that comes through the Holy Spirit. It is a power that is in operation all day long, all the time, and comes through the Holy Spirit. Paul says "Be strong in the Lord and in the power of his might." And so that is a lot of energy, spiritual energy there we're talking about. The Lord does not run out of energy. There may be an energy crisis in every other way, oil, coal, all these things that you can think about; but there is no energy crisis when it comes to the Lord.

We are all encouraged to be strong, and to use this energy that is from the Lord. What is it to be directed for or toward? It is to be used so that we will be able to stand against the wiles of the devil. And in addition to this power and might that comes from the Lord, we are to put on the armor that He has provided for us.

Now our danger is not in the people that we meet every day. Some mistakenly think that if someone says an ugly thing about you or to your face, or says something that hurts you and may bring the tears, they are there to destroy your soul. They may even say things like, "It's your fault. You did this thing to me. You offended me. You hurt me." It isn't the person who's saying this to you who is guilty. He is not the one who is trying to destroy your soul. The guilty one is the enemy. He is the one who put these thoughts in you neighbor's mind and heart; he is the instigator of all of this cruelty and wicked talk. Harmful devices whatever they might be all come from Satan.

~ Lesson 2 ~
We Fight Unseen Forces ~ Examples from Daniel and Job
◆Satan uses forces that we can't see with the naked eye.◆

The Lord revealed it to Paul that we, our enemy is ...*not against flesh and blood, but against principalities, against powers, against the rulers of the darkness of this world, against spiritual wickedness in high places. [Ephesians 6:12b] In high places* is a phrase Paul uses, perhaps five times in his letter to the Ephesians. Sometimes he calls it the *heavenlies,* or *up in heaven*, up somewhere out of what might be our reach, but not out of the reach of Satan.

Therefore, our enemy is the one who is leading against us all of these forces of darkness, spiritual wickedness in high places. It is Satan and the wicked spirits and the wicked angels that are his helpers. We have places in the scripture that help us understand this. We have at least two places that give us an insight into what goes on in the heavenlies, and what we mean by Satan working in that area and working against us.

One very particular instance is in **Daniel 10**. We find that Daniel had had a revelation from the Lord, a great and mighty revelation about the end times and about the Jews, and also about the antichrist. And he said it made him ill for several days. He could hardly stand it. And when he prayed; he prays a wonderful prayer. He is concerned about his people, about the Jews. He prays this prayer:

And now, O Lord, our God, that hast brought thy people forth out of the land of Egypt with a mighty hand, and hast gotten thee renown as at this day; we have sinned, we have done wickedly. O Lord, according to all thy righteousness, I beseech thee, let thine anger and thy fury be turned away from thy city Jerusalem, thy holy mountain: because for our sins and for the iniquities of our fathers, Jerusalem and thy people are become a reproach to all that are about us. Now therefore, O our God, hear the prayer of thy servant, and his supplications, and cause thy face to shine upon thy sanctuary that is desolate for the Lord's sake. O my God, incline thine ear and hear; open thine eyes, and behold our desolations, and the city which is called by thy name: for we do not present our supplications before thee for our righteousness, but for thy great mercies. O Lord, hear; O Lord, forgive; O Lord, hearken and do; defer not, for thine own sake, O my God: for thy city and thy people are called by thy name.
[**Daniel 9:15-19**]

After the vision that Daniel had into the future and the terrible things that are to come about on the earth, he prays for Jerusalem. You just heard his prayer, "Oh Lord, Oh Lord!" he prays. "Won't you forgive?" The Lord revealed many prophecies, some which have been fulfilled and some which we are waiting breathlessly to be fulfilled. He showed Daniel about the Antichrist. What will the Lord do for Jerusalem, and what will he do for the Jews?

Daniel prayed and pleaded with the Lord and then he waited for the answer. And he waited, and he waited, and he waited. And the Bible says [**Daniel 10:3**] he waited twenty-one days. At the end of twenty-one days he had the most marvelous vision of Jesus. *I lifted up my eyes and looked, and behold, a certain man clothed in linen . . . and his body was like beryl and his face as the appearance of lightening, and his eyes as lamps of fire, and his arms and his feet like in color to polished brass, and the voice of his words like the voice of a multitude.* [**Daniel 10:5-6**] We know that this is Christ.

John the Revelator also beheld part of this vision. [**Revelation 1:13-15**]. This was the same description of Jesus in Daniel. Daniel said in **Daniel 10:7** that only he saw this vision. The men that were with him saw nothing; however, there was a great quaking that fell upon them so that they fled and hit themselves. They didn't see it but they knew and sensed the presence of Christ and they fled.

Therefore I was left alone and saw this great vision, and there remained no strength in me. I retained no strength. Then he heard a voice, and then he fell asleep and he woke up when a hand touched him. He says, it set him upon my knees and upon the palms of my hands. [**Daniel 10:8-10**]

And he said unto me, Oh, Daniel, a man greatly beloved, understand the words that I speak unto thee. An angel was there and had touched him, and these were the words he told Daniel. *I stood trembling while he talked to me, and the voice said, "Fear not." And He says that you prayed and did set thine heart to understand and to chasten thyself before God, He said, thy words were heard. And he said, I was sent with an answer to your prayer. But, he said, the prince of the kingdom of Persia withstood me one and twenty days.* **Satan who inspired the Persians with their wickedness held up this angel. Satan himself withstood him**. And he says, *"Lo, Michael, one of the chief princes, came to help me, and now I am come to make thee understand what shall befall thy people in the later days."* [**Daniel 10:11-14a**]

Here is something that goes on in the heavenlies and that is what we need strength for:
- to have faith and
- to be strong and hold on and
- trust the Lord, because we have an enemy that works against us.

There are rulers of darkness in this world, and spiritual wickedness in high places, and the enemy would dare to try to intercept an answer coming from the Lord or being sent from the Lord.

Indeed the enemy did intercept this answer for twenty-one days, although the Lord heard and sent the answer the first day. So we want to be strong and have power and might to be strong against this kind of an enemy that works and we don't **SEE** him work. We can't see him with the naked eye, and we may pray and wonder:

Why doesn't the Lord answer prayer and why hasn't He heard me?
He has and it may be the enemy or the powers of spiritual wickedness in high places that are holding up the answer to your prayer.

How many times has Job's life been an inspiration to all of us? We think, if Job would hold on and be true to the Lord, and not sin with his mouth, and if Job could say, *"Though he slay me, yet will I trust him,"* [**Job 13:15**] with all he went through, then can't we hold on a little bit and stand a little bit of persecution or suffering or trial, whatever it might be?

Job did not know what was going on in high places and the kind of workings Satan was bringing against him. However, Job belonged to the Lord, and the Lord used him. He even said to Satan, "Have you noticed my servant Job?" Job could be relied on because he was steady. He loved the Lord, and he was not going to doubt the Lord, and the Lord knew his heart.

You read in the very first chapter how all these things happened to come to Job. Did the Lord put this kind of suffering on him? Did the Lord make him sick? Did the Lord take away his possessions? Did the Lord cause his wife to tell him to curse the Lord and die? No, it was Satan.

We find out in **Job 1:6** that there was a day when the sons of God came to present themselves before the Lord, and Satan came also among them. It is believed that this was somewhere in *high places* and Satan has freedom right now of the air and the earth and the regions below the earth. Satan is traveling all around and the Bible says he came amongst them.

And the Lord spoke to him, "Where have you been, and whence comest thou?" Where did you come from? *And he answered the Lord, "From going to and fro in the earth and from walking up and down in it."* This means he had to have been going up and down in the earth. *The Lord says, "In your travels have you noticed, have you considered my servant Job that there's none like him in the earth, a perfect and upright man?"* Satan answered the Lord and said, *"Well do you think he serves you for nothing? He's getting something out of it. He knows you have put a hedge around him and he knows that you're taking care of him and you're at his side. You've blessed the work of his hands and his substance is increased."* [**Job 1:6-10**]

And so Satan said, "Let me touch him and you'll see, he'll doubt." So the Lord says, *"He is in your power, but only upon himself put not thine hand."* Job did not doubt the Lord when he lost all of his possessions and his sons and daughters. The four corners of the house fell on them and they were dead. Job did not doubt the Lord, or he did not sin, or charge the Lord foolishly. [**Job 1:11-22**]

Then Satan made another suggestion. He says in [**Job 2:5**], *"Let me touch his body, make him sick, then he will doubt."* And the Lord said, "Yes, but you cannot kill him." Satan did all he could to destroy the faith Job had in the Lord and yet Job sinned not. He was steady. He had the power and the might that we are talking about.

Take unto you the whole armor of God that ye may be able to withstand in the evil day, and having done all, stand.
[Ephesians 6:13]

The words *in the evil day*, does not have reference to the judgment or even the time of tribulation. It refers to the day when Satan or some of his evil forces – the rulers of darkness, as the Bible calls them may come against us. We may have an evil day when Satan will come against us, or we may have evil days, maybe one after another. **It is possible to stand through the might and the power of the Holy Spirit, and the Lord has made provision, and armor for us.**

There is no reason to doubt the Lord. I believe it helps us to hold on and have faith and trust Him when we understand a little bit of the workings of Satan against us. Although we have no idea what he may be saying about us, bringing against us, or what may be going on in the heavenlies against us, but we can rest assured that the Lord is on our side. The Lord will bring us through victorious, whatever the struggle may be if we have faith and hold on to Him. We must put on the armor of God that we may be able to stand against the fiery darts of the enemy.

May the Lord bless you as you turn your face towards Him and be encouraged whether your problem is physical, some kind of unseen battle or a fierce temptation, Find your strength and power in Jesus Christ and in His Spirit. May the Lord bless you!

NOTES

Chapter 18
Spiritual Warfare Against Principalities

The Apostle Paul instructs us to put on our spiritual armor because our battle in this world is a spiritual one. It is a warfare that involves the trickery and power of the devil, as opposed to a human battle. The devil will use human beings to carry out his schemes. They are just being used by these entities for the purposes of accomplishing evil. Evil spirits are the true power behind those who oppose the things of God (knowingly or unknowingly).

For our wrestling is not against flesh and blood, but against the principalities, against the powers, against the world-rulers of this darkness, against the spiritual hosts of wickedness in the heavenly places.
[Ephesians 6:12]

~ Lesson 1 ~
What is a Principality?
◆Our Spiritual Warfare is Against Principalities◆

The Greek word ***arche***, meaning chief or ruler, helps us to understand the concept of the word **principalities**. These principalities are ruling devil spirits possessing executive authority or governmental rule in the world. As we will see, this ruling power usually involves a particular nation, people or race.

There are evil angels ruling the kingdoms of the world that oppose the truth of God. And Satan is the chief prince or ruler, of both the world system and its organization of demons, as noted in the gospel of Matthew. In Matthew **12:24**, the devil is called ***Beelzebub*** meaning **lord of the dwelling**. These wicked spirits are subject to and operate under Satan's dominion. They, like their chief prince, direct, control, rule, and carry out the present darkness of this world.

The *American Heritage Dictionary* defines **principalities** as:

1. A territory ruled by a prince or from which a prince derives his title.
2. The position, authority, or jurisdiction of a prince; sovereignty

The idea of prince devil spirits ruling or controlling a region is supported in the Old Testament book of Daniel 10. An angel visits Daniel in response to his prayer to God. This angel, who was sent by God to answer Daniel's prayer, was delayed for 21 days because of a battle that took place between God's angel and *a prince of the kingdom of Persia.*

Daniel reveals the angel's message in the following: *Then said he (the angel) unto me, "Fear not, Daniel: for from the first day that thou didst set thine heart to understand, and to chasten (humble) thyself before thy God, thy words were heard, and I am come for thy words. But the prince of the kingdom of Persia withstood me one and twenty days: but, lo, Michael, one of the chief princes, came to help me; and I remained there with the kings of Persia."* **[Daniel 10:12,13]**

The spiritual battle, for this angel, was of such magnitude that Michael, the archangel of God and designated prince of Israel, assisted the angel in battle. Another enemy of God, the prince of Greece, is also mentioned: *Then said he (the angel), "Knowest thou wherefore I come unto thee? And now will I return to fight with the prince of Persia: and when I am gone forth, lo, the prince of Grecia shall come. But I will shew thee that which is noted in the scripture of truth: and there is none that holdeth with me in these things, but Michael your prince."* [**Daniel 10:20, 21**]

The book of Daniel gives us an excellent example of how these unseen spiritual entities fight to increase and maintain their realms of influence and control in order to hinder God's purposes. These princes are named after the nations or rather their principalities in which they rule.

It is Satan's purpose to deceive these nations and to keep them from obtaining knowledge of God's truth and salvation through His Son, Jesus Christ. In the **Revelation 20**, Satan is depicted as a deceiver of nations. The Greek word for **deceive** is *planaho* and according to Strong's Greek Dictionary, this word means: to cause to roam from safety, truth or virtue, go astray, seduce, wander, and to be out of the way.

~ Lesson 2 ~
Our Lack of Discernment = Success for Satan
Satan's major success in deceiving a nation is due to a lack of discernment on the part of the people.

The people are blind to the invisible forces of supernatural evil that are operating and influencing their visible human agents of political, social, religious and philosophical programs. Satan's greatest victory would be to convince the world that he just doesn't exist. However, God signifies the devil as the author of sin, sickness and death, and warns us to be alert and vigilant because the devil, as a roaring lion roams about seeking whom he may devour [**1 Peter 5:8**].

The devil controls the kingdoms of the world
and we are not to underestimate his influence and power, nor believe that this is the will of God. God is telling us to stand against these evil forces by equipping ourselves with the power of God, and looking unto Christ as our example.

Luke 4:5-7 And the devil, taking Him (Jesus) up into an high mountain, shewed unto him all the kingdoms of the world in a moment of time. And the devil said unto him, All this power will I give thee, and the glory of them: for that is delivered (to surrender or yield up) unto me; and to whomsoever I will give it. If thou therefore wilt worship me, all shall be thine.

Definition: *kingdoms* – properly royalty, that is (abstractly) rule, or (concretely) a realm (literally or figuratively)

Revelation 11:15 And the seventh angel sounded; and there were great voices in heaven, saying, "The kingdoms of this world are become the kingdoms of our Lord, and of his Chris; and he shall reign forever and ever."

Until [**Revelation 11:15**] is fulfilled, we can only conclude, as the Apostle Paul instructs, is that our wrestling involves principalities or peoples or regions under the influence and deception of Satan. Satan is the prince or ruler of the kingdoms of this world. The Bible also describes it as the kingdom of darkness, which is where we have our spiritual warfare. Do not be fooled, Satan can and does prosper evil people in the world.

♦Our Spiritual Warfare is Against Powers and World Rulers of Darkness♦

The Greek word for **powers** is *exousia*, which means derived or conferred authority; the warrant or right to do something, or delegated influences of control. Although the word powers, is left unclear as to Paul's precise meaning in the verse, this expression is used elsewhere in scripture to infer the powers that be in authority.

In keeping with the context of this verse, it would include all high-ranking evil supernatural powers and the power of sin and evil in operation in the world. The fruits of this type of evil can probably be seen in drug cartels, gross poverty, plagues, terrorism and other heinous crimes against humanity, and even toward the animal kingdom.

Some Christian authors also associate world rulers with magic and demonic pagan gods such as the Ephesians' Artemis. This seems to be in line with the pagan culture of ancient times where temples were dedicated to these demonic pagan deities.

Let us not forget Molech, the national god of the Ammonites in Old Testament history. The priests would place the sacrificial children into the brass hands of the image. Then these helpless victims would slip into the fire below. It is described in scripture as the 'abomination of the nations'. [**2 Kings 16:3** ASV]

♦ Our Spiritual Warfare is Against Spiritual Wickedness in Heavenly Places ♦

The Greek word for **wickedness** is *poneria* and means depravity, particularly in the sense of malice and mischief, plots, sins, and iniquity.

The *American Heritage Dictionary* defines **malice** as:

1. A desire to harm others or to see others suffer; extreme ill will or spite.
2. Law – The intent, without just cause or reason, to commit a wrongful act that will result in harm to another.

Since Satan is the prince of the power of the air, these wicked spirits in high places are often understood to be the collective organization of all of Satan's devil spirits. These malevolent spirits work evil and mischief and operate in our atmosphere. They operate as close to the very air we breathe and reach to realms beyond. All kinds of spiritual filth are propagated in these realms for the purpose of humanity's deception and subsequent destruction. Prior to becoming a Christian we too walked according to the prince of the power of the air.

Ephesians 2:2, 3 *Wherein time past ye walked according to the course of this world, according to the prince of the power of the air, the spirit that now worketh in the children of disobedience; Among whom also we all had our conversation in times past in the lusts of our flesh, fulfilling the desires of the flesh and of the mind; and were by nature the children of wrath, even as others.*

As Christians we are delivered from the power of the prince of the air, and from the sinful nature that once ruled our path in life. When we received God's Holy Spirit at the moment of our conversion to Christ, we were translated from the kingdom of darkness to the kingdom of God's light. We are continually delivered and empowered by God as we walk according to His Word and Spirit that He has given us. As we do this, we take our seat in the heavenlies with Christ.

Ephesians 2:5-7 *Even when we were dead in sins, hath quickened us together with Christ, (by grace ye are saved;) and hath raised us up together and made us sit together in heavenly places in Christ Jesus: That in the ages to come he might shew the exceeding riches of his grace in his kindness toward us through Christ Jesus.*

Jesus is also called a Prince. However, He is the Prince of Peace and of Life [**Isaiah 9:6; Acts 3:15**]. His kingdom plays no part in this present world's system of darkness. He told his disciples, *"Hereafter I will not talk much with you: for the prince of this world cometh, and hath nothing in me."* [**John 14:30**] He continued in **John 18:36**…*"My kingdom is not of this world: if My kingdom were of this world, then would my servants fight, that I should not be delivered to the Jews: but now is my kingdom not from hence.*

Jesus is not speaking against the Jews, for Jesus and His followers were Jewish. He is speaking against the hypocritical religious authorities who would have Jesus killed versus lose their sphere of control over the people of God. Their own belly was their god.

The details of God's plan, His provision of escape from Satan's kingdom of darkness through faith in Christ was kept a mystery from the beginning of time. It wasn't until the revelation of the Son of God on earth and His complete victory in His death and resurrection for the salvation of humanity that the mystery of salvation through Christ is revealed in us.

1 Corinthians 2:7-10 *But we speak the wisdom of God in a mystery, even the hidden wisdom, which God ordained before the world unto our glory. Which none of the princes of this world knew: for had they known it, they would not have crucified the Lord of glory. But as it is written, eye hath not seen, nor ear heard, neither have entered into the heart of man, the things which God hath prepared for them that love him. But God hath revealed them unto us by the his Spirit: for the Spirit searcheth all things, yea, the deep things of God.*

In other words, if God's enemies knew that the Lord's death would bring the Kingdom of God and His power into the hearts of every believer, with His gift of the Holy Spirit, they would not have crucified Him.

❖ WHO IS YOUR PRINCE? For the Christian, Jesus Christ is our Prince of Peace and Life and we will reign with Him forevermore.

❖ WHAT IS THE MYSTERY REVEALED? The mystery revealed is…Christ in you, the hope of glory. [**Colossians 1:26, 27**]

Jesus Christ came as a light in the world. He was a light that the kingdom of darkness tried to extinguish.

Through the sacrifice of Christ, the Son of God and God's gift of the Holy Spirit given to every believer, and through the manifold wisdom of God, the kingdom of light continues to grow.

1 Corinthians 2:8 *Which none of the princes of this world knew: for had they known it, they would not have crucified the Lord of glory.*

NOTES

Chapter 19
God Is Saying To Us: "Fear NOT!"

Luke 10:19 Behold I give unto you power to tread on serpents and scorpions, and over all the power of the enemy.

⇒GOD IS RAISING UP A FEARLESS PEOPLE⇐

God is going to have a people today who are STRONG, COURAGEOUS and FEARLESS even in the midst of great opposition, trial and danger…during the fiercest onslaughts of the enemy, and even in the face of death. FEAR NOT. BE STRONG AND OF GOOD COURAGE are not simply words of encouragement; they are given as a COMMAND by God to His people. FEAR NOT!

- God told Abram: **Fear not**, Abram: I am thy shield, and they exceeding great reward. [**Genesis 15:1**]

- He told Isaac: **Fear not,** for I am with thee, and will bless thee, and multiply thy seed for my servant Abraham's sake. [**Genesis 26:24**]

- God said to Jacob: **Fear not** to go down into Egypt; for I will there make of thee a great nation. [**Genesis 46:3**]

- He told Moses: **Fear ye not**, stand still, and see the salvation of the Lord. [**Exodus 14:13**]

- God told Joshua: Have I not commanded thee? Be strong and of a good courage; **be not afraid,** neither be thou dismayed: for the LORD thy God, is with thee whithersoever thou goest. [**Joshua 1:9**]
- God told Jehoshaphat and the children of Israel as they went to fight their enemies: Ye shall not need to fight in this battle: set yourselves, stand ye still, and see the salvation of the LORD with you, O Judah and Jerusalem: **fear not**, nor be dismayed; tomorrow go out against them: for the LORD will be with you. [**2 Chronicles 20:17**]

- God said to Israel: **Fear not**: for I have redeemed thee, I have called thee by they name; thou art mine. When thou passest through the waters, I will be with thee; and through the rivers, they shall not overflow thee; when thou walkest through the fire, thou shalt not be burned; neither shall the flame kindle upon thee. For I am the LORD thy God, the Holy One of Israel… [**Isaiah 43:1-3**]

- He told Daniel, **Fear not**: peace be unto thee, be strong, yea, be strong. [**Daniel 10:19**]

We Must P.U.S.H
Pray Until Something Happens

Paul told the Romans, "The God of peace will soon crush Satan under your feet." [**Romans 16:20** (NIV)] Whose feet was Paul referring to? THE CHURCH! Through Christ we have been given the *dunamis* power of God, and it is OUR FEET God want to use to tread on Satan. It is OUR FEET He is going to use to CRUSH Satan!

God wants us to GET SPIRITUALLY VIOLENT…PURSUE Satan and the evil spirits that are attacking us in our minds…and FIGHT against them until they are totally destroyed. He wants us to expose them, one by one, and put our feet on their necks.

As we go out onto the battlefield of our hearts and minds to destroy the spirit of fear, I want everyone to see themselves as the captains of Joshua's army. By faith take the victory Christ has already won over Satan and his demon spirits. We must put our feet where Christ's is…on the neck of every enemy…every fear in our lives. As Commander in Chief over God's army, Christ's command to us as we go into battle is the same as Joshua's was to his soldiers – FEAR NOT!

NOTES

Chapter 20
If the Strongman is NOT Bound
~ Lesson 1 ~

The Strongman Must Be Bound

It doesn't matter how much scriptural knowledge you have, even if you can quote the whole Bible. If Jesus doesn't come down and bind the strongman and the powers of hell working in our lives, we won't make it! We have to have the Kingdom of God to come to us and be in us. In **Luke 11:20** Jesus said, "*if I with the finger of God cast out devils, no doubt the kingdom of God is come upon you.*" **Luke 17:21** says, "*behold, the kingdom of God is within you.*" But we have a part to play in this binding. We have to believe what God has said, His testimony, and speak it in faith!

[Confession: Father, in the name of Jesus Christ, I come against every demon power that has attached itself to my life and I announce that in Jesus name, you are defeated in my life. I belong to the Lord Jesus Christ; His blood has purchased me; and I command you to loose me in Jesus' name. I thank you, Father, for the authority you have given me as a believer. I stand on the strength of your Word and I will not turn back. I have given you my life and I will walk with you until you complete the work you have begun in me and I thank you, in Jesus name, Amen.]

Most who go to church, any church, to hear the Word of God, are never taught anything about the warfare or their part in it. So when all hell breaks loose, you find them testifying to the power of the enemy and talking about quitting and saying, "It's too hard, I can't make it, I didn't bargain for this, or the devil is doing this to me and that to me."

No matter how much scripture you know it doesn't stop the powers of hell from attacking you. Satan even tried to tempt Jesus, the Son of God. The victory Jesus got over him in the wilderness was not a one-time victory. When Satan left off from his temptation, scripture says it was only *for a season*, or until an *opportune time*. One battle and victory doesn't end the warfare.

It's a life-long warfare!

It's the devil's job to test and tempt us and he only does that which God has given him and allows him to do! He only does and can do what the Father allows him to do, nothing more. Salvation is warfare, not just going to church and having covered dish dinners. And, we must be those who press through and overcome and not as those who draw back unto perdition [**Hebrews 10:38-39**].

Don't think that more knowledge will raise you up to a place in Christ where you're no longer subject to the battle or that Satan can no longer tempt you. All you have to do is look at all those who have fallen to know the reality of this. When a person comes to the place of pride in his spiritual position or place of ministry he is ripe for spiritual deception and a fall from the place of being protected and delivered by the power of God and into the hands of Satan.

But, God has promised us **1 Corinthians 10:13**, *There hath no temptation taken you but such as is common to man: but God is faithful, who will not suffer you to be tempted above that ye are able; but will with the temptation also make a way to escape, that ye may be able to bear it.*". And, He said He would never leave us or forsake us, as long as we walk in obedience. If we forsake Him, then He will forsake us [**2 Chronicles 15:2**].

Psalms 149:5 – *Let the saints be joyful in glory: let them sing aloud upon their beds.* **If they feel like it?** No, but just do it. **Hebrews 13:15** – B*y him therefore let us offer the sacrifice of praise to God continually, that is, the fruit of our lips giving thanks to his name.* But, if you praise God half-heartedly, you're offering Him a blemished sacrifice. If your mind is not on Him when you pray or praise and it's just mechanical repetitions, it's unacceptable for it's a blemished sacrifice. What happens when you really praise God?

Psalms 149:6 – *Let the high praises of God be in their mouth, and a two edged sword in their hand...* When you put His praise in your mouth, it becomes as a sharp, two-edged sword in your hand. We are talking about a supernatural weapon for warfare that God has given to us. **For what? Psalm 149:7** – *To execute vengeance upon the heathen, and punishments upon the people...* When you praise God from your heart, you execute God's vengeance upon your enemies, speaking of the powers of hell. Remember our warfare is not with people who are your enemies but the spirits behind them [**Ephesians 6:12**]. Your praise puts God's vengeance on your behalf into motion.

You have to remember that you're no match for demon powers in your flesh or abilities. What, if when you come before God, you don't "feel" like praising? **Isaiah 61:3** – *To appoint unto them that mourn in Zion, to give unto them beauty for ashes, the oil of joy for mourning, the garment of praise for the spirit of heaviness...* There is a 'spirit' of heaviness and darkness. It's a spirit, a devil, attaching itself to your life. The solution is to put on praise as a garment. Depression, oppression, etc., are spirits, birds of prey; that come down upon the sacrifice – us. Remember the fowls that came down to eat up Abram's sacrifice in Genesis 15, after he prepared the animals to make a covenant with God? **Genesis 15:11** says Abram drove the fowls away from his sacrifice. Today, we are the sacrifice.

Romans 12:1 – *I beseech you therefore, brethren, by the mercies of God, that ye present your bodies a living sacrifice, holy, acceptable unto God, which is your reasonable service.* Sacrifice has to do with worship. When your life becomes a sacrifice, the birds of prey come against you. But God inhabits the praises of His people. True praise, in spirit and in truth, brings God's presence. But, God will not give His presence to a blemished sacrifice. Our praise must be from a pure, sincere heart.

Psalms 149:7-8 – *To execute vengeance upon the heathen, and punishments upon the people; To bind their kings with chains, and their nobles with fetters of iron...* to bind the powers of hell, but pull down the strongholds of hell.

Ephesians 6:12 – *For we wrestle not against flesh and blood, but against principalities, against powers, against the rulers of the darkness of this world, against spiritual wickedness in high places.* **Psalms 149:8-9** – *To bind their kings with chains, and their nobles with fetters of iron; To execute upon them the judgment written: this honour have all his saints. Praise ye the LORD.* Judgment against the powers of darkness! They have been defeated.

Hebrews 2:14 – *Forasmuch then as the children are partakers of flesh and blood, he also himself likewise took part of the same; that through death he might destroy him that had the power of death, that is, the devil...* **Colossians 2:15** – *And having spoiled principalities and powers, he made a show of them openly, triumphing over them in it.* Satan has no power over you any longer; unless you believe he does - his power was broken at Calvary! The power of sin over you has been broken!

Romans 6:14 – *For sin shall not have dominion over you: for ye are not under the law, but under grace.* Behind every besetting sin is a strongman, a devil. God will not move in your life to deliver you until you begin to walk in obedience. God gives the anointing of the Holy Spirit to those who obey Him [**Acts 5:32**]. What you profess is meaningless if you are not a doer of the Word.

The Holy Spirit is also called the Oil of God.

It's the anointing that breaks the yoke. **Isaiah 10:27** – *And it shall come to pass in that day, that his burden shall be taken away from off thy shoulder, and his yoke from off thy neck, and the yoke shall be destroyed because of the anointing.* The yoke is a shackle, as a yoke put on oxen; it's a symbol of authority. It's Satan's power over you to control your life through temptation and sin habits. God only gives the oil of the Spirit to those who obey Him. Jesus said, "*Why call ye me, Lord, Lord, and do not the things which I say?*" [**Luke 6:46**] There is a big difference between calling Jesus Lord and giving Him the Lordship of your life to sit on the throne of your heart.

Remember the ten virgins. All had religion.

Five were hearers that walked in bondage and darkness, under Satan's yoke of sin. Five had the yoke of sin in their life broken by the oil of the Holy Spirit. Five were set free and delivered. They walked in obedience to what they heard. That brings God's presence and anointing and deliverance in our lives. Do you believe God?

~ Lesson 2 ~
It Does Happen in the Natural as a Result of the Spiritual

Let's look at Abraham and remember, it's first the natural and then the spiritual. These things are happening to us in the spirit. God gave Abraham a promise. Has He given you the promise of His Word? But, then we find ourselves in a dilemma. God's Word says one thing, but we are experiencing something else contrary to that word. Why? Let's look at Abraham, a man and his wife beyond the years of having children.

Genesis 15:1-7a – *After these things the word of the Lord came unto Abram in a vision, saying, Fear not, Abram: I am thy shield, and thy exceeding great reward. And Abram said, Lord God, what wilt thou give me, seeing I go childless, and the steward of my house is this Eliezer of Damascus? And Abram said, Behold, to me thou hast given no seed: and, lo, one born in my house is mine heir. And, behold, the word of the Lord came unto him, saying, This shall not be thine heir; but he that shall come forth out of thine own bowels shall be thine heir. And he brought him forth abroad, and said, Look now toward heaven, and tell the stars, if thou be able to number them: and he said unto him, So shall thy seed be."*

God gave Him a promise. But, that isn't enough. We have to believe it.

And he believed in the Lord; and he counted it to him for righteousness. So, do you think that made everything go as smooth as a baby's bottom? No. But God gave him His righteousness, provision and protection! That's Jesus! He is our righteousness and everything we need Him to be in our lives… *And he said unto him, I am the Lord that brought thee out of Ur…* Come out of UR – come out of the place of idols and idolatry!

Colossians 3 tells us of that which is idols to us! **Colossians 3:5** – *Mortify therefore your members which are upon the earth; fornication, uncleanness, inordinate affection, evil concupiscence, and covetousness, which is idolatry...* Anything that comes between God, and us between obedience and us to His Word is idolatry. God brought us out of idolatry as He did Abraham. **Genesis 15:7** – *I am the Lord that brought thee out of Ur of the Chaldees, to give thee this land to inherit it.*

God gave him a promise! But, Abraham wants God to give him proof, another promise that He will inherit the land. **Genesis 15:8** – *And he said, Lord God, whereby shall I know that I shall inherit it?* We are saying, "God, how do I know I will really overcome? How can I know it?" So God said, "Let's get married; let's enter into a covenant." **Genesis 15:9, 10** – *And he said unto him, Take me an heifer of three years old, and a she goat of three years old, and a ram of three years old, and a turtledove, and a young pigeon. And he took unto him all these, and divided them in the midst, and laid each piece one against another: but the birds divided he not.*

Now some know church and religion for many years without knowing Christ personally. But, then, they were brought to a place of knowing that they needed to receive Christ for themselves. Each of us came to realize that we needed to know God for ourselves and that we couldn't make it on grandpa's religion or anything else. You asked Jesus to come into your life and forgive you. You accepted the finished works of Calvary and the blood sacrifice of the Lord Jesus and, thereby, entered into the blood covenant that the Father made with Jesus.

Then you probably thought everything would be wonderful from that point on. But, we didn't know something. We didn't know about the warfare. Then, Satan came on the scene in fury and many, then, run from walking with God. That's **Mark 4:14, 16-17** – *The sower soweth the word. … And these* *are they likewise which are sown on stony ground; who, when they have heard the word, immediately receive it with gladness; And have no root in themselves, and so endure but for a time: afterward, when affliction or persecution ariseth for the word's sake, immediately they are offended.*

God said, "*My people are destroyed for lack of knowledge*" [**Hosea 4:16**]. **Genesis 15:11** – *And when the fowls came down upon the carcasses, Abram drove them away.* What are the fowls of the air? Jesus taught us in **Mark 4:14-15** that it's Satan and the demon powers that war against us. Abraham received the Word, the promise of God. He cut the animals to make a blood sacrifice and entered into covenant with God. And, the powers of hell came to stop him, to stop and devour his sacrifice. Your life is your sacrifice, that which you promise and commit to God of your life.

♦ Satan will test and try to stop us. ♦

Our commitment will be tested and proven. From this natural story we see a spiritual principle. God doesn't show up to confirm and establish His covenant until Abraham has done his part and resisted the devil. He meant business with God. Most don't want to take the responsibility of having to do their part like Abraham had to do.

The two writers of the Bible that seemed to know most about the war and the way we fight in this war were David and Paul. They told us it's like being in the military. **Psalm 13:2** – *How long shall I take counsel in my soul, having sorrow in my heart daily? How long shall mine enemy be exalted over me?* Counsel in your soul; you're doing that as you hear God's Word. **Psalm 42:9** – *I will say unto God my rock, Why hast thou forgotten me? Why go I mourning because of the oppression of the enemy?* He said he was under oppression and he describes how he feels. **Psalm 42:10** – *As with a sword in my bones, mine enemies reproach me; while they say daily unto me, Where is thy God?* DAILY, he was under the attack of Satan, his enemies, saying, "You won't make it." Where is your victory? Where is the promise of God in your life?

Psalm 43:2 – *For thou art the God of my strength: why dost thou cast me off? Why go I mourning because of the oppression of the enemy?* Let's see David testimony. **Psalm 18:16** – *He sent from above, he took me, he drew me out of many waters.* Sent from above. WHAT? Maybe His angels, as described in Hebrews 1:7, 14 or Matthew 4:11! The Father sent angels to minister even to Jesus, when He walked as a man.

Psalm 18:16 – *He sent from above, he took me, he drew me out of many waters.* Waters…could that be the flood in **Isaiah 59:19b** and **Matthew 7:25** and **Revelation 12:15**? It's a flood of words, accusations, condemnations, doubts, and fears. Who is this flood coming against?

Revelation 12:17 – *And the dragon was wroth with the woman, and went to make war with the remnant of her seed, which keep the commandments of God, and have the testimony of Jesus Christ.* If you're not serious with God, but walk in compromise, this flood won't come against you. These are the only ones the devil is resisting and fighting, those who know and walk in the truth, who are a threat to his kingdom.

Psalm 18:16 – *He sent from above, he took me, he drew me out of many waters.* Now he explains he isn't talking about the physical waters at the beach. **Psalm 18:17-19** – *He delivered me from my strong enemy, and from them which hated me: for they were too strong for me. They prevented me in the day of my calamity: but the Lord was my stay. He brought me forth also into a large place; he delivered me, because he delighted in me.* God delights in the wise virgins who obey, not just those who go to church and hear His Word.

Was David talking about a conflict? **Psalm 118:8-10** – *It is better to trust in the Lord than to put confidence in man. It is better to trust in the Lord than to put confidence in princes. All nations compassed me about: but in the name of the Lord will I destroy them.* I will destroy the powers of hell. His enemies surrounded him, but he speaks his faith in God. **Psalm 118:11-13** – *They compassed me about; yea, they compassed me about: but in the name of the Lord I will destroy them. They compassed me about like bees; they are quenched as the fire of thorns: for in the name of the Lord I will destroy them. Thou hast thrust sore at me that I might fall: but the Lord helped me.*

The devils pushed him with violence. But, **Psalm 118:14** says *The LORD is my strength and song, and is become my salvation.* David gave two pictures of the powers of hell coming at us – as nations and bees. But God was his stay, his salvation. If the strongman in your life is not bound, you won't make it! What happens when we come to Jesus?

Isaiah 59:15a – *Yea, truth faileth; and he that departeth from evil maketh himself a prey...* Now what happens to a person who knows nothing about electricity who touches live, hot wires? Okay, what happens to a person who understands electricity and who touches those same wires? It doesn't matter whether you knew it or understood it or not, the same thing will happen. Same with **Isaiah 59:15**! What is a prey? A prey is the spoil of goods taken in war by force from an enemy. Another definition is: that which is seized by violence to be devoured, to be robbed, to be plundered. Animals of prey or beasts of prey are larger animals that love flesh such as lions, tigers, vultures or wolves. Example: a wolf on the sheep. A philosopher said, "Grief preys on the body and spirit while envy and jealousy preys on the health." To be a prey means to be devoured and plundered by that which is greater and stronger.

And, they told us that Christians couldn't have problems with demons. **Revelation 12:7-8** – And there was war in heaven: Michael and his angels fought against the dragon; and the dragon fought and his angels, And prevailed not; neither was their place found any more in heaven.

The devil didn't have the power to stay in heaven.

Revelation 12:9a – And the great dragon was cast out, that old serpent, called the Devil, and Satan... **Cast out!**

John 12:31 – Now is the judgment of this world: now shall the prince of this world be cast out. Satan was cast out of heaven to the earth and he has come down with fury to bring judgment.

Revelation 12:12, 9 Therefore rejoice, ye heavens, and ye that dwell in them. Woe to the inhabiters of the earth and of the sea! for the devil is come down unto you, having great wrath, because he knoweth that he hath but a short time. ... And the great dragon was cast out, that old serpent, called the Devil, and Satan which deceiveth the whole world: he was cast out into the earth, and his angels were cast out with him. This all took place at Calvary. At the same time something else happened.

Revelation 12:10a – And I heard a loud voice saying in heaven, Now is come salvation, and strength, and the kingdom of our God, and the power of his Christ...

We already quoted **Hebrews 2:14** and **Colossians 2:15**. Satan has been defeated!

Revelation 12:10b – for the accuser of our brethren is cast down, which accused them before our God day and night. But that isn't all. **Revelation 12:11** – And they overcame him by the blood of the Lamb, and by the word of their testimony; and they loved not their lives unto the death.

~ Lesson 3 ~
Walking in Victory - Dying to Self
The purpose of the blood, the purpose of the cross, is that we might overcome the devil and walk in the victory of Christ. But to achieve walking in that victory, we must die to self.

Revelation 12:13 – And when the dragon saw that he was cast unto the earth, he persecuted the woman which brought forth the man-child. Herod went after the baby Jesus to kill Him by killing all males under two years old.

Revelation 12:14 – And to the woman were given two wings of a great eagle, that she might fly into the wilderness, into her place, where she is nourished for a time, and times, and half a time, from the face of the serpent. Whenever the Lord rescues you from danger, you can say, symbolically, you were given the wings of eagles to escape. That term was used concerning God's bringing Israel out of Egypt in **Exodus 19:4** – And Moses went down from the mount unto the people, and sanctified the people; and they washed their clothes.

Revelation 12:15 – And the serpent cast out of his mouth water as a flood after the woman, that he might cause her to be carried away of the flood. It is a flood of words, to provoke you to the flesh so that your flesh, which causes you to sin, sweeps you away from the presence of God. And then Satan says, "make yourself a fig leaf covering" like Adam did. But, if you've sinned, run back to the blood sacrifice.

Revelation 12:16 – And the earth helped the woman, and the earth opened her mouth, and swallowed up the flood which the dragon cast out of his mouth. That simply is **Isaiah 54:17** – No weapon formed against you shall prosper.

Then we come to what pertains to us. We are God's sacrifice. We are new creatures in Christ

Jesus. **Revelation 12:17a** – And the dragon was wroth with the woman, and went to make war with the remnant of her seed… The woman is the church, the bride. "War" – are you using the weapons of your warfare? Many have head knowledge of them, but won't use them as spending time in praise and worship.

Revelation 12:17b – which keep the commandments of God, and have the testimony of Jesus Christ. Who does he make war with? The remnant of the church's seed! They are defined in the last part of the verse! The rest of the religious folk say to this remnant, "you're a bunch of Jesus freaks, you're fanatics." "I love the Lord", they say. "But you're just too fanatical, you've gone overboard."

The false church and governments are used by Satan to wage war against God's people. **Revelation 17:14** – These shall make war with the Lamb, and the Lamb shall overcome them: for he is Lord of lords, and King of kings: and they that are with him are called, and chosen, and faithful. You may be a prey, but you have the promise that if you do your part, God will set you free, free of lust, gossip and slander, pride, rebellion and all the sin that has so easily beset you.

Isaiah 59:15a – Yea, truth faileth; and he that departeth from evil maketh himself a prey… Prey? You become a sitting duck to a hunter. We are in a wrestling match like Jacob of old. We have been brought to that place and God wants us to be as determined as Jacob was and say, "Lord, I won't let you go until you bless me." How? **Acts 3:25** – Ye are the children of the prophets, and of the covenant which God made with our fathers, saying unto Abraham, And in thy seed shall all the kindreds of the earth be blessed. How does he do it?

Philippians 3:21b – … According to the working whereby he is able even to subdue all things unto himself. It's by the power of the Holy Ghost working in us. But, we fight to fight and sometimes we find ourselves becoming weary of the fight.

Isaiah 49:24 – Shall the prey be taken from the mighty, or the lawful captive delivered? The mighty one is Satan. But God gives us this promise to those who are asking, "will I ever be free?" **Isaiah 49:25a** – But thus saith the Lord, Even the captives of the mighty shall be taken away, and the prey of the terrible shall be delivered… How will we come to deliverance? **Isaiah 49:25b** – for I will contend with him that contendeth with thee, and I will save thy children.

♦ **The two things our flesh, religion, and demons HATE are praise, worship and prayer.** ♦

Luke 18:1 – *And he spake a parable unto them to this end, that men ought always to pray, and not to faint…* Not faint! Don't give up and lose hope. Yet many Christians say, "I feel like giving up."

Luke 18:2-5 – *Saying, There was in a city a judge, which feared not God, neither regarded man: And there was a widow in that city; and she came unto him, saying, Avenge me of mine adversary. And he would not for a while: but afterward he said within himself, Though I fear not God, nor regard man; Yet because this widow troubleth me, I will avenge her, lest by her continual coming she weary me.* There are those who say if you pray for something more than once, you have no faith. If so, why did Jesus pray twice for the blind man and three times the same thing in the garden of Gethsemane?

Luke 18:6-8 – *And the Lord said, Hear what the unjust judge saith. And shall not God avenge his own elect, which cry day and night unto him, though he bear long with them? I tell you that he will avenge them speedily. Nevertheless when the Son of man cometh, shall he find faith on the earth?* Will you have the faith to cause you to keep coming to God and hanging on until He answers? The lady was asking for legal protection, for the judge to bind her adversary. Are you asking God to bind your adversary, the strongman coming against you? You won't get free by ten minutes of prayer before bed.

Matthew 17:14 – *And when they were come to the multitude, there came to him a certain man, kneeling down to him…* He humbled Himself before God in prayer. In **Psalm 35:13**, David said, "*I humbled my soul with fasting!*" When you're asked to fast, does your flesh rejoice and get excited? Or does it start thinking of all kinds of goodies you love to eat? **Matthew 17:15** – *Lord, have mercy on my son: for he is a lunatic, and sore vexed: for ofttimes he falleth into the fire, and oft into the water.* Often falls… How often do you fall into the fire and water, the flood of Satan's words?

~ Lesson 4 ~
Jesus Bound the Strongman

Matthew 17:16-18 – *And I brought him to thy disciples, and they could not cure him. Then Jesus answered and said, O faithless and perverse generation, how long shall I be with you? how long shall I suffer you? bring him hither to me. And Jesus rebuked the devil; and he departed out of him: and the child was cured from that very hour.*

Jesus bound the strongman in His life. Think about it. Are there things that were once a part of your life that you once enjoyed and loved before coming to Christ that if the devils waved in front of you now, would not so much as get your attention? Are there things in your life now that when tempted, you'd say, "God, I don't have the strength to overcome that." That's a strongman in your life. That's what this message is about. Satan will never stop tempting, harassing and pushing us violently to sin again, until he is bound by the Lord Jesus Christ. Our job is to pray daily and even fast until God comes on the scene.

Abraham had to keep driving the birds, the devils, away until the time when God cut the covenant. **Genesis 15:12, 17-18a** – *And when the sun was going down, a deep sleep fell upon Abram; and, lo, an horror of great darkness fell upon him. ... And it came to pass, that, when the sun went down, and it was dark, behold a smoking furnace, and a burning lamp that passed between those pieces. In the same day the Lord made a covenant with Abram...* That's the same way it is with us. Abraham had to come to a place of deep sleep. We have to enter the Sabbath rest and cease from our works and labors in the flesh. God has to bring us into that rest. God does it by His Spirit. And that oil of the Spirit is only given to the obedient. And only then is the yoke of the enemy broken. **Isaiah 10:27** – *And it shall come to pass in that day, that his burden shall be taken away from off thy shoulder, and his yoke from off thy neck, and the yoke shall be destroyed because of the anointing.*

♦**Until you do your part in obedience, God will not establish you.**♦

Matthew 17:18-19 – *And Jesus rebuked the devil; and he departed out of him: and the child was cured from that very hour. Then came the disciples to Jesus apart, and said, "Why could not we cast him out?"* Privately, apart, they came to him. Why? They had a reputation. They were His disciples. They should know. They had gotten embarrassed before? Peter ate lots of 'shoe sandwiches'.

Matthew 17:20 – *And Jesus said unto them, Because of your unbelief: for verily I say unto you, If ye have faith as a grain of mustard seed, ye shall say unto this mountain, Remove hence to yonder place; and it shall remove; and nothing shall be impossible unto you.* God doesn't give that faith and His presence and anointing to all or cheaply. The fire of the Holy Ghost only comes upon the sacrifice that stays on the altar! It consumes the sacrifice. We need that fire! Jesus baptizes with the Holy Ghost and fire [**Matthew 3:11**].

Matthew 17:21 – *Howbeit this kind goeth not out but by prayer and fasting.* We are talking about strongmen in our life that keeps throwing us in the fire and then water. It's like lust that will heat you up in passion, and then slam you down, and then the flood of words that comes and condemns us afterward. **Mark 9:28** – *And when he was come into the house, his disciples asked him privately, "Why could not we cast him out?"* Why could we not bind this devil? **Mark 9:29** – *And he said unto them, "This kind can come forth by nothing, but by prayer and fasting."* If you're not willing to pay the price, you will not be delivered from this strongman!

Think now about the cross. Think about Jesus and where you are in your walk with Him. Think about the things throwing you down, the flood of words that easily bring you under condemnation. The things by which Satan seems to just pick on you at will and you find yourself back in this whirlpool, this cesspool, over and over again. Think about it. Let's pray.

[**Prayer:** Dear Father, I'm a prey to demon spirits because I have chosen with my heart to turn from evil. The enemy has surrounded me, but my faith is not in the enemy. My faith is in you, your strength, your power, and your authority. And I submit myself before you today and ask you to place into my soul, by the Holy Spirit, a desire for fasting and prayer. I ask you to send forth from heaven the strength that you gave to Elijah, the prophet; that you walked in when you were on the earth, Lord Jesus. When I came to you and gave you my life I really meant it. I never planned to go back to evil, to practice sin. I fell because I had no knowledge and I found myself on a spiritual roller coaster. Deliver me for Jesus sake, in Jesus name I ask.]

Psalm 149:5-6 – *Let the saints be joyful in glory: let them sing aloud upon their beds. Let the high praises of God be in their mouth, and a two-edged sword in their hand...* The praises of God in your mouth becomes as a two-edged sword in your hand; a weapon in God's hand against demon powers in your life. Hebrews tells us about a two-edged sword. Why do we need this sword? Is it because we are in a war with the powers of hell? The sword is our weapon of offense to attack the enemy.

Psalm 149:7 – *To execute vengeance upon the heathen, and punishments upon the people...* Here the heathen and people are types and shadows of demons. They are the enemies of God of His people. When we praise God, His presence comes among us.

That's **Psalms 22:3** – *But thou art holy, O thou that inhabitest the praises of Israel."* When we praise God, our enemies are punished and, remember, we are not in a battle against flesh and blood.

2 Corinthians 10:3-4 – *For though we walk in the flesh, we do not war after the flesh: (For the weapons of our warfare are not carnal, but mighty through God to the pulling down of strong holds;)...* **Psalm 149:7-8** – *All they that see me laugh me to scorn: they shoot out the lip, they shake the head, saying, He trusted on the Lord that he would deliver him: let him deliver him, seeing he delighted in him.* Who are these Kings?

Ephesians 6:12 – *For we wrestle not against flesh and blood, but against principalities, against powers, against the rulers of the darkness of this world, against spiritual wickedness in high places.*

Psalm 149:9 – *To execute upon them the judgment written: this honour have all his saints. Praise ye the Lord.* The judgment written! That means it is finished and done. It's eternally settled in heaven.

Hebrews 2:14 – *Forasmuch then as the children are partakers of flesh and blood, he also himself likewise took part of the same; that through death he might destroy him that had the power of death, that is, the devil...* Jesus rendered him powerless, powerless to stop us from inheriting eternal life. This is an honor God has given to His saints.

We have seen that salvation is a great wrestling match. Jacob wrestled all night and some of us have been wrestling and it is coming to the wee hours of the morning and the dawning of The Lamb is upon us. Jacob wrestled and said, "I will not let you go until you bless me." [**Genesis 32:24-26**] God's blessings are **Acts 3:26**. Jacob cried and made supplication unto God because he wanted to be changed. Jacob knew he couldn't change himself. We, too, are helpless to change ourselves. If God doesn't do it, it won't be done and we will end of in hell.

Jeremiah 17:14 – *Heal me, O Lord, and I shall be healed; save me, and I shall be saved: for thou art my praise.* We can't save ourselves. He does it by His power working in us. **Philippians 3:21** – *Who shall change our vile body, that it may be fashioned like unto his glorious body, according to the working whereby he is able even to subdue all things unto himself.* We have to be re-born by the Spirit of God. He has to change our nature and character as Jacob of old.

Genesis 32:27-28 – *And he said unto him, "What is thy name?" And he said, "Jacob." And he said, "Thy name shall be called no more Jacob, but Israel: for as a prince hast thou power with God and with men, and hast prevailed."* He became Israel, 'the God ruled man', or 'a prince with God'. He wrestled with God. We are wrestling and striving to be over comers like Jacob. Only the over comers inherit all things [**Revelation 21:7**]. What things? They are the things that God has prepared for those who love Him.

1 Corinthians 2:9 – *But as it is written, Eye hath not seen, nor ear heard, neither have entered into the heart of man, the things which God hath prepared for them that love him.* We are in the wee hours of the morning, struggling for our lives and, if we don't work out our salvation before God with fear and trembling, and if God doesn't bind the strongman in our lives, we are doomed for hell. There were five wise and five foolish virgins. Only five made it to heaven. The other five went to hell. Only the wise had the oil of obedience. **Acts 5:32** says He gives the Holy Spirit to those who obey Him. **Hebrews 5:9** – *And being made perfect, he became the author of eternal salvation unto all them that obey him...* If you're not doing what God has commanded you to do, He will not move any longer with you. God only moves in your life when you're walking in obedience.

Genesis 15:6 – *And he believed in the Lord; and he counted it to him for righteousness.* You're here because you claim to be a believer. You claim to have given Him your life. But many are divorcing God and don't know it. Why did Jesus die? **2 Corinthians 5:15** – *And that he died for all, that they which live should not henceforth live unto themselves, but unto him which died for them, and rose again.* God wants a peculiar people, a people for His own possession [**1 Peter 2:9**]. We are His possession because He has bought and purchased us with His own blood.

Acts 20:28 – *Take heed therefore unto yourselves, and to all the flock, over the which the Holy Ghost hath made you overseers, to feed the church of God, which he hath purchased with his own blood.* Therefore, we are His bondservants, slaves. And slaves have no rights. They simply live to please their master. Many want everyone and even God to notice what they are doing. They almost want God to praise them. But, look at this parable Jesus gave of a servant.

Luke 17:7-10 – *But which of you, having a servant plowing or feeding cattle, will say unto him by and by, when he is come from the field, "Go and sit down to meat?" And will not rather say unto him, "Make ready wherewith I may sup, and gird thyself, and serve me, till I have eaten and drunken; and afterward thou shalt eat and drink?" Doth he thank that servant because he did the things that were commanded him? I trow not. So likewise ye, when ye shall have done all those things which are commanded you,* *say, "We are unprofitable servants: we have done that which was our duty to do."* Doing all we are commanded is just doing what we should do.

So God made Abram a promise and he believed it. Then Abram asked this question in **Genesis 15:8** – *And he said, "Lord God, whereby shall I know that I shall inherit it?"* God's answer was, 'Let's cut a covenant'. Let's get married. Abram cut the pieces of the sacrifice and then something happened... **Genesis15:11** – *And when the fowls came down upon the carcasses, Abram drove them away.* It's first the natural and then the spiritual. Today we are the sacrifice [**Romans 12:1**].

When the fowls came upon the sacrifice, it was Abram's responsibility to drive them away. When the powers of hell come against us, it is our responsibility to drive them away. Yet most of God's people give in to devils, to the pressures and temptations and turn their backs on God and blame Him and accept what the devil is saying and doing. What a mockery of God's grace to be so ready, so quick to backslide and turn back from God. Many because they had no knowledge of this warfare called salvation. *God said my people perish for lack of knowledge* [**Hosea 4:6a**].

However, many with knowledge still turn from God and back to sin. And, so God rejects them from being a priest unto Him. **Hosea 4:6b** – *because thou hast rejected knowledge, I will also reject thee, that thou shalt be no priest to me...* It's the same reason Saul was rejected from being king. **1 Samuel 15:23** – *For rebellion is as the sin of witchcraft, and stubbornness is as iniquity and idolatry Because thou hast rejected the word of the Lord, he hath also rejected thee from being king.*

We have been called to reign in life as kings and priests unto God. **Revelation 1:5-6** – *And from Jesus Christ, who is the faithful witness, and the first begotten of the dead, and the prince of the kings of the earth. Unto him that loved us, and washed us from our sins in his own blood, and hath made us kings and priests unto God and his Father; to him be glory and dominion forever and ever. Amen.*

~ Lesson 5 ~
Our Lives Become Prey for the Enemy When We Belong to Jesus

Genesis 15:11-12 – *And when the fowls came down upon the carcasses, Abram drove them away. And when the sun was going down, a deep sleep fell upon Abram; and, lo, an horror of great darkness fell upon him. Abram fought off the birds of prey until a deep sleep fell upon Him, until He came into the rest of God* [**Hebrews 3 – 4**]. When you gave your life to Jesus, you became a prey. It's like a large flesh eating animal preying upon a smaller one, like a hawk on a chicken or a wolf on a sheep. It's to be plundered and devoured by one stronger than you. You are in a war against all hell. But, God is your help and your stay.

Isaiah 59:14 – *And judgment is turned away backward, and justice standeth afar off: for truth is fallen in the street, and equity cannot enter."* We are in this time today. **Isaiah 59:15** – *Yea, truth faileth; and he that departeth from evil maketh himself a prey: and the Lord saw it, and it displeased him that there was no judgment.* Truth fails and so there is no uprightness. But, the moment you turn from evil to truth, the devils come against you. David said they came against him like bees.

Isaiah 49:24 – *Shall the prey be taken from the mighty, or the lawful captive delivered? We say, "Is it really possible that God will ever deliver me?"* How many remember a time when you were fighting a battle against something that was stronger than you? It might have been depression, lust, anger, or whatever. And, you can look back and see how God delivered you and be thankful that that battle is over. But, now God is working on something else and the battle goes on. The war goes on and God building our lives goes on. We are His building, His workmanship, but that work won't be finished until we are in His presence. And God has promised to deliver us and He is faithful to His promise.

Isaiah 49:25a – *But thus saith the Lord, "Even the captives of the mighty shall be taken away, and the prey of the terrible shall be delivered..."* We, like Abram, before God gave Him the name Abraham, had a part to play – something to do. We have to fight off the birds of prey and we do that when we praise and worship God. When you are being attacked and feel beat down, that's the time for a sacrifice of praise unto God because He inhabits the praise of His people [**Psalms 22:3**]. We don't go by our 'feelings'. **Isaiah 61:3** – *To appoint unto them that mourn in Zion, to give unto them beauty for ashes, the oil of joy for mourning, the garment of praise for the spirit of heaviness; that they might be called trees of righteousness, the planting of the Lord, that he might be glorified.*

You praise God until He is satisfied and comes down into our midst and binds the strongman. Most go to church and just watch as if they have come to see a performance, being nothing more than spectators. But, this is a battle we all have to get involved in.

Isaiah 49:25a – *But thus saith the Lord, "Even the captives of the mighty shall be taken away, and the prey of the terrible shall be delivered..."* That is decreed. It is an established fact! How is Satan bound? **Isaiah 49:25b** – *for I will contend with him that contendeth with thee, and I will save thy children.* God will do it! **Isaiah 49:26** – *And I will feed them that oppress thee with their own flesh; and they shall be drunken with their own blood, as with sweet wine: and all flesh shall know that I the Lord am thy Saviour and thy Redeemer, the mighty One of Jacob. Jacob, not Israel.*

We are to fight and stand until God comes on the scene.

Until you do your part, God is not going to move. We are co-laborers together with Him [**1 Corinthians 3:9**]. God's remnant is soldiers, not picnickers, bikers and party throwers. We need the attitude of Gideon's 300 and the workers of Nehemiah. Soldiers who are alert, who eat and drink with their eyes open and watching, as those who worked with their sword on their sides or in one hand, [**Judges 7:6**; **Nehemiah 4:17-18**].

~ Lesson 6 ~
Christianity is not a Party or Picnic, but Warfare.

Hosea 10:12 – *Sow to yourselves in righteousness, reap in mercy; break up your fallow ground: for it is time to seek the Lord, till he come and rain righteousness upon you.* How long do you seek Him – until…

1 Peter 4:1 – *Forasmuch then as Christ hath suffered for us in the flesh, arm yourselves likewise with the same mind: for he that hath suffered in the flesh hath ceased from sin…* What is that same mind?

1 Peter 4:2 – *That he no longer should live the rest of his time in the flesh to the lusts of men, but to the will of God.* This is the purpose of an offering in the flesh. Your flesh will feel it and squeal like a stuck pig.

1 Peter 5:8a – *Be sober, be vigilant; because your adversary the devil…* Sober! The only way to be of a sober spirit is by prayer. If you don't pray, you will be drunk on the spirit of this world or dead religion.

Matthew 26:41 – *Watch and pray, that ye enter not into temptation: the spirit indeed is willing, but the flesh is weak.* If you're not praying, you will enter into temptation like Peter. **1 Peter 5:8** – *your adversary the devil, as a roaring lion, walketh about, seeking whom he may devour…* Roaring lion, a predator that eats flesh, like the birds of prey that came against Abram's sacrifice. Simply put, devils devour flesh.

1 Peter 5:9-10 – *Whom resist stedfast in the faith, knowing that the same afflictions are accomplished in your brethren that are in the world. But the God of all grace, who hath called us unto his eternal glory by Christ Jesus, after that ye have suffered a while, make you perfect, establish, strengthen, settle you.* Grace is God's power, presence and anointing to overcome, not grease as in, "I can do anything and slide by. God don't see my sin." It's still whatsoever a man sows that shall he also reap [**Galatians 6:7-8a**].

Nothing has changed. **Romans 11:8** is still true! *(According as it is written, God hath given them the spirit of slumber, eyes that they should not see, and ears that they should not hear;) unto this day.* But, after you suffer, resisting the urges of your flesh, God will begin a four-fold work in your life.

1 Peter 5:10 – *But the God of all grace, who hath called us unto his eternal glory by Christ Jesus, after that ye have suffered a while, make you perfect, establish, strengthen, settle you.* Called! Did God call you? Then you were called to suffer with Him.

1 Peter 2:21 – *For even hereunto were ye called: because Christ also suffered for us, leaving us an example, that ye should follow his steps…* But, in the end, God will perfect you, bring you to maturity and establish you in holiness and make you an over comer and strengthen you to stand against the devil and settle, literally, "to lay a basis for", i.e., "to lay a foundation"!

The Lord Jesus will not bind the strongman in your life until you cry out for Him to bind him. If your attitude is, "I don't feel like praying". You're saying, "I don't feel like being delivered".

Matthew 17:15 – *Lord, have mercy on my son: for he is a lunatic, and sore vexed: for ofttimes he falleth into the fire, and oft into the water.* Some in the church today are spiritual lunatics. They are thrown into different fires of their lusts and habits. Then, after they give into these fires, the devils come with all the words (flood) of condemnation. They are thrown into the water; in the fire, then into the water.

In **Mark 9** is a parallel of this story.

Mark 9:28 – *And when he was come into the house, his disciples asked him privately, "Why could not we cast him out?"* They came *privately*, because they didn't want others to hear the Lord's answer. This is the same thing Matthew said, privately. Could it be they didn't want to look bad in front of others or be humbled in front of others and ashamed by His answer? Usually you can't cast the strongman out of your own life.

Mark 9:29 – *And he said unto them, This kind can come forth by nothing, but by prayer and fasting.*

~ Lesson 7 ~
What is Our Part in Deliverance

Nothing else can bring deliverance – not running around after some man with power to give you instant deliverance like the foolish virgins.

Deuteronomy 7:22 says *God delivers us from our enemies, little by little.* You have a part to play in this; it's called, ***working out your salvation***

[**Philippians 2:12**]. You have to do your part. Here it is prayer and fasting. It is the narrow way that God designed for us to walk in. We don't know why He so designed and ordered our spiritual walk and the requirements necessary for us to get victory, but because He alone is God, it was His choice to make. There is no devil more powerful or harder for God to cast out than another, or harder for Him to deal with. They all bow to God's will and have to go when He says go, including Lucifer. But where men are concerned, God gave some more power or authority than others and so it takes more effort on our part to get victory over some than others.

Mark 14:41a – *And he cometh the third time, and saith unto them, "Sleep on now, and take your rest..."* We have all met this devil, the demon of sleep. You could have slept all night and when you go to pray, he hits you. For some it works the same when they go to read the Bible. In service, they can sing, shout. However, when the word beings, off they go. Are you determined enough to fight back? Stand up, get a drink of cold water, but don't just let him keep putting you to sleep. This is only a baby devil. But when you stand against the devil coming against you, then God will send an angel to establish you. He will tell the devil to leave you. But you have to show God you mean business. This was the only time that Jesus asked his disciples outright to pray with Him.

Mark 14:41b – *it is enough, the hour is come; behold, the Son of man is betrayed into the hands of sinners.* It is enough. The day of Jesus' coming is upon us and some of us are taking our rest. **Mark 14:38** is a warning that we not enter into temptation. *Watch ye and pray, lest ye enter into temptation. The spirit truly is ready, but the flesh is weak.*

Today there is little preaching on fasting and prayer. No one's flesh likes to do it. **Mark 2:19-20** – *And Jesus said unto them, "Can the children of the bride chamber fast, while the bridegroom is with them? As long as they have the bridegroom with them, they cannot fast. But the days will come, when the bridegroom shall be taken away from them, and then shall they fast in those days."* God will bring us to the place where we have to fast. When you find yourself in a hard place, you will pray when you would not have otherwise.

In **Psalms 35:13**, David said, "I humbled my soul with fasting", his feelings and emotions. But if God can't get you to pray by the wooing of His Spirit, then He will send hard places in your life to force you to pray. God is trying to get His people to heaven, but some are like a child having a temper tantrum, kicking and screaming against God's efforts to save them. When we fight against God, He sends His arrows (demons) against us. If we won't come the easy way, by the Spirit, God will try to bring us by the hard way because He loves us that much.

Job 36:13 – *But the hypocrites in heart heap up wrath: they cry not when he bindeth them.* This is one of the ways God passes judgment on us. It is like having a savings account and putting everything you can

into it to get out every possible bit of interest. When God sends judgment to bring us to repentance and we don't cry out to Him, we store up interest in our account to receive more of God's wrath.
Job 36:14 – *They die in youth, and their life is among the unclean.* Youth, they don't grow to maturity. What does God desire to do?

Job 36:15-16 – *He delivereth the poor in his affliction, and openeth their ears in oppression. Even so would he have removed thee out of the strait into a broad place, where there is no straitness; and that which should be set on thy table should be full of fatness.* Straight, God wants to remove us from the hard place we are in of being under His judgment and bring us to a broad place, a place of rest, peace and safety from the powers of hell that are devouring our lives. **Fatness** means the very best. God wants to put us in the place of giving us the best heaven has, a place of His blessing, anointing and presence. Sometimes God sends us hard places to get us to pray and cry out to Him. Because He loves us as a parent, He does what is best for us, though it is sometimes not enjoyable, as correction never is easy on our flesh.

Psalms 72:12-14 – *For he shall deliver the needy when he crieth; the poor also, and him that hath no helper. He shall spare the poor and needy, and shall save the souls of the needy. He shall redeem their soul from deceit and violence: and precious shall their blood be in his sight.* When you cry out to Him, He delivers you from the power of the devils coming against you. **Psalms 69:33** – *For the Lord heareth the poor, and despiseth not his prisoners.* His prisoners! When God's people, who are in prison cry out, He hears them.

Psalms 68:19-20 – *Blessed be the Lord, who daily loadeth us with benefits, even the God of our salvation. Selah. He that is our God is the God of salvation; and unto God the Lord belong the issues from death.* Satan is trying to bring us to spiritual death; but God gives us an escape. **Psalms 102:18-20** – *This shall be written for the generation to come: and the people which shall be created shall praise the Lord. For he hath looked down from the height of his sanctuary; from heaven did the Lord behold the earth; To hear the groaning of the prisoner; to loose those that are appointed to death...*

God is listening for the groan of the prisoner, one going through a hard place. Why? Because it gives Him pleasure? No, because He wants to set them free from the bondage they got themselves into because of sin. It is a bondage that will bring death if they're not delivered.

Matthew 6:9-10 – *After this manner; therefore pray ye: Our Father which art in heaven, Hallowed be thy name. Thy kingdom comes. Thy will be done in earth, as it is in heaven.* Thy kingdom comes! What does that mean to you for God's Kingdom to come to you. **Matthew 12:28** – *But if I cast out devils by the Spirit of God, then the kingdom of God is come unto you.* Jesus has to bind the strongman in your life. When God's Kingdom comes to you, when you pray that, you're praying for His authority, power and dominion to come into your life and bind the strongman and set you free.

Matthew 12:29 – *Or else how can one enter into a strong man's house, and spoil his goods, except he first bind the strong man? and then he will spoil his house.* God binds the strongman and brings His presence and life into your life. Remember **Isaiah 49** – Can the prey be taken from the mighty man, Satan? We were Satan's house or dwelling before we came to Christ. He enters Satan's house and binds him and He makes our house, a temple, a place for the dwelling of His Holy Spirit, the temple of God. But how does He do it? Little by little!

Do you want every sin habit in your life broken?

Then ask for His Kingdom to come into your life. **Mark 3:27** – *No man can enter into a strong man's house, and spoil his goods, except he will first bind the strong man; and then he will spoil his house.* Our home, our life was Satan's property until Jesus delivered us. But some of us are still fighting a few giants in our land, our heart, and have not taken possession of it. **Luke 11:20-21** – *But if I with the finger of God cast out devils, no doubt the kingdom of God is come upon you. When a strong man armed keepeth his palace, his goods are in peace…*

These are lives that Satan's hold on is secure. There's no battle. **Luke 11:22** – *But when a stronger than he shall come upon him, and overcome him, he taketh from him all his armour wherein he trusted, and divideth his spoils.* When Jesus comes, He strips Satan of his armor, his weapons and authority in our life and sets us free. The finger of God represents His Kingdom coming into your life to cast demons out of your life and it also can bring demons to your life. Blessing and cursing, deliverance and bondage both come by the finger of God.

Exodus 8:16-19 – *And the Lord said unto Moses, "Say unto Aaron, Stretch out thy rod, and smite the dust of the land, that it may become lice throughout all the land of Egypt." And they did so; for Aaron stretched out his hand with his rod, and smote the dust of the earth, and it became lice in man, and in beast; all the dust of the land became lice throughout all the land of Egypt. And the magicians did so with their enchantments to bring forth lice, but they could not: so there were lice upon man, and upon beast.* Up until now the magicians repeated all the miracles that Moses performed. We have the truth and power of God too, our religion is as good as your; however, God upped the ante until everyone had to admit it was Him and there was a difference in their religion and power of their god.

♦Jesus is the one who binds the strongman and drives him out.♦

Matthew 12:39-41 – *But he answered and said unto them, An evil and adulterous generation seeketh after a sign; and there shall no sign be given to it, but the sign of the prophet Jonas: For as Jonas was three days and three nights in the whale's belly; so shall the Son of man be three days and three nights in the heart of the earth. The men of Nineveh shall rise in judgment with this generation, and shall condemn it: because they repented at the preaching of Jonas; and, behold, a greater than Jonas is here.* Jesus is the one greater than Jonah. He said they repented, but you have only grown harder at the preaching and call for repentance.

Today men say, "**I don't have to repent again, I repented ten years ago**", and they think they got their ticket punched to heaven because of a one-time magical prayer they call a confession or profession of faith that is supposed to make them eternally saved and cover all sins, past, present and future so they can even die by suicide and go to heaven. That is not rightly dividing the Word of God.

Matthew 12:42 – *The queen of the south shall rise up in the judgment with this generation, and shall condemn it: for she came from the uttermost parts of the earth to hear the wisdom of Solomon; and, behold, a greater than Solomon is here.* The Queen of Sheba traveled a great distance to hear truth. Many have an opportunity to receive it without inconvenience and yet won't repent. What happens to that life?

Matthew 12:43-44 – *When the unclean spirit is gone out of a man, he walketh through dry places, seeking rest, and findeth none. Then he saith, I will return into my house from whence I came out; and when he is come, he findeth it empty, swept, and garnished.* This life was made clean obviously washed from sin, delivered and living a morally upright life. But they were not a doer of the word, but took their salvation for granted.

Matthew 12:45 – *Then goeth he, and taketh with himself seven other spirits more wicked than himself, and they enter in and dwell there: and the last state of that man is worse than the first. Even so shall it be also unto this wicked generation.* All they wanted was to see signs and wonders, but they didn't want Jesus for Himself.

Matthew 12:38 – *Then certain of the scribes and of the Pharisees answered, saying, "Master, we would see a sign from thee."* That's how many are today.

Matthew 11:28 – *Come unto me, all ye that labour and are heavy laden, and I will give you rest.* Are you weary of sin habits and darkness in your life? Do you have a yoke of bondage in your life around your neck?

Matthew 11:29 – *Take my yoke upon you, and learn of me; for I am meek and lowly in heart: and ye shall find rest unto your souls.* This is God's divine exchange. Everyone is a slave. The question is who is your master.

Romans 6:16 – *Know ye not, that to whom ye yield yourselves servants to obey, his servants ye are to whom ye obey; whether of sin unto death, or of obedience unto righteousness?* **Matthew 11:30** – *For my yoke is easy, and my burden is light.* Light! Jesus is light and light dispels darkness. His light breaks the yoke of darkness. How does He do it?

Deuteronomy 7:1 – *When the Lord thy God shall bring thee into the land whither thou goest to possess it, and hath cast out many nations before thee, the Hittites, and the Girgashites, and the Amorites, and the Canaanites, and the Perizzites, and the Hivites, and the Jebusites, seven nations greater and mightier than thou…*

All the giants then were physical. But they are types and shadows of what we face and fight today in the spirit. Is God trying to bring us into the land, into the place of His presence and provision for our lives? What do we have to do to overcome to possess our land? Many nations! God has to deliver us from many demon powers working in our lives. But He only does it for those who cry out to Him. If He doesn't bind and cast these demons out of your life, you're doomed to die. What do we have to get victory over?

- ❖ Hittites are a spirit of fear and dread.
- ❖ Girgashites are a turning back spirit, a spirit of apostasy, giving up and going back to the pleasures of the world.
- ❖ Amorites are a spirit of gossip, slander and bragging.
- ❖ Canaanites are a spirit of greed and money, anything for money, trickery, lies, selling the body.
- ❖ Perizzites means *unwalled place*, a spirit of lukewarmness and compromise.

It's **Isaiah 5**. This spirit reminds you of the things you enjoyed as a sinner, gets you to give into lusts, fantasizing, etc. **2 Corinthians 10:4-5** told us to cast down every thought contrary to the word of God. When you don't and you give into to this temptation, it brings more of the powers of hell against you. When you fail to obey God's Word and cast down those thoughts and imaginations contrary to the Word of God, this causes God to remove His presence from your life and remove the hedge of protection around us

⟹God is working with His vineyard in **Isaiah 5**.

- ❖ <u>Hivites</u> are a spirit of bright lights, the attractions of the world, everything to attract attention to self, to be seen. But, God doesn't want you to do anything to attract attention to yourself. These are all things we have to walk through, to take possession of the land, our hearts.
- ❖ <u>Jebusites</u> are a spirit of guilt and condemnation. This is a powerful devil. When you fall, this devil comes to keep you down. We have to look at God's word and promise.

Romans 8:1 – *There is therefore now no condemnation to them which are in Christ Jesus, who walk not after the flesh, but after the Spirit.* The Holy Spirit convicts of sin to bring repentance. Satan condemns you to destroy you and make you give up trying by telling you that you will never get victory and that you're a failure. Just remember **1 John 1:9** – *If we confess our sins, he is faithful and just to forgive us our sins, and to cleanse us from all unrighteousness.* If you fall and sin, just run back to the cross, the blood is for your cleansing. Jesus is our high priest.

Proverbs 24:16 – *For a just man falleth seven times, and riseth up again: but the wicked shall fall into mischief.* Rise up.

Isaiah 52:2 – *Shake thyself from the dust; arise, and sit down, O Jerusalem: loose thyself from the bands of thy neck, O captive daughter of Zion.* God said these seven nations were greater than us.

Deuteronomy 7:1b … *seven nations greater and mightier than thou…* We are in a war against an enemy we can't see, but we can sometimes feel them. If God doesn't bind them, we won't make it.

Deuteronomy 7:17-20 – *If thou shalt say in thine heart, These nations are more than I; how can I dispossess them? Thou shalt not be afraid of them: but shalt well remember what the Lord thy God did unto Pharaoh, and unto all Egypt; The great temptations which thine eyes saw, and the signs, and the wonders, and the mighty hand, and the stretched out arm, whereby the Lord thy God brought thee out: so shall the Lord thy God do unto all the people of whom thou art afraid. Moreover the Lord thy God will send the hornet among them, until they that are left, and hide themselves from thee, be destroyed."* Are there still devils hiding in your life, hiding out? God works to expose the darkness in us so that we will cry out to Him and He can cleanse us and set us free.

Deuteronomy 7:21 – *Thou shalt not be affrighted at them: for the Lord thy God is among you, a mighty God and terrible.* When a devil tells you that you're not free, don't fear. Just tell him Jesus has promised to set you free and give you the victory, even it it's little by little.

Deuteronomy 7:22 – *And the Lord thy God will put out those nations before thee by little and little: thou mayest not consume them at once, lest the beasts of the field increase upon thee.* These nations listed in verse one represent the "beasts of the field", demon powers. They say, "Christians can't have demon problems."

Do you think Christians who gossip and slander have the spirit of Christ?

**Why do you think Christians walk in lust and unforgiveness and a hundred other things?
There is a warfare they didn't tell us about.**

But let us keep pressing on in faith and rest in **Deuteronomy 7:23-24** – *But the Lord thy God shall deliver them unto thee, and shall destroy them with a mighty destruction, until they be destroyed. And he shall deliver their kings into thine hand, and thou shalt destroy their name from under heaven: there shall no man be able to stand before thee, until thou have destroyed them.*

NOTES

NOTES

Chapter 21
Scriptures For Victorious Living

♦Scriptures On God's Favor♦

- **Genesis 39:3, 4** And his master saw that the Lord was with him and that the Lord made all he did to prosper in his hand. So Joseph found favor in his sight…

- **Job 10:12** You have granted me life and favor, and Your care has preserved my spirit.

- **Psalm 5:12** For You, O Lord, will bless the righteous; with favor You will surround him as with a shield.

- **Psalm 23:5, 6** You prepare a table before me in the presence of my enemies; You anoint my head with oil; my cup runs over. Surely goodness and mercy shall follow me all the days of my life; and I will dwell in the house of the Lord forever.

- **Psalm 30:5** For His anger is but for a moment, His favor is for life; weeping may endure for a night, but joy comes in the morning.

- **Numbers 6:25, 26** The Lord make His face shine upon you, and be gracious to you; the Lord lift up His countenance upon you, and give you peace.

- **Psalm 8:4-6** What is man that You are mindful of him, and the son of man that You visit him? For You have made him a little lower than the angels, and You have crowned him with glory and honor. You have made him to have dominion over the works of Your hands; You have put all things under his feet.

- **Psalm 103:4, 5** Who redeems your life from destruction, who crowns you with loving kindness and tender mercies, who satisfies your mouth with good things, so that your youth is renewed like the eagle's.

- **Jeremiah 29:11** For I know the thoughts that I think toward you, says the Lord, thoughts of peace and not of evil, to give you a future and a hope.

- **Jeremiah 33:3** Call to Me, and I will answer you, and show you great and mighty things, which you do not know.

- **John 17:22, 23** And the glory which You gave Me I have given them, that they may be one just as We are one: I in them, and You in Me; that they may be made perfect in one, and that the world may know that You have sent Me, and have loved them as You have loved Me.

❖ **Acts 2:46, 47** So continuing daily with one accord in the temple, and breaking bread from house to house, they ate their food with gladness and simplicity of heart, praising God and having favor with all the people. And the Lord added to the church daily those who were being saved.

❖ **Romans 5:15** … For if by the one man's offense many died, much more the grace of God and the gift by the grace of the one Man, Jesus Christ, abounded to many.

❖ **Romans 6:14** For sin shall not have dominion over you, for you are not under law but under grace.

❖ **Romans 5:17** For if by the one man's offense death reigned through the one, much more those who receive abundance of grace and of the gift of righteousness will reign in life through the One, Jesus Christ.

❖ **2 Corinthians 8:9** For you know the grace of our Lord Jesus Christ, that though He was rich, yet for your sakes He became poor, that you through His poverty might become rich.

❖ **2 Corinthians 9:8** And God is able to make all grace abound toward you, that you, always having all sufficiency in all things, may have an abundance for every good work.

❖ **Ephesians 1:3** Blessed be the God and Father of our Lord Jesus Christ, who has blessed us with every spiritual blessing in the heavenly places in Christ…

❖ **Ephesians 1:7, 8** In Him we have redemption through His blood, the forgiveness of sins, according to the riches of His grace which He made to abound toward us in all wisdom and prudence.

❖ **2 Thessalonians 2:16, 17** Now may our Lord Jesus Christ Himself, and our God and Father, who has loved us and given us everlasting consolation and good hope by grace, comfort your hearts and establish you in every good word and work.

❖ **1 Timothy 1:14** And the grace of our Lord was exceedingly abundant, with faith and love which are in Christ Jesus.

❖ **Hebrews 4:16** Let us therefore come boldly to the throne of grace, that we may obtain mercy and find grace to help in time of need.

❖ **Titus 3:4-7** But when the kindness and the love of God our Savior toward man appeared, not by works of righteousness which we have done, but according to His mercy He saved us, through the washing of regeneration and renewing of the Holy Spirit, whom He poured out on us abundantly through Jesus Christ our Savior, that having been justified by His grace we should become heirs according to the hope of eternal life.

❖ **2 Peter 1:2, 3** Grace and peace be multiplied to you in the knowledge of God and of Jesus our Lord, as His divine power has given to us all things that pertain to life and godliness, through the knowledge of Him who called us by glory and virtue…

❖ **Phil. 3:10** That I may know him, and the power of his resurrection, and the fellowship of his sufferings, being made conformable until his death

◆Scriptures On Guidance & Leading◆

- ❖ **Psalm 16:11** God will show me the path of life.

- ❖ **Psalm 23:1** The Lord is my shepherd, I shall not lack.

- ❖ **Psalm 32:8** God will instruct me and teach me in the way I should go. He will guide me with His eye.

- ❖ **Psalm 37:23** My steps are ordered by the Lord.

- ❖ **Psalm 119:105** Your word is a lamp to my feet and a light to my path.

- ❖ **Proverbs 3:5, 6** I trust in the Lord with all my heart and lean not on my own understanding. In all my ways I acknowledge Him and He directs my paths.

- ❖ **Isaiah 30:21** I shall hear a word behind me, saying, "This is the way, walk in it," whenever I turn to the right or the left.

- ❖ **Isaiah 48:17** Thus says the Lord, my Redeemer, the Holy One of Israel: "I am the Lord your God, Who teaches you to profit, Who leads you by the way you should go."

- ❖ **Isaiah 58:11** The Lord will guide me continually.

- ❖ **John 7:17** I desire to do God's will so I shall know whether it is from God.

- ❖ **John 8:12** I follow Jesus so I shall not walk in darkness, but I have the light of life.

- ❖ **John 10:3-5** I hear Jesus' voice and He calls me by name and leads me out. Jesus goes before me and I follow him, for I know his voice. I will by no means follow a stranger.

- ❖ **John 16:13** The Spirit of truth has come and He is guiding me into all truth. He will tell me things to come.

- ❖ **Romans 8:14** I am led by the Spirit of God for I am a son of God.

- ❖ **Philippians 2:13** It is God Who works in me both to will and to do for His good pleasure.

- ❖ **Colossians 3:15** I let the peace of God rule in my heart.

- ❖ **Colossians 4:12** I will stand perfect and complete in all the will of God.

❖ **<u>Hebrews 13:21</u>** The God of peace will make me complete in every good work to do His will, working in me what is well pleasing in His sight, through Jesus Christ.

♦Scriptures On Hearing God♦

❖ **John 10:27** [ESV] My sheep hear my voice, and I know them, and they follow me.

❖ **Proverbs 20:27** [ESV] The spirit of man is the lamp of the Lord, searching all his innermost parts.

❖ **Isaiah 30:21** [ESV] And your ears shall hear a word behind you, saying, "This is the way, walk in it," when you turn to the right or when you turn to the left.

❖ **Isaiah 55:3** [ESV] Incline your ear, and come to me; hear, that your soul may live.

❖ **Jeremiah 33:3** [ESV] Call to me and I will answer you, and will tell you great and hidden things that you have not known.

❖ **1 Kings 19:11-13** [ESV] And he said, "Go out and stand on the mount before the Lord." And behold, the Lord passed by, and a great and strong wind tore the mountains and broke in pieces the rocks before the Lord, but the Lord was not in the wind. And after the wind an earthquake, but the Lord was not in the earthquake. And after the earthquake a fire, but the Lord was not in the fire. And after the fire, the sound of a low whisper. And when Elijah heard it, he wrapped his face in his cloak and went out and stood at the entrance of the cave. And behold, there came a voice to him and said, "What are you doing here, Elijah?"

❖ **Luke 11:28** [ESV] But he said, "Blessed rather are those who hear the word of God and keep it!"

❖ **John 6:63** [ESV] It is the Spirit who gives life; the flesh is no help at all. The words that I have spoken to you are spirit and life.

❖ **John 8:47** [ESV] Whoever is of God hears the words of God. The reason why you do not hear them is that you are not of God.

❖ **John 10:27** [ESV] My sheep hear my voice, and I know them, and they follow me.

❖ **John 14:26** [ESV] But the Helper, the Holy Spirit, whom the Father will send in my name, he will teach you all things and bring to your remembrance all that I have said to you.

❖ **John 16:13** [ESV] When the Spirit of truth comes, he will guide you into all the truth, for he will not speak on his own authority, but whatever he hears he will speak, and he will declare to you the things that are to come.

- ❖ **<u>Acts 10:15</u> [ESV]** And the voice came to him again a second time, What God has cleansed and pronounced clean, do not you defile and profane by regarding and calling common and unhallowed or unclean.

- ❖ **<u>Romans 8:14</u> [ESV]** For all who are led by the Spirit of God are sons of God.

- ❖ **<u>Romans 8:16</u> [ESV]** The Spirit himself bears witness with our spirit that we are children of God…

- ❖ **<u>1 Corinthians 2:16b</u> [NIV]** …But we have the mind of Christ.

- ❖ **<u>Ephesians 1:18</u> [KJV]** The eyes of your understanding being enlightened; that ye may know what is the hope of his calling, and what the riches of the glory of his inheritance in the saints…

- ❖ **<u>Colossians 1:9</u> [ESV]** And so, from the day we heard, we have not ceased to pray for you, asking that you may be filled with the knowledge of his will in all spiritual wisdom and understanding.

- ❖ **<u>Hebrews 4:12</u> [ESV]** For the word of God is living and active, sharper than any two-edged sword, piercing to the division of soul and of spirit, of joints and of marrow, and discerning the thoughts and intentions of the heart.

◆Scriptures On Peace◆

Speak these scriptures out of your mouth and do the things that are pleasing to God. When you receive His faith in your heart you will also receive His peace in your heart. Peace is the inward indicator that He is fully involved on your behalf. Peace is the emotion of faith.

❖ **John 14:27** Peace I leave with you; my peace I give you. I do not give to you as the world gives. Do not let your hearts be troubled and do not be afraid.

❖ **Romans 5:1** Therefore, since we have been justified through faith, we have peace with God through our Lord Jesus Christ…

❖ **Isaiah 53:5** But he was pierced for our transgressions, he was crushed for our iniquities; the punishment that brought us peace was upon him, and by his wounds we are healed.

❖ **2 Thessalonians 3:16** Now may the Lord of peace himself give you peace at all times and in every way. The Lord be with all of you.

❖ **Isaiah 26:3** You will keep in perfect peace him whose mind is steadfast, because he trusts in you.

❖ **Psalm 34:14** Turn from evil and do good; seek peace and pursue it.

❖ **Colossians 3:15** Let the peace of Christ rule in your hearts, since as members of one body you were called to peace. And be thankful.

❖ **Philippians 4:7** And the peace of God, which transcends all understanding, will guard your hearts and your minds in Christ Jesus.

❖ **Numbers 6:25, 26** The Lord make his face shine upon you and be gracious to you; the Lord turn his face toward you and give you peace.

❖ **Psalm 122:6** Pray for the peace of Jerusalem: May those who love you be secure.

❖ **Psalm 147:14** He grants peace to your borders and satisfies you with the finest of wheat.

❖ **Romans 12:18** If it is possible, as far as it depends on you, live at peace with everyone.

❖ **Psalm 119:165** Great peace have they who love your law, and nothing can make them stumble.

❖ **Galatians 5:22** But the fruit of the Spirit is love, joy, peace, patience, kindness, goodness, faithfulness.

❖ **Psalm 4:8** I will lie down and sleep in peace, for you alone, O Lord, make me dwell in safety.

❖ **Proverbs 16:7** When a man's ways are pleasing to the Lord, he makes even his enemies live at peace with him.

❖ **Isaiah 32:17** The fruit of righteousness will be peace; the effect of righteousness will be quietness and confidence forever.

❖ **John 16:33** I have told you these things, so that in me you may have peace. In this world you will have trouble. But take heart! I have overcome the world.

❖ **Psalm 29:11** The Lord gives strength to his people; the Lord blesses his people with peace.

❖ **Romans 15:13** May the God of hope fill you with all joy and peace as you trust in him, so that you may overflow with hope by the power of the Holy Spirit.

◆Scriptures To Strengthen Your Faith◆

❖ **Deuteronomy 31:6** Be strong! Be courageous! Do not be afraid of them! For the Lord your God will be with you. He will neither fail you nor forsake you.

❖ **Joshua 1:6-9** Be strong and courageous, for you shall give this people possession of the land which I swore to their fathers to give them. Only be strong and very courageous; be careful to do according to all the law which Moses My servant commanded you; do not turn from it to the right or to the left, so that you may have success wherever you go. This book of the law shall not depart from your mouth, but you shall meditate on it day and night, so that you may be careful to do according to all that is written in it; for then you will make your way prosperous, and then you will have success. Have I not commanded you? Be strong and courageous! Do not tremble or be dismayed, for the Lord your God is with you wherever you go.

❖ **2 Chronicles 20:17** But you will not need to fight! Take your places; stand quietly and see the incredible rescue operation God will perform for you, Oh people of Judah and Jerusalem! Don't be afraid or discouraged! Go out there tomorrow, for the Lord is with you!

❖ **Psalm 4:8** I will lie down in peace and sleep, for though I am alone, Oh Lord, you will keep me safe.

❖ **Psalm 32:7-9** You are my hiding place from every storm of life; You even keep me from getting into trouble! You surround me with songs of victory. I will instruct you (says the Lord) and guide you along the best pathway for your life; I will advise you and watch your progress. Don't be like a senseless horse or mule that has to have a bit in its mouth to keep it in line!

❖ **Psalm 34:17-19** Yes, the Lord hears the good man when he calls to Him for help, and saves him out of all his troubles. The Lord is close to those whose heart is breaking; He rescues those who are humbly sorry for their sins. The good man does not escape all troubles – he has them, too. But the Lord helps him in each and every one.

❖ **Psalm 37:7** Rest in the Lord; wait patiently for Him to act. Don't be envious of evil men who prosper.

❖ **Psalm 37:8-11** Stop your anger! Turn off your wrath. Don't fret and worry – it only leads to harm. For the wicked shall be destroyed but those who trust the Lord shall be given every blessing. Only a little while and the wicked shall disappear. You will look for them in vain. But all who humble themselves before the Lord shall be given every blessing, and shall have wonderful peace.

❖ **Psalm 40:1-3** I waited patiently for God to help me; then He listened and heard my cry. He lifted me out of the pit of despair, out from the bog and the mire, and set my feet on a hard, firm path and steadied me as I walked along. He has given me a new song to sing, of praises to our God. Now many will hear of the glorious things He did for me, and stand in awe before the Lord, and put their trust in Him.

❖ **Psalm 112:6-8** Such a man will not be overthrown by evil circumstances. God's constant care of him will make a deep impression on all who see it. He does not fear bad news, nor live in dread of what may happen. For he is settled in his mind that Jehovah will take care of him. That is why he is not afraid, but can calmly face his foes.

❖ **Proverbs 3:5, 6** Trust the Lord completely; don't ever trust yourself. In everything you do, put God first, and He will direct you and crown your efforts with success.

❖ **Isaiah 26:3, 4** He will keep in perfect peace all those who trust in Him, whose thoughts turn often to the Lord! Trust in the Lord always, for in the Lord, Jehovah, is your everlasting strength.

❖ **Isaiah 40:31** Those who hope in the Lord will renew their strength. They will soar on wings like eagles; they will run and not grow weary, they will walk and not be faint.

❖ **Isaiah 41:10** Fear not, for I am with you. Do not be dismayed. I am your God. I will strengthen you; I will help you; I will uphold you with My victorious right hand.

❖ **Isaiah 41:13, 14** I am holding you by your right hand – I, the Lord your God – and I say to you, don't be afraid; I am here to help you. Despised though you are, fear not, Oh Israel; for I will help you. I am the Lord, your Redeemer; I am the Holy One of Israel.

❖ **Isaiah 54:10** For the mountains may depart and the hills disappear, but My kindness shall not leave you. My promise of peace for you will never be broken, says the Lord Who has mercy upon you.

❖ **Habakkuk 2:1, 3** I will climb my watchtower now, and wait to see what answer God will give to my complaint. But these things I plan won't happen right away. Slowly, steadily, surely, the time approaches when the vision will be fulfilled. If it seems slow, do not despair, for these things will surely come to pass. Just be patient! They will not be overdue a single day.

❖ **John 14:1-3** Let not your heart be troubled. You are trusting God, now trust in Me. There are many homes up there where my Father lives, and I am going to prepare them for your coming. When everything is ready, then I will come and get you, so you can always be with Me where I am. If this weren't so, I would tell you plainly.

- ❖ **John 14:18** No, I will not abandon you or leave you as orphans in the storm – I will come to you.

- ❖ **John 14:27** I am leaving you with a gift – peace of mind and heart! And the peace I give isn't fragile like the peace the world gives. So don't be troubled or afraid.

- ❖ **Romans 8:24, 25** We are saved by trusting. And trusting means looking forward to getting something we don't yet have – for a man who already has something doesn't need to hope and trust that he will get it. But if we must keep trusting God for something that hasn't happened yet, it teaches us to wait patiently and confidently.

- ❖ **Romans 8:28** And we know that all that happens to us is working for our good if we love God and are fitting into His plans.

- ❖ **Romans 8:31, 32** What can we ever say to such wonderful things as these? If God is on our side, who can ever be against us? Since He did not spare even His own Son for us but gave Him up for us all, won't He also surely give us everything else?

- ❖ **Philippians 4:6, 7** Don't worry about anything; instead, pray about everything; tell God your needs, and don't forget to thank Him for His answers. If you do this, you will experience God's peace, which is far more wonderful than the human mind can understand. His peace will keep your thoughts and your hearts quiet and at rest as you trust in Christ.

- ❖ **Philippians 4:11-13** Not that I was ever in need, for I have learned how to get along happily whether I have much or little. I know how to live on almost nothing or with everything. I have learned the secret of contentment in every situation, whether it be a full stomach or hunger, plenty, or want; for I can do everything God asks me to with the help of Christ Who gives me the strength and power.

- ❖ **Hebrews 10:35-38** Do not let this happy trust in the Lord die away, no matter what happens. Remember your reward! You need to keep on patiently doing God's will if you want Him to do for you all that He has promised. His coming will not be delayed much longer. And those whose faith has made them good in God's sight must live by faith, trusting Him in everything. Otherwise, if they shrink back, God will have no pleasure in them.

- ❖ **Hebrews 13:5-7** Stay away from the love of money; be satisfied with what you have. For God has said, "I will never, never fail you nor forsake you." That is why we can say without any doubt or fear, "The Lord is my Helper and I am not afraid of anything that mere man can do to me." Remember your leaders who have taught you the Word of God. Think of all the good that has come from their lives, and try to trust the Lord as they do.

❖ **James 1:2-4** Dear brothers, is your life full of difficulties and temptations? Then be happy, for when the way is rough, your patience has a chance to grow. So let it grow, and don't try to squirm out of your problems. For when your patience is finally in full bloom, then you will be ready for anything; strong in character, full and complete.

❖ **James 5:7, 8** Now as for you, dear brothers who are waiting for the Lord's return, be patient, like a farmer who waits until the autumn for his precious harvest to ripen. Yes, be patient. And take courage, for the coming of the Lord is near.

❖ **1 Peter 5:7** Let Him have all your worries and cares, for He is always thinking about you and watching everything that concerns you.

About the Author

Dr. Henry Lewis and Patricia Lewis is the President and Co- President of an Apostolic International ministry called **Joshua International** .They have been married for 43 years and have two children and 6 grandchildren. Henry Lewis is a Sicilian Scottish Jew. His descendants come from Italy, Scotland and S Africa. Patricia is Canadian French, Native American and German. Descendants are traced from Canada, Paris, Switzerland, Russia, UK, Netherlands, Ireland and Germany.

Henry is a descendent of the famous Author and Pastor **Andrew Murray**. One of Andrew Murray's descendants were named after him who pastored in Fall River, MA

Dr. Lewis has authored 12 books which is still increasing. The first book called 'The Unholy Anointing' which later was changed to ' A Quest for Spiritual Power' is now translated in Arabic and in French. Over 7000 copies sold in Arabic. All books are sold on Amazon under H.A.Lewis.

Henry is a sought-after speaker and author, teaching at churches and conferences along with numerous TV guest media outlets teaching on subjects such as: spiritual warfare, revival, transformation, revelation, transforming prayer. Henry teaches amongst international prophetic leaders in many countries and holds three Doctorates in Counseling, Theology and Christian Education.

Charisma magazine shared his testimony as a former political occult leader in 2000. 750,000 Hindus accepted Christ after this article was translated in their language.

Henry's faith foundational friends are with : Dr. Leonard Heroo (Apostle and President of Zion Bible Institute & School of the Prophets), Evangelist Robert Schambach, Prophet David Wilkerson, Derek Prince, Lester Sumrall, Frank Hammond etc. Their passion and faith put a deep thirst for the knowledge and truth of God's word in them which resulted in having a deeper relationship with his Lord and Savior, Jesus Christ – and not a religion – so he could hear and know the voice of God.

Dr. Henry Lewis is ordained with the Assemblies of God. Henry is also ordained Rabbi through Asher Intrater from the Revive Israel Ministries

He is available for speaking

Activate the Kingdom of God Within You
YOU are the Lion of Judah

For More Information

Dr. H.A.Lewis
Joshua International

P.O. Box 1799
Maricopa, AZ 85139

Email: Info@halewis.org
Email: Info@ joshua-edu.org

To order or inquire of additional products, visit us online

Website: www.halewis.org
Visit us on facebook

Book Cover Artist: Debbie Wheat
Contact: izayu54@yahoo.com

Book Co-coordinators

Grace Miller
Patricia Lewis

Books

A Quest for Spiritual Power - Redeemed from the Curse - Testimonial
A Quest for Spiritual Power - Redeemed from the Curse - Arabic
Choisi Par Le Maitre: En quête de puissance spirituelle - French translation
A Quest for Spiritual Power - Arabic translation
Nimrod - How religions began and how it applies today
Spiritual Opposition to the Five Fold Ministry
The Secret Names of the Strongmen - study material & prayer manual
Jezebel - human or the spirit of baal?
The Dispensation of the Lion and the lamb
The Return of the Days of Noah
The War between the Unseen Kingdoms

Available on Amazon

https://www.amazon.com/-/e/B01L7UBNDE

H.A.Lewis

Recommended Authors

Andrew Murray
Derek Prince
Frank Hammond
David Jeremiah
Lester Sumrall
Charles Spurgeon
Tony Evans
Leonard Ravenhill
David Young Cho
Watchman Nee
Dr. Roy Hicks
Aimee Semple Mc Phearson
Stanley H. Frodsham
David Ravenhill
David Wilkerson
Smith Wigglesworth
T.B.Barrett
A.A.Boddy
Cecil Polhill
Robert A Brown
W.J. Williams
John G. Lake
D.L. Moody
George Mueller
George Stormont
R.A.Torrey
William J Seymour
David Brenner
John Wesley
Charles & Frances Hunter
Kenneth Hagin Sr.

Recommended Reading

1. <u>Communion With God</u> by: Mark and Patti Virkler
2. <u>Spirit Born Creativity</u> by: Mark Virkler
3. <u>The Fourth Dimension II</u> by: David Young Cho
4. <u>Hearing God</u> by: Peter Lord
5. <u>Celebration of Discipline</u> by: Richard Foster
6. <u>Communion With The Holy Spirit</u> by: Watchman Nee
7. <u>Hear His Voice</u> by: Douglas Wead
8. <u>Hearing His Voice</u> by: John Patrick Grace
9. <u>The Way Into The Holiest</u> by: Derek Prince
10. <u>The Soul's Sincere Desire</u> by: Glenn Clark
11. <u>The Gentle Breeze Of Jesus</u> by: Mel and Nona Tari
12. <u>Abide in Christ</u> by: Andrew Murray
13. <u>God's Chosen Fast</u> by: Arthur Wallis
14. <u>Whatever Happened to Hope</u> by: Dr. Roy Hicks
15. <u>With Signs Following</u> by: Stanley H. Frodsham
16. <u>Our Authority Over Sickness And The Devil</u> by: Gardner
17. <u>The Two Covenants and the Second Blessing</u> by Andrew Murray
18. <u>The Full Blessing of Pentecost</u> by Andrew Murray
19. <u>Pentecostal Pioneers Remembered</u> by Keith Malcomson
20. <u>The Prayer Ministry of the Church</u> by Watchman Nee
21. <u>Gathered In His Name</u> by Watchman Nee
22. <u>Man has been given power to make way for, or to obstruct the power of God</u> by Watchman Nee
23. <u>Let the Lion Roar</u> - Video -Francoise Frank
24. <u>The Two Babylon's</u> by Alexander Hyssop